D0916565

ℰℛ

EDITIONS RÉVEIL

Grégoire Chabot

UN JACQUES CARTIER ERRANT

Jacques Cartier Discovers America

Trois Pièces / *Three Plays*

The University of Maine Press / Le Centre Franco-Américain
Orono, Maine 1996

Un Jacques Cartier Errant/Jacques Cartier Discovers America is the first publication in the series EDITIONS RÉVEIL, co-published by the University of Maine Press and Le Centre Franco-Américain of the University of Maine.

The English translations of Grégoire Chabot's plays were completed in 1996 with a grant from the Maine Humanities Council. The author and publisher thank the Council for its support.

First Edition 1996

This book has been smyth-sewn for permanence. The paper used in this publication meets the minimum requirements of the American National Standard for Information Sciences—Permanence of Paper for Printed Library Materials, ANSI Z39.48-1984. Manufactured in the United States of America.

Book design and cover artwork by Michael Alpert

ISBN: 0-89101-087-4

TABLE DES MATIÈRES

Table of Contents

INTRODUCTION

The certainty that everything Franco-American was totally useless to me and the life I wanted to create kept gradually building up in me when I was a kid. It reached its apogee in 1955, when I was about 10, right in the middle of an otherwise enjoyable episode of "Disneyland."

Werner von Braun, the German rocket scientist who chose American $$$ over the USSR's dictatorship of the proletariat at the end of the Second World War, was using graphs, charts, cartoons, and a bunch of other visual aids to explain how the English-speaking U. S. was destined to conquer space. And with his charts and graphs, he was also defining what I perceived to be a future full of hope, adventure, success, and optimism. According to von Braun and practically every one else who showed up on the black and white TV which had recently moved into the living room of our apartment in Waterville, Maine, everything was possible for a specific and select group—those who lived in the good old U. S. of A. and spoke English. Proud, supremely confident, their eyes and goals set on a distant star, the members of this group faced a bright and limitless future.

How different their outlook was from that of the Francos who surrounded me. They rejected everything modern, avoided anything new at all costs, and refused (or were terrified) to raise their eyes, even if it were just to glance quickly at the horizon. Their main goal seemed to be to perpetuate a past that was comfortable to them and which promised them salvation at the end of their days.

At the age of 10, while watching Werner von Braun and his rockets, I realized that what I wanted was the future and adventure, rather than the past and salvation. And judging from everything I has seen and heard in my ten short years of life, the future and adventure spoke only English.

I'm telling you all this because it helps provide an answer for the first question many people ask when they learn that I write in French, even though I live in the biggest and most populous English-speaking

La certitude croissante que la Franco-Américanie ne pouvait m'offrir absolument rien dans la vie atteignit son apogée en 1955, quand j'avais dix ans. C'était, si je ne me trompe, au beau milieu du programme "Disneyland" que je regardais à la télé.

Werner von Braun, savant allemand qui avait préféré l'argent américain à la dictature du prolétariat de l'U.R.S.S. après la Deuxième Guerre Mondiale, était en train de m'expliquer, avec l'aide de tableaux, schémas, et dessins animés, comment les Etats-Unis anglophones allaient conquérir l'espace. Et avec les dessins et les tableaux, c'était un avenir plein d'espoir, d'aventure, de succès, et d'optimisme qui se déroulait devant moi. Selon von Braun et plusieurs autres comme lui qui habitaient la télé dans le salon de notre appartement à Waterville, Maine à l'époque, tout était possible à un certain groupe d'élus—les gens qui vivaient aux Etats et qui parlaient anglais. Fiers, pleins de confiance, les yeux fixés sur une étoile lointaine, les membres de ce groupe contemplaient un avenir sans limites.

Quel contraste, pensais-je, aux Francos qui rejetaient tout ce qui était moderne, avaient peur du nouveau, et évitaient, à tout prix, les changements. Pessimistes, résignés à leur sort de colonisés, refusant (ou étant terrifiés) de lever les yeux même pour jeter un petit coup d'oeil à l'horizon, ils s'efforçaient de perpétuer un passé qui leur était confortable et qui leur assurait le salut.

A dix ans, en regardant Werner von Braun et ses fusées, je me rendis compte que c'était l'avenir et l'aventure plutôt que le passé et le salut, qui m'intéressaient. Selon tout ce que j'avais vu et entendu pendant mes dix courtes années de vie, l'avenir se faisait en anglais exclusivement.

Je vous raconte tout ceci parce que ça aide à répondre à la grande question qu'on me pose quand on apprend que j'écris en français au sein du plus grand pays anglophone du monde, i.e., "Pourquoi?" Ça

country in the world, i.e., "Why?" My pre-adolescent decision also helps provide some historical context, allowing me to talk about what was going on in my head—and in the wacky world of Franco-Americans—about twenty years ago when I started the process of writing which ended up creating the three plays which you'll find on the pages that follow.

The certainty I felt at ten was so strong that it stayed with me for the better part of twenty years. Even today, I don't have to search too far or too hard to find it . . . or even revive it. It accompanied me to Assumption Prep for my high school career. It advised me to major in English during the year I spent at Boston College. In a strange twist, it even told me to choose French as the major for my B.A. and M.A. If I was going to speak French, it whispered to me, then I would speak it like a true Frenchman from France whom the Anglos respected, not like a Franco-American hick whom they constantly put down, assuming they were even aware of his miserable existence.

But at the start of the 70s, the process of anglicization, which was the key to my future, had slowed alarmingly. In spite of my best efforts at assimilation, I was still different—in thought, word, and deed (through my fault, through my fault, etc.)—from the members of the dominant culture. To make matters worse, I felt that my life was constantly off key.

That's when I started to re-examine my Franco identity to see if it might not be more comfortable and livable. This process of ethnic rediscovery was going great guns for a couple of years. I accepted everything Franco without question and without reservation. Being Franco was great and it was fun. It stayed great and fun until the 1974 "Congrès du Comité de Vie Franco-Américaine" in Manchester, New Hampshire.

That's when I realized that fate had a little surprise in store for me.

At the Congrès in Manchester, I was among the dozen or so "young Francos" who attended. At the Congrès in Manchester, I rediscovered the bleak pessimism, the paralyzing fatalism, the obsession with the past, and a whole collection of other Franco ethnic traits that were neither great nor fun. At the Congrès in Manchester, I realized that, as a

me donne aussi l'occasion de parler de ce qui se passait dans mon cerveau et dans la Franco-Américanie il y a une vingtaine d'années, quand j'ai commencé le processus d'écriture qui créa les trois pièces que vous retrouverez sur les pages qui suivent.

La certitude que j'ai ressentie à dix ans était tellement forte qu'elle resta avec moi pour une vingtaine d'années. Même aujourd'hui, je n'ai pas besoin de chercher trop loin ou trop fort pour la retrouver. Elle m'accompagna à l'Assomption pour mes quatre ans d'école secondaire. Elle me conseilla de me spécialiser en "English" pendant l'année que j'ai passée à Boston College. C'était même cette certitude qui m'aida à choisir le français comme spécialisation pour mon B.A. et M.A. Si j'allais parler le français, ma certitude me chuchota à l'oreille, je le parlerais comme un Français de France que les Américains anglophones respectaient, pas comme un rustre Franco-Américain mal instruit qu'ils méprisaient, s'ils se rendaient même compte de son existence.

Mais au début des années 70, la confiance que le processus d'anglicisation auquel je tenais tellement allait réussir commença à s'évaporer. En dépit de tous mes efforts, je restais toujours "différent"—en pensée, parole, et action (par ma faute, par ma faute, etc.)—des membres de la société dominante. Qui pis est, j'avais l'impression que je faussais constamment.

Je commençai, donc, à explorer mon identité franco pour voir si je m'y sentais plus confortable. La redécouverte de mon ethnicité marcha assez bien pour une couple d'années. J'acceptais tout et ne critiquais rien. Etre Franco, c'tait beau, pi c'tait le fun. Ça resté beau pi fun jusqu'au Congrès du Comité de Vie Franco-Américaine à Manchester en 1974.

C'est là que je me suis rendu compte que le sort réservait une p'tite surprise pour moué.

Au Congrès à Manchester, j'étais parmi une dizaine de "jeunes Francos" qui ont assisté à la réunion. Au Congrès à Manchester, j'ai retrouvé le pessimisme noir, le fatalisme paralysant, l'obsession avec le passé, et tout un tas d'autres traits de notre ethnicité qui n'étaient ni beaux, ni le fun. Au Congrès à Manchester, je vis clairement qu'on

group, we were at death's door when I heard an endless series of speeches from people who kept congratulating themselves for preserving and perpetuating "notre belle langue et notre belle culture"—at the very moment when every Franco under the age of forty, except for our little group, was trying to get as far away from anything Franco as possible. At the Congrès in Manchester, I was reminded very clearly why I had tried so hard to assimilate into the dominant culture for so long.

That's when I realized something that scared me to death. I wasn't entirely comfortable or happy either as a Franco or as an American. It simply wasn't possible for me to adapt to an existing identity. My father's generation (and those that preceded his), knew that it was Franco more than it was American. The generations that would follow would clearly be more American than Franco. My generation seemed to be lost somewhere in an identity netherland.

As a result, I felt I had three choices. I could resign myself to being miserable by choosing one of the false identities available—Franco or American. Or, I could alternate between the two in a state of perpetual schizophrenia. Unfortunately, selecting either of these two choices had been responsible for driving most of the generations of Francos that preceded me to drink.

The third choice was to create a newer and more appropriate identity—one that I could perhaps share with others of my generation who were having as much trouble as I was simply trying to "find" themselves. Naturally, that's the choice I made—not out of some heroic impulse or a commitment to the "cause" of saving the French language in New England, but simply because the idea of living an entire lifetime without a clear and comfortable sense of identity scared the hell out of me.

If I were going to create a new Franco-American identity for myself, I wanted to do it on a positive note. Among the Franco traits that remained great and fun even after the debacle of the 1974 Congrès was the impressive talent and creativity that could be found in a surprisingly large cross section of the Franco population. Just go to most Franco gatherings and you'll see exactly what I mean.

In 1974, I felt that this creative spirit had not disappeared from the Franco scene. Instead, it had been imprisoned for years in a series of

était un groupe en train de mourir quand j'entendis toute une série de beaux discours de gens qui se félicitaient d'avoir préservé et perpétué notre belle langue et notre belle culture—au même moment où tous les jeunes Francos, sauf notre petit groupe, faisaient leur possible pour s'assimiler une fois pour tout. Au Congrès à Manchester, je me souvins, encore une fois, pourquoi j'avais tant essayé de m'angliciser et de m'américaniser.

C'est à ce moment-là que j'ai eu peur en crime. Je venais de me rendre compte que je ne me sentais entièrement à l'aise ni comme Franco, ni comme Américain. J'avais perdu la possibilité comfortable de m'adapter à ce qui existait déjà. La génération de mon père (et celles qui l'avaient précédée) savait qu'elle était plutôt franco qu'américaine. Les générations qui suivraient seraient clairement plus américaines que francos. J'avais l'impression que moué pi mes chums, on était perdu dans le milieu en quèque part.

Donc, je n'avais que trois choix. Je pouvais me résigner à être misérable en choississant une fausse identité entre les deux qui se présentaient. Ou je pouvais alterner entre les deux dans une sorte de schizophrénie perpétuelle. Hélas, ces deux choix étaient responsables pour le fait que la plupart des oncles et cousins qui m'avaient précédé s'étaient mis à boire.

Le troisième choix était de me créer une identité nouvelle et réelle—une que je pourrais peut-être partager avec mes contemporains qui avaient autant de difficultés que moué à se "trouver." C'est ainsi que j'ai choisi—pas parce que j'étais courageux ou parce que c'était une sorte de "cause" glorieuse pour sauver le français en Nouvelle-Angleterre, mais plutôt parce que j'avais peur en maudit de passer une vie entière sans identité.

Je voulais commencer la création de "mon" identité avec un élément très positif. Ce que j'avais trouvé extraordinairement beau pi le fun chez les Franco, c'était l'esprit créateur qui se trouvait chez plusieurs membres du groupe. Vous n'avez qu'à assister à une soirée franco pour voir ce que je veux dire.

En 1974, j'avais l'impression que le groupe n'avait pas oublié l'existence de cet esprit. Mais il l'avait emprisonné dans une série de discours

deathly boring and blindly self-congratulatory speeches that were the mainstays of the Congrès du Comité de Vie and all other events sponsored by the Franco elite. The time had come to free this creative spirit, at least in me.

This would have a number of positive results. First, it would help me create a personalized Franco-American identity by rediscovering one of the most positive Franco traits and putting it to use. Then, if others began writing and composing and singing on a regular basis, we could perhaps contemplate the future of the Franco-American group with some optimism. A future isn't maintained, or conserved, or protected. It must be actively created day after day, even if we must face the frightening thought that the results might be impossible to calculate and foresee. This essential process required the liberation of the Franco creative spirit.

Even if we couldn't "save" the traditional Franco-American reality which was then—and still is—alive only because of heroic efforts and advanced life support systems, we might at least ensure that it wouldn't die without leaving us a few last words that could inspire us more than the platitudes which it had taken to mumbling over and over again in its dotage.

The liberation of my creative spirit really got started in 1975. I was able to write a series of skits for the two half-hours per month allotted to Francos on the "Tout en Français" radio program at WFCR, the public radio station at the University of Massachusetts in Amherst. Don Dugas, who was then a U.Mass faculty member, had fought successfully for the air time, token though it seemed. With his encouragement and help—especially in playing the perpetual interviewer, I created such memorable characters as Mathias Barnabé (the poet laureate of East Vassalboro); Philias Berthiaume, Ph.D.; and Super Grenouille, among others.

Don Dugas was also the key to the creation of "Un Jacques Cartier Errant" in the Spring of 1976. Don had moved to the National Materials Development Center for French and Portuguese in Bedford, NH., where he quickly got to work setting up a colloquium that would provide a radically different atmosphere and point of view from the ones we found at the Congrès in 1974.

Part of the colloquium would be an evening of entertainment, highlighting new Franco-American creative efforts. He asked Paul Paré and

ennuyeux qu'on prononçait à longueur de journée au Congrès du Comité de Vie et à d'autres réunions. Il fallait maintenant libérer cet esprit créateur, du moins chez moi.

Ceci pourrait avoir des effets multiples. D'abord, ça m'aiderait à formuler une identité personnelle en retrouvant et utilisant un des meilleurs traits de notre ethnicité. Ensuite, si d'autres se mettaient à écrire et à composer et à chanter, on pourraient enfin être un peu optimiste à propos de l'avenir de la Franco-Américanie. Un avenir ne se "maintient" pas. Il ne se "conserve" pas. Il ne se "protège" pas. Il se crée d'une façon active, et souvent imprévisible, chaque jour. Ce processus exige la libération de l'esprit créateur.

Même si on n'arrivait pas à "sauver" la Franco-Américanie traditionelle qui était, à ce moment-là, et reste toujours sur son lit de mort, on pourrait du moins s'assurer qu'elle ne mourrait pas sans nous laisser quelques dernières paroles qui sauraient inspirer mieux que les platitudes qu'elle s'était mise à répéter sans cesse, gâteuse qu'elle était devenue.

La libération de mon esprit créateur commença pour de bon en 1975. J'écrivis une série de saynètes pour la demi-heure bimensuelle franco-américaine du programme "Tout en Français" au poste de radio WFCR de l'Université du Massachusetts à Amherst. Don Dugas, qui était professeur à UMass à l'époque, avait réussi à avoir ces demi-heures. Avec son aide et son encouragement—surtout en jouant le rôle de mon "Interviewer" perpétuel pour les saynètes—je créai les personnages de Mathias Barnabé (poète officiel villageois de East Vassalboro); Philias Berthiaume, PhD; et Super Grenouille, parmi d'autres.

C'est aussi Don Dugas qui rendit la création de "Un Jacques Cartier Errant" possible au printemps, 1976. Rendu au National Materials Development Center for French and Portuguese à Bedford, NH, Don eut l'idée d'avoir un colloque qui servirait de contrepoint au Congrès de 1974.

Il tenait à avoir une soirée au cours du colloque qui mettrait en vedette le nouvel esprit créateur franco-américain. Il demanda à Paul

me if we could perhaps come up with something to help fill the evening. The result was Paul's one act play—"Les Trois Anges," and my "Un Jacques Cartier Errant." As it was finally constituted, the program included songs from the group Psaltery, made up of Lil Labbé and Don Hinckley, and two of my radio skits in addition to the plays. That was an extraordinary night for me, because it proved that works written and performed by Francos could entertain and even touch an audience—even one that included "real" Frenchmen and Québécois. That realization set my head spinning. To this day, it hasn't stopped.

"Un Jacques Cartier Errant" was a perfect first play for me. It explains why it is so important for Francos of my generation to create a new identity. The play also introduces two themes that dominate my work.

The first is the idea that we have both the right and the obligation to scrutinize the expectations/values/messages, etc., presented to us by our Franco side and our American side before deciding to accept them and perpetuate them. It's the only real way to find an identity of our own—and have any hope of advancing the Franco fact.

The second theme is best expressed by the character of Ti-Jean. "Until we find our own song to sing . . . and a real voice to sing it with," Francos are doomed to fade away into oblivion, simply because they decided to perpetuate everything and create nothing.

Together, these two themes give an overview of the process that I continue to use to create a future and an identity. Occasionally and surprisingly, the process works. Gradually, I am transforming myself into a Marie-Marthe who has gone beyond the character in the play and no longer needs to lip sync to Maurice Chevalier tapes to express her creativity. Instead, I have started using my own voice, while still constantly fighting the need to preface every utterance with an apology.

Paré et à moi d'écrire quelque chose qu'on pourrait présenter. Donc, quand elle eut lieu au début juin, 1976, cette soirée se composa de chansons de Lil Labbé et Don Hinckley (Psaltery), "Les Trois Anges" de Paul Paré, deux de mes saynètes de la radio, et "Un Jacques Cartier Errant." Pour moi, ce fut une soirée extraordinaire qui démontra très clairement qu'il était possible de divertir et toucher une assistance (y avait même des Français de France, pi des Québécois là-dedans) avec des oeuvres franco-américaines, interprétées par des artistes franco-américains. Wow. J'vous dis que j'en avais fait du voyageage psychique en deux ans.

Pour moi, "Un Jacques Cartier Errant" était parfaite comme première pièce. D'abord, elle expliqua pourquoi il était tellement important pour les Francos de ma génération de se créer une nouvelle identité. Elle présenta d'une façon bien plus intéressante et amusante, tout ce que j'essaie de dire dans cette introduction. Ensuite, elle lança deux thèmes qui se retrouvent dans toutes les oeuvres dramatiques que j'ai écrites jusqu'à présent.

Le premier, c'est l'idée qu'on a le droit et le devoir d'examiner de près les demandes/valeurs/messages, etc. de notre "côté" franco ET de notre "côté" américain avant de les perpétuer. C'est la seule façon de se trouver une identité valable, et d'avancer notre côté franco en même temps.

Le deuxième thème c'est, comme le dit le personnage de Ti-Jean dans la pièce, que "jusqu'à temps qu'on peut trouver notre chanson, pi la chanter nous-autres-même," notre groupe sera voué au dépérissement et à l'oubli, simplement parce qu'il aura tout perpétué sans ne jamais rien créer.

Ensemble, ces deux thèmes donnent un aperçu du processus que j'utilise toujours pour me créer un avenir et une identité, et qui réussit quelque fois à réaliser son but. Peu à peu, je deviens une Marie-Marthe qui n'a plus besoin des tapes de Maurice Chevalier pour s'exprimer, mais qui commence, de temps à autre, à utiliser sa propre voix . . . sans sentir le besoin de s'excuser à chaque fois qu'il va pour dire quelque chose.

NOTES ON THE PLAYS

"Un Jacques Cartier Errant" was written in 1976 and presented for the first time in June, 1976 at St. Anselm's College as part of a colloquium sponsored by the National Materials Development Center (NMDC) for French and Portuguese. The Center also published the play in paperback in 1977.

"Chère Maman" was written in 1978 and published by the NMDC in 1979.

"Sans Atout," written in 1980, was first performed at a colloquium sponsored by the Canadian-American Center at the University of Maine at Orono in the Summer of 1981.

The English translations of all three plays were done in the Summer of 1995. Generally, there is a one-to-one correspondence between the original French dialog and its translation. However, my primary goal was to maintain the integrity of the message found within each play, plus create a readable and enjoyable English text. Therefore, I did not hesitate to vary from the original whenever I felt it necessary to achieve this goal.

In preparing the French version of the plays for this publication, I tried to stay as true to the original text as possible. I did my best to resist the temptation of making wholesale changes in works written almost twenty years ago to reflect the wiser and more mature person I think I have become. My "wiser and more mature" side, I kept telling myself, should write something new if it wants to be reflected.

So, besides correcting a few misprints, the only change I made to "Un Jacques Cartier Errant" is in the section where Joséphine talks about Marie-Marthe's lip syncing. The Maurice Chevalier songs are now on tape rather than on records, simply because vinyl has pretty much disappeared in 1995.

In "Chère Maman," I have clarified the meaning of certain lines and changed a couple of Franco-American localisms after a number of Franco readers told me they had no idea what the lines meant. I have

NOTES À PROPOS DES PIÈCES

"Un Jacques Cartier Errant" fut écrite en 1976 et présentée pour la première fois au colloque du National Materials Development Center (NMDC) for French and Portuguese au début juin 1976, au Collège St. Anselm à Manchester, NH. La pièce fut aussi publiée par le Center en 1977.

"Chère Maman" fut écrite en 1978 et publiée par le NMDC en 1979.

"Sans Atout," écrite en 1980, eut sa première à un colloque du Centre d'Etudes Canadiennes à l'Université du Maine à Orono en 1981.

En préparant les pièces pour ce volume, j'ai trouvé que c'était très difficile de ne rien changer dans un texte que j'avais écrit il y a une vingtaine d'années. C'était pénible de faire face à la personne dans sa trentaine que j'étais et que j'ai retrouvée partout dans le texte. J'aurais plutôt voulu que l'oeuvre reflète l'homme plus mûr et plus sage que j'espère être devenu.

J'ai essayé de ne pas succomber à la tentation de faire des tas de changements. Je crois que si je veux vous présenter mon côté "mûr et sage," c'est à moi d'écrire quelque chose de nouveau aujourd'hui.

Donc, à part de corriger quelques fautes d'orthographe, le seul changement que j'ai fait dans "Un Jacques Cartier Errant" se trouve quand Joséphine parle des pantomimes de Marie-Marthe. Maintenant, les chansons de Maurice Chevalier se trouvent sur un "tape," plutôt que sur un "récord" comme elles l'étaient dans le texte original, simplement parce qu'il n'y a presque plus de "récords" en 1995.

Dans "Chère Maman," j'ai changé certaines tournures de phrases que plusieurs lecteurs à qui j'ai parlé avaient de la difficulté à comprendre. J'ai aussi ajouté la mention dans le dialogue que Connie reste

also added a line to indicate that Connie lives across the street from her old maid aunts, which explains why they are able to see Jerry coming to pick her up.

The changes in "Sans Atout" are more numerous and significant. But most of them were made, at least in my mind, after the play's first performance in 1981. This means that they are contemporary with the play and not imposed arbitrarily 20 years later. At that moment, having seen the play performed, I became acutely aware that:

1. Juliette's monologue in Act I was much too long and somewhat repetitive. It has been pared down considerably in this version.

2. Too much of the action was going on . . . and being lost . . . in the kitchen which I had placed in the wings. The kitchen is now part of the stage setting.

3. The role of the television was not clear enough. I have therefore added some suggestions to ensure that the TV becomes a leading character in the play.

I also feel more free to make changes in "Sans Atout" since the play has not been previously published.

ACKNOWLEDGMENTS

Plays don't get written or performed or published without the help of a whole bunch of people. Here's a partial list of my bunch to whom I express my profound thanks.

To three members of the generation that preceded me—Don Dugas, Robert Paris, and Norm Dubé—who faced a much more difficult and bitter struggle, because the institutions and mind-sets they were fighting against were so much more deeply entrenched at the time. Their example and active support before, during, and after their stay at the NMDC were vital to me.

To those who were part of the premieres of "Un Jacques Cartier Errant" in 1976 and "Sans Atout" in 1981—especially Paul Paré for being a creative sounding-board, Julien Olivier for bringing Ti-Jean to life, René Plante for a combination of guts and enthusiasm as both

juste à côté des vieilles filles . . . ce qui aide à expliquer pourquoi celles-ci voient ce qui se passe entre Connie et Jerry.

Les changements dans "Sans Atout" sont plus nombreux et plus sérieux. Mais la plupart ont été faits, du moins dans mon esprit, après la première de la pièce en 1981. Donc, ce sont des changements qui sont contemporains à l'écriture de la pièce. A cette époque, ayant vu la pièce sur la scène, je me suis rendu compte que:

1. Le monologue de Juliette dans le premier acte était trop long et se répétait souvent. Je l'ai donc coupé.

2. Beaucoup trop se passait dans la cuisine que j'avais mis dans les coulisses. La cuisine fait maintenant partie de la mise-en-scène.

3. Le rôle de la télévision n'était pas assez clair. J'ai donc ajouté des suggestions pour être certain que la télé devienne un des personnages principaux de la pièce.

Il faut dire aussi que "Sans Atout" n'avait jamais été publiée et n'existait que comme manuscrit. Je me sentais donc libre de faire plus de changements.

DES GROS MERCIS

Des pièces ne s'écrivent pas et ne se font pas présenter ni publier sans l'aide de toute une gang de monde. Voici une liste partielle de ma gang à qui j'envoie des gros mercis.

A trois membres de la génération qui m'a précédé—Don Dugas, Robert Paris, et Normand Dubé—qui ont connu une lutte bien plus difficile et amère, parce que les institutions et façons de penser auxquelles ils faisaient la guerre étaient, à l'époque, beaucoup plus fortes. Leur exemple et leur encouragement actif avant, pendant, et après qu'ils étaient au NMDC furent essentiels.

A ceux qui ont contribué aux premières d'"Un Jacques Cartier Errant" en 1976 et "Sans Atout" en 1981—surtout Paul Paré pour avoir osé écrire lui étou, Julien Olivier pour son Ti-Jean extraordinaire, René Plante pour son courage et son enthousiasme comme metteur-en-

director and actor, and Ray Pelletier for having put "Sans Atout" on the colloquium's agenda.

To Henri Poirier who produced one of the only (perhaps THE only) copies of the manuscript of "Sans Atout" when I had no idea what I had done with the original or any copies I might have had. Without his diligence in keeping his copy since 1981, the play would never have made it into this volume (or any other volume, for that matter).

To Yvon Labbé and FAROG for a list of stuff too long to include here. Without him and the many FAROGists I dealt with over the years, many of the pages that follow would be blank.

To Michael Alpert of the University of Maine Press for having recognized the importance of the Franco-American fact in Maine, and for finally providing those of us who dare write a better chance of being read.

To Jim Bishop of the Centre Franco-Américain at the University of Maine, who decided in November of 1994 that it was essential to find a way to publish my plays and the works of other Francos. In less than a year, he was able to work out an agreement for a Franco-American book series between the Centre and the University of Maine Press. It's frightening what Francos can do when they set their minds to it.

Finally, to my daughters Michelle and Hillary, who always seem to provide inspiration and support when I need it most.

G.R.C.
Newburyport MA
December 14, 1995

scène et comédien, et Ray Pelletier pour avoir mis "Sans Atout" au programme.

A Henri Poirier pour avoir gardé une des seules (peut-être LA seule)
copies du manuscrit de "Sans Atout" depuis 1981. Sans sa prévoyance,
la pièce serait sans doute perdue parce que je n'avais aucune idée où
se trouvaient ni mon original, ni mes copies.

A Yvon Labbé et FAROG pour une liste de stuff trop longue pour
mettre icit. Sans lui et eux, beaucoup des pages suivantes seraient
blanches.

A Michael Alpert et les Presses de l'Université du Maine pour avoir
reconnu l'importance du fait franco dans le Maine et pour avoir enfin
donné aux Francos qui osent écrire la possibilité d'être publiés.

A Jim Bishop du Centre Franco-Américain, qui décida, en
novembre de 1994, qu'il fallait trouver une façon de publier mes pièces
et les oeuvres d'autres Francos, et qui réussit, en moins d'un an, à créer
un accord pour toute une série franco-américaine entre le Centre et
les Presses de l'Université du Maine. C'est épeurant ce que les Francos
peuvent faire quand y se mettent quèque chose dans tête.

Enfin, à mes filles Michelle et Hillary qui sont toujours là avec l'inspiration et l'appui qu'il me faut.

G.R.C.
Newburyport MA
14 décembre, 1995

UN JACQUES CARTIER ERRANT

Jacques Cartier Discovers America

Pièce en un acte / A Comedy in One Act

CAST OF CHARACTERS

BARMAN (JOSEPH), *a Franco-American in his early fifties*

JOSÉPHINE, *Joseph's wife, in her early fifties*

TI-JEAN CÔTÉ, *a mill worker, in his mid thirties*

JACQUES CARTIER, *Francophone phantasm*

LÉO, *Joséphine's brother, in his late forties*

SETTING

The play takes place in a bar in a working class neighborhood of one of the major Franco-American centers of New England (e.g. the West End of Manchester, New Hampshire). When the play opens, the BARMAN *is behind the bar washing glasses and generally tidying up.* JOSÉPHINE, *his wife, is sitting at a table stage right. She could be reading the paper or knitting.* TI-JEAN *enters left, crosses to the bar, and sits on a stool. The* BARMAN *greets him like a regular.*

BARMAN: Hey, Côté! How's it going?

TI-JEAN: *(Tired and fed up)* It's not! Dammit, it's hot out there!

BARMAN: *(Giving him a beer)* Here ya go! This oughta help a bit.

TI-JEAN: You'd think they'd give us the day off in weather like this. It was a hundred and thirty in that damn mill today. Four people fainted from the heat.

BARMAN: *(Sermonizing)* You'll earn your bread by the sweat of your brow, my son.

PERSONNAGES

BARMAN (JOSEPH), *un Franco-Américain, dans la cinquantaine*

JOSÉPHINE, *sa femme. Une Franco-Américaine, dans la cinquantaine*

TI-JEAN CÔTÉ, *un travailleur au moulin, dans la trentaine*

JACQUES CARTIER, *fantôme francophone*

LÉO, *frère de Joséphine, dans la quarantaine*

MISE EN SCÈNE

La pièce se passe dans un bar dans le quartier ouvrier (e.g. le "West End" de Manchester, NH) d'un des grands centres franco-américains de la Nouvelle Angleterre. Au lever du rideau, le BARMAN *se trouve derrière le bar. Il est en train d'essuyer des verres.* JOSÉPHINE, *sa femme, est assise à une table à droite. Elle lit le journal ou tricotte.* TI-JEAN *entre de gauche, traverse au bar, et s'asseoit. Le* BARMAN *le salue comme s'il le connaissait depuis longtemps.*

BARMAN: Allô, Côté! Comment ça va?

TI-JEAN: *(Fatigué et "tanné")* Parle-moué-z-en pas. Maudit qui fait chaud!

BARMAN: *(Lui donnant une bière)* Tiens, ça, ça va te faire du bien.

TI-JEAN: Tu penserais qui nous aurait donné la maudite journée off. Y faisait 130 au moulin après-midi. Y n'a quatre qui ont perdu connaissance.

BARMAN: *(Sermonisant)* Tu gagneras ton pain à la sueur de ton front, mon gars.

TI-JEAN: Great, but by the time I get to eat my bread, it's all drenched with sweat and covered with mold.

JOSÉPHINE: Don't complain. At least you're lucky enough to have a job. There's a lot of people who can't seem to find work these days . . . like my poor brother Léo.

BARMAN: *(Aside. To* TI-JEAN*)* Her "poor brother Léo" hasn't been able to find work for the past thirty years.

JOSÉPHINE: *(Who heard the aside)* That's not true. My little brother worked hard all of his life.

BARMAN: Oh, that's right. I forgot. You can really work up a sweat standing in line at the unemployment office week after week to get your check.

JOSÉPHINE: Well, Léo can't take just any old job that comes along. He's an educated man.

BARMAN: Now, that's true. How much time did he spend in college, Joséphine? A week?

JOSÉPHINE: Three months. But he learned a lot.

BARMAN: Yep. They even kicked him out because he was studying too hard. *(To* TI-JEAN*)* He kept trying to get every girl on campus to help him out with his anatomy homework.

JOSÉPHINE: *(Gets up. Angry)* Well, I don't have to sit here and listen to you insult my family. I could say a few things about those brothers of yours, Joe, but I've got better things to do than spend all day spreading lies about other people.

JOSÉPHINE *exits right. Pause. The* BARMAN *and* TI-JEAN *cross down to the center table and sit, just as* JOSÉPHINE *reappears.*

Ti-Jean: Ouais, mais moué, ma sueur tombe sur mon maudit pain pi y moisit avant que j'aie la chance de le manger.

Joséphine: Au moins t'as une job, toué. Regarde mon pauvre p'tit frère, Léo. De c'temps-cit, y a pas de travail pour lui.

Barman: *(A voix basse à* Ti-Jean*)* Ça fait trente ans qui y a pas de travail pour lui.

Joséphine: *(Qui a entendu)* C'est pas vrai, ça. Y a travaillé fort, mon p'tit frère.

Barman: Ah, oui. J'y avais pas pensé. C'est tough de rester en ligne des heures de temps à l'unemployment chaque semaine pour avoir son chèque.

Joséphine: Ben, y peut pas travailler n'importe où lui, Léo. Y est éduqué.

Barman: C'est vrai, ça. Combien de temps qui a passé au collège, bonnefemme? Une semaine?

Joséphine: Trois mois. Mais y a appris à plein.

Barman: Ouais. Ils l'ont même mis à porte parce qui étudiait trop. *(A Ti-Jean)* Y essayait de repasser ses leçons de biologie avec toutes les filles des environs.

Joséphine: *(Se lève. Enragée)* Ah, ben chu pas pour rester icit pour t'entendre insulter ma famille. J'pourrais en dire des affaires à propos de la tienne, toué, bonhomme, mais ch't'une femme charitable.

(Elle sort à droite. Un temps. Le Barman *et* Ti-Jean *descendent à la table au centre et s'asseoient.* Joséphine *revient.)*

JOSÉPHINE: You know, I don't remember seeing your brothers in church these past few Sundays. *(She exits right again.)*

BARMAN: *(Without looking at* JOSÉPHINE*)* That's because they'd rather spend the time with their families.

JOSÉPHINE: *(Entering again)* I suppose that's why they're in some sleazy bar every night?

BARMAN: It keeps them off the streets.

JOSÉPHINE: I really feel sorry for their poor wives.

BARMAN: Don't! They know where to find them if they want them.

JOSÉPHINE: And you have the nerve to bad mouth my little brother who wouldn't even hurt a fly. It's just not fair that he's having such a hard time.

She exits.

BARMAN: *(Aside. To* TI-JEAN. *Showing his fist)* I wouldn't mind making times just a little harder . . .

JOSÉPHINE: *(From offstage)* What did you say?

BARMAN: *(To off)* I said I'd like to spend time helping him find work, for starters.

JOSÉPHINE: *(From off)* He can get along just fine without any help from you.

BARMAN: *(To off)* Yeah. Now, if he could just get along without chasing after every married woman in town, we'd all be better off.

Silence. After a moment, the BARMAN *crosses left and listens. He looks at his watch, comes back to the table and sits.*

JOSÉPHINE: J'te dis que tes frères, là, j'les voué pas à l'église souvent. *(Elle sort de nouveau.)*

BARMAN: *(Sans se tourner)* Y aiment rester avec leurs familles, c'est tout.

JOSÉPHINE: *(Elle revient.)* J'suppose que c'est pour ça qui sont dans les bar rooms à toutes les soirs?

BARMAN: *(Même jeu)* Au moins y courent pas les rues.

JOSÉPHINE: Ça me fait d'la peine pour leurs pauvres femmes.

BARMAN: Ben, y savent où les trouver si elles veulent les voir.

JOSÉPHINE: *(Le laisse presque pas finir)* Pi tu parles de mon p'tit frère qui a jamais fait de mal à personne. Y n'arrache, lui.

Elle sort.

BARMAN: *(A voix basse)* J'aimerais ben y arracher une couple d'affaires, moué.

JOSÉPHINE: *(Qui a entendu. Des coulisses)* Quoi c'est que tu dis?

BARMAN: *(Aux coulisses)* J'ai dit que j'aimerais ben l'aider dans ses affaires, moué.

JOSÉPHINE: *(Des coulisses)* Y peut ben s'en passer de ton aide, toué, vieux snoreau!

BARMAN: *(Aux coulisses)* Asteur, si y pouvait se passer des femmes des voisins, ça irait ben!

Silence. Après un temps, le BARMAN *traverse à gauche. Il écoute. Il regarde sa montre, revient à la table, et s'assoit de nouveau.*

BARMAN: *(To* TI-JEAN. *As if making an announcement)* Ah, the start of the soaps!

TI-JEAN: Is she really into them?

BARMAN: Into them?!? She spends an hour and a half telling me about them every night. I guess that there's a really important episode on today, because Elizabeth, who just married Paul, has a little boy from a first marriage. And when he was born, they noticed that the poor kid wasn't quite right . . . if you catch my drift. *(The rest of the conversation can be very muted as* JACQUES CARTIER *enters left.)* At three months, he was already a professor of sixteenth century French literature. Well, right away, Elizabeth put him in a college somewhere and tried to forget the whole mess. But now she's afraid that if she has another kid with Paul, they'll run into the same problem.

TI-JEAN: Man, that's depressing!

BARMAN: No kidding. But Elizabeth has a secret that . . .

During the dialogue above, JACQUES CARTIER *enters left. The* BARMAN *and* TI-JEAN *do not notice him and continue their conversation. He looks around and appears to be in ecstasy.*

CARTIER: Ah! What boundless wonder, gratitude, and joy to find myself in this beautiful country that I once discovered and explored . . . this savage land where I, with these very hands, sewed the seeds of a new French civilization. And now, Milord, you have allowed me to see for myself the hardy and bountiful plants that have sprung up from those tiny seeds. Thanks to this kindest of gifts, I, your unworthiest of servants, can finally walk among my own people. I can once again feel this sacred soil under my feet . . . this soil which, for centuries, has been nourished with the blood of our martyrs, the sweat of our peasants' honest toil, and the tears of the loving mothers who gave us birth. Oh, Lord! My cup overflows with happiness! *(He gets down on one knee.)* Please, let me die in this moment of extimate ultasy . . . *(He hesitates.*

BARMAN: *(A* Ti-Jean*)* Tiens! La v'là pris avec ses histoires.

Ti-Jean: Ses histoires?

BARMAN: Ouais, tu sais. A TV toutes les après-midi. A me conte ça chaque soir. Ça d'l'air que c'est ben important aujourd'hui, parce qu'Elizabeth, qui est mariée à Paul, a déjà eu un p'tit garçon de son premier mariage. Pi quand y est venu au monde, y ont trouvé que le pauvre petit, y était pas ben, si tu sais c'que j'veux dire. *(Le reste de la conversation peut se passer à voix basse pendant que* Jacques Cartier *entre de gauche.)* A trois mois, y était déjà un professeur de français. Ben, Elizabeth l'a mis tout de suite dans un collège en quèque part pi a essayé d'oublier ça. Mais asteur, a l'a peur que si a l'a un autre bébé avec Paul, y va avoir le même défaut.

Ti-Jean: Ça, c'est décourageant.

BARMAN: Là, tu l'as dit. Mais Elizabeth, elle, a un secret . . .

Pendant ce dialogue, Jacques Cartier *entre de gauche. Il regarde autour de lui et doit paraître au comble du bonheur. Mais il reste invisible au* Barman *et à* Ti-Jean *qui continuent leur conversation à voix basse.*

CARTIER: Ah! Quelle joie, quelle allégresse, quel bonheur de me trouver dans ce beau pays que j'ai découvert, que j'ai exploré . . . ce pays sauvage où j'ai moi-même semer les graines d'une nouvelle civilisation française. Et maintenant, Dieu, vous m'avez permis de retourner voir les plantes hardies, vigoureuses, et fructueuses que sont devenues ces graines minuscules. Vous m'avez octroyé le don de revenir parmi les miens, de marcher sur ce sol sacré que nos martyrs ont aspergé de leur sang . . . les habitants, de leurs sueurs . . . et les femmes, de leurs larmes. Ah! c'est trop, Seigneur! *(Il tombe à genoux.)* Laissez-moi mourir dans ce moment d'extrême suprase . . . *(Il hésite. Se reprend)* Dans ce moment d'extrase surpême . . . *(Même jeu)* Dans ce moment de grande joie. *(Pause)* Quelle belle fin cela aurait fait. *(Il revient à soi. Se lève)* Dommage

Tries again) In this moment of estisum ultimy . . . *(He hesitates.)* In this moment of great joy! *(Pause. In admiration of his own words)* Aaaah, what a way to go! *(He gets up.)* Pity I'm already dead. *(He notices* TI-JEAN *and the* BARMAN.*)* Ah, what do I espy, but two valiant colonists. I wonder? Do I dare? *(He makes up his mind.)* Of course! What better way to fully slake my thirst for knowledge about this new and glorious French nation. *(Crosses to the bar)* My good man, a bottle of your finest wine, if you will!

BARMAN: *(Without looking. He still doesn't see* CARTIER.*)* Sorry, mac. This is a tavern. We don't serve wine. Only beer.

During the next few lines, TI-JEAN *and* BARMAN *finally notice* CARTIER. *They should be surprised, but not excessively.*

CARTIER: Hmmm, a rather crude drink for one accustomed to the nectar of the gods. You're sure you don't have any wine?

BARMAN: I'm afraid . . . Hmm, wait a minute. *(He crosses right. To offstage)* Joséphine!?!

JOSÉPHINE: *(From off)* What do you want? Elizabeth is getting ready to tell Paul about her baby.

BARMAN: Do you have any of that wine of yours left?

JOSÉPHINE: I think so.

BARMAN: Good, bring it on down. We've got a special request from a customer. *(He goes behind the bar.)*

JOSÉPHINE: *(From off)* Hold on a minute! *(She enters right with a bottle of Mogen David 20/20 or other highly sweetened wine.)* Who in the world would want . . . *(She notices* CARTIER. *Whispers to the* BARMAN*)* Holy Mother of God!! Who's THAT?!?

que je suis déjà mort. *(Il aperçoit* Ti-Jean *et le* Barman.) Mais voici deux valeureux colons. Puis-je? Osai-je? Devrais-je? *(Il se décide.)* Oui! Quelle meilleure façon d'apprendre l'état actuel de cette glorieuse et nouvelle civilisation française. *(Se dirige vers le bar)* Monsieur, une bouteille de votre meilleur vin, s'il vous plaît!

BARMAN: *(Sans regarder. Il ne voit pas* Cartier.) Ça me fait ben d'la peine, Monsieur, mais on n'a pas de vin. C't'une taverne icit. On a ainque d'la bière.

Pendant les lignes suivantes, Ti-Jean *et le* Barman *devraient se tourner et apercevoir* Cartier. *Ils devraient être surpris, mais pas excessivement.*

CARTIER: De la cervoise? Boisson un peu rude pour quelqu'un accoutumé aux mets célestes. Vous êtes certain que vous n'avez pas de vin?

BARMAN: Ah, oui, Mons . . . Oh, attendez. *(Il va à la porte à droite. Aux coulisses)* Joséphine!?!

JOSÉPHINE: *(Des coulisses)* Quoi c'est que tu veux? J't'après regarder mes histoires!

BARMAN: As-tu encore de ce vin-là que tu boué?

JOSÉPHINE: J'pense que oui.

BARMAN: Bon, ben descends-le. Y un Monsieur icit qui en veut. *(Il se met derrière le bar.)*

JOSÉPHINE: *(Des coulisses)* Attends une minute! *(Elle entre de droite avec une bouteille de Mogen David 20/20 ou un autre vin très sucré.)* Quel sorte de mautadit . . . *(Elle aperçoit* Cartier. *Au* Barman *à voix basse)* Torvis!! Qui c'est que c'est ça!?!

BARMAN: *(Shrugs his shoulders. Gives* CARTIER *a glass of wine)* There you go! Let me know what you think. My wife won't drink anything else.

CARTIER: Ah, I cannot thank you enough, my good man. *(He raises his glass.)* Madam . . . Sirs . . . to his majesty, the king!!! *(He drinks the wine in one gulp. When the taste finally registers, he grimaces noticeably.)*

BARMAN: Not too bad, eh, for wine?

CARTIER: The taste is certainly . . . euh . . . unique.

BARMAN: Another glass?

CARTIER: *(Very quickly)* Ah, no . . . euh . . . no, thank you. That's done very nicely for the moment. But, you sirs . . . and you, dear madam . . . you must doubtless wonder who I am.

BARMAN: Well, I did think of asking.

JOSÉPHINE: It's really none of our business, but . . .

CARTIER: Fear not, humble settlers. I am ready to answer all of your questions . . . whether they be expressed or implied. First of all, let me introduce myself. I am the explorer who first discovered this wonderful land!

BARMAN: You're Christopher Columbus?

During the next few lines, JACQUES CARTIER *will try to help* JOSÉPHINE *and the* BARMAN *guess his identity. He can't believe that these "humble settlers" don't recognize him.*

CARTIER: Euh, no. *(He thinks a bit.)* It is I who transplanted the virile and valiant French race onto this foreign soil.

BARMAN: *(He thinks he knows.)* The Marquis de Lafayette!

BARMAN: *(Hausse les épaules. Donne un verre de vin à* CARTIER*)* Bon, Monsieur. Vous m'en direz des nouvelles. Ma femme, elle, c'est ainque ça qu'a boué.

CARTIER: Ah, je vous remercie infiniment, Monsieur. *(Il lève son verre.)* Madame, Messieurs, à sa Majesté, le Roi! *(Il boit le vin tout d'un trait. Il grimace perceptiblement.)*

BARMAN: Pas pire, hein, pour du vin?

CARTIER: Il faut admettre que le goût est . . . euh . . . inoubliable.

BARMAN: Un autre p'tit verre?

CARTIER: *(Très rapidement)* Ah, non . . . euh . . . non, merci. Ça suffit vraiment pour le moment. Mais vous, Messieurs . . . et vous, ma chère dame . . . vous vous demandez sans doute qui je suis.

BARMAN: C'est vrai que la question nous est venue à l'idée.

JOSÉPHINE: C'est pas vraiment de nos affaires, mais . . .

CARTIER: N'ayez pas peur, chers colons. Je suis prêt à répondre à toutes vos questions, qu'elles soient exprimées ou sous-entendues. D'abord, je suis l'explorateur qui a découvert ce pays!

BARMAN: Vous êtes Christophe Colomb?

Au cours du dialogue suivant, JACQUES CARTIER *essaie d'aider à* JOSÉPHINE *et au* BARMAN *à deviner son identité. Il ne peut pas croire que ces "colons" ne le reconnaissent pas.*

CARTIER: Euh, non. *(Il réfléchit un peu.)* C'est moi qui a transplanté la race hardie et vigoureuse de la France sur ce sol étranger.

BARMAN: *(Il pense qu'il sait.)* Le Marquis de Lafayette!

CARTIER: *(Becoming annoyed)* Thanks to me, the fragile flower of French civilization was able to take root and flourish in this hostile land.

JOSÉPHINE: St. Francis Xavier?

CARTIER: *(Gives up)* And it is I, JACQUES CARTIER, who has received a boon from God Himself . . . a boon that has allowed me to return to Earth to see what has happened to my New France!

BARMAN: Ah, so you're Jacques Cartier. Joséphine, THAT'S Jacques Cartier!

JOSÉPHINE *(With growing excitement)* Jacques Cartier? Jacques Cartier? Jacques Cartier right here in my house? Oh, wait 'til Evelyn hears about this! *(She exits right.)*

BARMAN: Sorry, Mister Cartier, but you've got to understand that Evelyn always has the mayor or the governor or some other important character at her house. My wife's been waiting for twenty years to tell her that someone important showed up here.

CARTIER: Well . . . er . . . certainly. But I would have spoken with her further . . . to determine the status and role of women here in New France.

BARMAN: Don't worry. She'll be back! But I'm afraid I may have some bad news for you, Mister Cartier.

CARTIER: Please, have no fear! Speak your mind freely! I am here to listen and learn.

BARMAN: Well, it's simple really. You're not in New France, here.

CARTIER: I beg your pardon?

BARMAN: You're not in New France.

CARTIER: *(Un peu irrité)* C'est moi qui a apporté ici, dans ce terrain hostile, la fleur fragile de la civilisation française.

JOSÉPHINE: St. François Xavier?

CARTIER: *(Abandonnant le jeu)* Et c'est à moi, JACQUES CARTIER, que le Bon Dieu a octroyé le don de revenir sur terre pour voir ce qui est arrivé à ma Nouvelle-France!

BARMAN: Ah, comme ça, c'est vous, Jacques Cartier. Bonnefemme, c'est Jacques Cartier, ça!

JOSÉPHINE *(De plus en plus enthousiasmé)* Jacques Cartier? Jacques Cartier? Jacques Cartier icit? Oh, attends que j'dise ça à Evelyn! *(Elle sort à droite.)*

BARMAN: Faut que vous l'excusez, Monsieur Cartier. Evelyn, elle, a toujours, le maire, ou le gouverneur, ou quèqu'un d'important comme ça chez eux. Ça fait vingt ans que ma femme attend pour y annoncer qu'on a quèqu'un de fameux icit.

CARTIER: Euh, oui, évidemment. Mais j'aurais voulu lui parler d'avantage . . . pour voir comment les femmes s'arrangent ici en Nouvelle-France.

BARMAN: Occupez-vous pas. A va revenir! Mais j'ai ben peur que j'ai des p'tites nouvelles pour vous, M. Cartier.

CARTIER: Mais n'ayez pas peur. Allez-y. Je suis ici pour vous écouter.

BARMAN: Ben, c'est pas mal simple. Vous êtes pas en Nouvelle-France, icit.

CARTIER: Pardon?

BARMAN: Vous êtes pas en Nouvelle France.

CARTIER: *(Who doesn't believe him)* If I'm not in New France, my good man, perhaps you would have the kindness to tell me exactly where I am . . . if such information is yours to give.

BARMAN: Smack dab in the middle of New England.

CARTIER: New ENGLAND?

BARMAN: Afraid so.

CARTIER: New ENGLAND?!? But that's terrible! Awful! Abominable! What am I to do!?! I have been traitorously handed over to mine enemies. New ENGLAND! Oh, I should have known better than trust the heavenly host!

BARMAN: I'm sorry, Mister Cartier.

CARTIER: The fault lies not with you, my good man. I really should have expected it with all the problems we've had to deal with up there.

BARMAN: Up there?

CARTIER: *(Points skyward with his finger)* Yes. You know. Up there.

BARMAN: *(Understands)* Oh, up THERE. *(Pause)* I always thought you weren't supposed to have any problems, up THERE.

CARTIER: Ah, my good man, if only you knew! First of all, the angels, archangels, and principalities are on strike . . . and the demands they are making are both excessive and ludicrous. Then, the guardian angels are refusing to do any guarding at all unless they can choose the people they're assigned to. But that, sir, is minor compared to this damned cherubs' lib movement. It's gotten so we have to do everything ourselves. Washing, ironing, cooking, heavenwork . . . they refuse to lift so much as a finger to help us. And now, to make matters even worse, they set me down right in the middle of New ENGLAND. *(Pause)* Could I possibly have another glass of that wine?

CARTIER: *(Qui a beaucoup de difficulté à le croire)* Mais si je ne suis pas en Nouvelle-France, Monsieur, j'aimerais bien savoir au juste òu je suis.

BARMAN: Au beau milieu de la Nouvelle-Angleterre.

CARTIER: La Nouvelle-ANGLETERRE?

BARMAN: Oui.

CARTIER: La Nouvelle-ANGLETERRE?!? Ah, mais c'est affreux! Absolument affreux! Que vais-je faire?!? Me voilà délivré entre les mains de mes ennemis. La Nouvelle-ANGLETERRE! Ah, les anges, je vous en veux!!!

BARMAN: Ça me fait ben d'la peine, M. Cartier.

CARTIER: Vous n'êtes pas le responsable, Monsieur. Vraiment, j'aurais du m'en attendre avec toutes les difficultés qu'il y a actuellement là-haut.

BARMAN: Là-haut?

CARTIER: *(Indiquant du doigt)* Oui. Vous savez. Là-haut.

BARMAN: *(Qui comprend)* Ah, oui, là-haut. *(Un temps)* J'savais pas qui y en avait, des difficultés, là-haut.

CARTIER: Ah, oui, je vous assure, Monsieur. D'abord, les anges, les archanges, et les principautés sont en grève et ils font des demandes absolument impossibles. Ensuite, avec ce mouvment de libération des chérubins, il faut tout faire soi-même. Lavage, repassage, ménage . . . elles refusent de faire quoi que ce soit. C'est même rendu à un point où plusieurs d'elles refusent de porter de soutiens-ailes. Avez-vous déjà vu ça, une cherubin sans soutiens-ailes? Kaflip, kaflop, kaflip, kaflop. C'est dégoûtant, Monsieur, absolument dégoûtant. Et maintenant, avec tout ça, ils me conduisent en Nouvelle-ANGLETERRE. *(Un temps)* Monsieur, si je pouvais avoir encore un verre de ce vin?

BARMAN: Of course. *(He hurries to pour* CARTIER *a glass.* CARTIER *drinks it in one gulp and grimaces at the taste.)* But the news isn't all bad, Mister Cartier.

CARTIER: What do you mean?

BARMAN: Well, for example, everybody you've met so far today—my wife, myself, and Ti-Jean over there—we all speak French.

CARTIER: You do?

BARMAN: Oui, Monsieur! And so do quite a few others.

CARTIER: *(His face brightens.)* Then, it must be that France conquered this territory in my absence, and that now, this entire savage continent is under the benevolent protection of his majesty, the king of France!

BARMAN: I'm afraid not.

CARTIER: No?

BARMAN: No.

TI-JEAN: *(Gets up and crosses to the bar)* Unfortunately, Mister Cartier, you might even say that the exact opposite happened.

CARTIER: But surely, you can't mean that . . .

BARMAN: Afraid so.

CARTIER: How long ago?

TI-JEAN: Over two hundred years.

CARTIER: *(Stunned by the news. Indicates his empty glass)* My good man, if I could impose once again. *(The* BARMAN *fills his glass. He drinks it in one*

BARMAN: Ah oui, certainement, Monsieur. *(Se dépêche pour lui donner un verre de vin)*

CARTIER: *(Il boit le vin d'un trait. Grimace. Pause. Tout à coup, son visage s'éclaircit)* Mais attendez! Vous dites que je suis en Nouvelle-Angleterre, Monsieur?

BARMAN: Oui, c'est correcte, ça.

CARTIER: Et vous et votre femme et ce monsieur-là *(il indique* TI-JEAN*)*, vous parlez tous notre belle langue?

BARMAN: Ça ben l'air à ça.

CARTIER: Il se doit donc que la France ait conquis ce pays-ci et que maintenant, tout ce grand continent sauvage soit sous la protection de sa Majesté, le Roi de France!

BARMAN: Non.

CARTIER: Non?

BARMAN: Non.

TI-JEAN: *(Se lève et va au bar)* En effet, M. Cartier, si vous me permettez, on pourrait même dire que c'est le contraire qui est arrivé.

CARTIER: Mais vous ne voulez certainement pas dire que . . .

BARMAN: Oui, exactement.

CARTIER: Depuis?

TI-JEAN: Plus que deux cents ans.

CARTIER: *(Assommé par les nouvelles. Indiquant le verre vide)* Monsieur, s'il vous plâit. *(Le* BARMAN *lui donne encore du vin qu'il boit d'un trait. Grimace)*

gulp. He grimaces at the taste. Pause. He sighs.) And I had such high hopes . . . hopes of seeing a thriving and expanding French colony. *(Pause)* So, you've been living under the terrible yoke of English oppression for over two hundred years?!?

BARMAN: Well, not really. We're Americans.

CARTIER: Americans? Americans? What in heaven's name are Americans?

TI-JEAN: Listen, Mister Cartier. It would probably take too long to give you all the details. But let's say that a long time ago, there was a war. And after the war, a bunch of people signed a piece of paper and Zap! . . . before they knew it, our ancestors became English citizens. Then later, here in New England, there was another war. Another bunch of people signed another piece of paper, and Zap! . . . before we knew it, we became Americans.

CARTIER: And these Americans, do they speak French or English?

BARMAN: English.

CARTIER: *(He shudders. Indicates that he wants another glass of wine, which he drinks in one gulp. He grimaces at the taste.)* I was afraid of that. But you said that you all speak French here.

TI-JEAN: Well, the French who were already here, or those who came here afterwards are called Franco-Americans. Some of them, like us, still speak French.

BARMAN: And that's the type of creature you see before you today!

CARTIER: *(Gets up suddenly. Takes out his sword)* Just a moment, my noble settlers. If there is still a race of francophone peoples here, all is not lost. Come! Take up your swords and follow me! Together, we will free this

Moi qui avait tant d'espoir de voir une colonie française florissante. *(Pause)* Vous vivez donc, depuis deux cents ans, sous le joug horrible de la domination anglaise?

BARMAN: Ben pas exactement. On est Américain.

CARTIER: Américain? Américain? Qu'est-ce que cela veut dire?

TI-JEAN: Écoutez, M. Cartier. Ça s'rait un peu long de toute vous expliquer ça. Mais disons qui a eu une guerre, eh? Pi après la guerre, on a signé un morceau de papier, pi bang! nos ancêtres, y sont devenus citoyens anglais. Après ça, icit en Nouvelle Angleterre, y a eu une autre guerre. On a signé un autre morceau de papier, pi bang! on est devenu Américain.

CARTIER: Et ces Américains, est-ce qu'ils parlent le français ou l'anglais?

BARMAN: L'anglais.

CARTIER: *(Il gémit. Indique qu'il veut un autre verre de vin. Il le boit d'un trait. Grimace)* Je m'en doutais. Mais, vous, vous parlez tous le français.

TI-JEAN: Ben les Français qui étaient icit ou ben qui sont venus icit après, on les appelle des Franco-Américains. Y en a qui parlent encore le français.

BARMAN: C'est c't'a sorte d'animal que vous voyez en avant de vous aujourd'hui!

CARTIER: *(Se lève tout à coup. Sort son épée)* Mais s'il y a encore des francophones ici, tout n'est pas perdu. Allons! Aux armes! Prenez vos épées et suivez moi! Nous allons libérer ce pays. Nous allons redonner au

country! Fighting side by side, we will give back to the king, the land that is rightfully his. *(He rushes out stage left. Pause. He comes back when he notices that no one is following him.)* What's wrong? Don't you long for the return of French rule?

BARMAN: Well, it's nothing personal, Mister Cartier . . .

TI-JEAN: Listen, Mister Cartier. I've read a little bit about my family's history. The first Côté was a trapper and woodsman under French rule. He worked night and day, and struggled like hell just to get by. My great grandfather was a farmer when the English were in charge. He worked night and day, too, and struggled like hell just to get by. My grandfather came down here to work in the mills for the Americans. He worked night and day, and struggled like hell just to get by. I work in the mills too. But I don't earn enough there, so I have to have a night job. Want to know how I'm doing? Like every one of my ancestors, I'm struggling like hell just to get by. If you think that the return of French rule is going to stop three hundred and fifty years of struggling like hell, I'm afraid you've got a big . . . and unpleasant surprise in store for you.

CARTIER: *(Points his sword at TI-JEAN)* Those are the words of a traitor, sir. Words that I will ignore for the moment, given the critical nature of your unfortunate situation. *(With a little too much sarcasm)* But, if you show so little respect for our king, and if you refuse to act for the cause of justice, truth, and honor which is . . . and has always been . . . the cause of France, why do you still deign to speak our beautiful language?

BARMAN: It's probably because we didn't have a choice.

TI-JEAN: And that won't last too much longer either.

CARTIER: What do you mean?

TI-JEAN: French is disappearing . . . and fast.

Roi ce qui lui appartient! *(Il se précipite vers la porte à gauche et sort. Pause. Il revient quand il s'aperçoit que personne ne le suit.)* Mais, qu'est-ce qu'il y a? Ne souhaitez-vous pas le retour du régime français?

BARMAN: Ben, on veut pas vous faire d'la peine, M. Cartier...

TI-JEAN: Écoutez, là, M. Cartier. J'ai lu un peu l'histoire de ma famille. Le premier Côté, y était coureur de bois sous le régime français. Y travaillait nuit et jour, pi y crevait. Mon arrière grand-père était un habitant sous le régime anglais. Lui étou, y travaillait nuit et jour, pi y crevait. Mon grand-père est venu icit travailler au moulin sous le régime américain. Y travallait nuit et jour, pi y crevait. Moué, j'travaille au moulin, étou. Ça me donne pas assez cher, ça fait que j'ai une autre job le soir. Pi savez-vous quoi c'est que je fais, moué? J'crève! Si vous vous imaginez que le retour du régime français va arrêter trois cent cinquante ans de crevage, j'ai peur que vous vous trompez ben mal.

CARTIER: *(Il menace* TI-JEAN *avec son épée.)* Ça, ce sont de paroles de trâitre, Monsieur. Paroles que je vais laisser passer sous silence pour le moment, étant donné l'aspect critique de la situation dans laquelle vous vous trouvez. *(Avec une ironie un peu trop appuyée)* Mais si vous méprisez tellement notre souverain, le Roi, ... et si vous refusez d'agir pour la cause de la justice, de la vérité, et de l'honneur qui est et qui a toujours été la cause de la France ... pourquoi parlez-vous toujours notre belle langue?

BARMAN: C'est facile. On avait pas le choix.

TI-JEAN: Pi ça durera plus ben longtemps non plus.

CARTIER: Que voulez-vous dire?

TI-JEAN: Le français disparaît.

CARTIER: But how? . . . Why?

BARMAN: That's easy. The younger generations had a choice and they chose English.

CARTIER: But that's horrible. It's heresy! It's sacrilege! It's unforgivable!

TI-JEAN: You think they should have chosen French?

CARTIER: Well of course they should have chosen . . .

TI-JEAN: *(Interrupting)* Why?

CARTIER: Really, gentlemen, as the language of the richest and most powerful country in the world, French is absolutely essential. It's spoken everywhere. If your "younger generations" want to succeed in the world, they must know how to speak French.

BARMAN: I'm afraid a couple of things have changed over the years, Mister Cartier.

CARTIER: What do you mean?

TI-JEAN: Well, for one thing, France isn't the richest and most powerful country in the world any more.

CARTIER: That, sir, is simply not possible!

BARMAN: Oh, I'm afraid it's true. It's the good old U. S. of A. They even teach it in school.

TI-JEAN: And that means that just about everybody speaks English now.

BARMAN: For young people, French isn't really very useful, Mister Cartier. Especially here.

CARTIER: Mais comment? . . . Pourquoi?

BARMAN: C'est ben facile. Les jeunes aujourd'hui, y ont eu un choix, eux-autres. Pi y ont choisi l'anglais.

CARTIER: Mais c'est terrible, ça. C'est même impardonnable!

TI-JEAN: Ils auraient dû choisir le français?

CARTIER: Mais il va sans dire qu' . . .

TI-JEAN: *(Ne le laisse pas finir)* Pourquoi?

CARTIER: Mais voyons, comme la langue du pays le plus puissant et le plus riche du monde, le français est absolument indispensable. Presque tout le monde le parle. Si vos jeunes veulent faire quoi que ce soit de bien dans le monde, ils devront parler français.

BARMAN: J'ai ben peur que les choses ont pas mal changé depuis votre temps, M. Cartier.

CARTIER: De quelle façon?

TI-JEAN: Ben, pour commencer, la France est pu le pays le plus puissant, pi le plus riche du monde.

CARTIER: Je ne vous crois pas, Monsieur!

BARMAN: Oh, c'est vrai. C'est l'Amérique. On l'enseigne même à l'école.

TI-JEAN: Pi ça, ça veut dire qu'asteur, presque tout le monde parle anglais.

BARMAN: Pour les jeunes, le français est pu vraiment utile, M. Cartier. Surtout icit.

CARTIER: But even if what you say is true . . . which I doubt most strongly . . . you must admit that French is one of the world's most beautiful languages. Young people should learn it for its aesthetic value.

TI-JEAN: And how much extra is that worth per hour on a paycheck, an aesthetic value? The boss here speaks English. If you want to understand what he's saying when he decides to cut your wages, you'd better speak English too.

CARTIER: But if that's the case, they should at least be bilingual, like myself.

TI-JEAN: *(Teasing)* And like MYself, too?

CARTIER: *(A little surprised)* Euh . . . of course.

TI-JEAN: And why in the world would they want to do that?

CARTIER: Come now, gentlemen. Speaking two languages is like being two different people.

BARMAN: Ooooh, think about how great that would be, Côté. If you were two different people, you could hold down four jobs, instead of only two.

TI-JEAN: *(He shakes his head.)* Two different people, huh? Well, Mister Cartier, I've been two different people for thirty-five years now. Want to know what it's gotten me? *(Doesn't let him answer)* Well, I'll tell you. First, my two different people went to parochial schools. There, they spoke mostly to my French person. But when he spoke, they laughed at his accent and his pronunciation and all the English words he used because he didn't have the words to say everything he wanted to say in French.

CARTIER: But you should have had teachers who were Franco-Americans like you to help you along.

CARTIER: Mais même si tout ce que vous me dites est vrai . . . ce que je doute fortement . . . vous ne pouvez pas nier que le français, c'est une des plus belles langues du monde. Que les jeunes l'apprennent pour sa valeur esthétique.

TI-JEAN: Pi combien que ça va donner sur leurs chèques chaque semaine, ça, une valeur esthétique? Le boss, lui, y parle anglais. Si on veut le comprendre quand y nous dit qui va baisser nos gages, on est aussi ben de l'savoir l'anglais, nous-autres étou.

CARTIER: Mais si ça, c'est le cas, ne pourraient-ils pas du moins être bilingues, comme moi, je le suis?

TI-JEAN: *(Se moquant un peu de lui)* Et comme moi, je le suis aussi?

CARTIER: *(Qui n'y avait pas pensé)* Euh . . . oui.

TI-JEAN: Et pi, quoi c'est que ça va donner, ça, être bilingue?

CARTIER: Et bien, si vous connaissez deux langues, vous êtes deux personnes.

BARMAN: Hé, ça, ça serait bon, Côté. Si t'étais deux personnes, tu pourrais avoir quatre jobs, au lieu d'ainque deux.

TI-JEAN: Deux personnes . . . deux personnes. Je va vous dire, là, M. Cartier. Moué, ça fait trente-cinq ans que chu deux personnes. Voulez-vous savoir quoi c'est que ça m'a donné? *(Il ne le laisse pas répondre.)* Ben, j'va vous le dire. Pour commencer, mes deux personnes sont allées à l'école paroissiale. Là, on parlait surtout à mon côté français. Mais en même temps, on riait de son accent, pi on riait de sa prononciation, pi on riait des mots anglais qui usait parce qui savait pas comment dire quoi c'est qui voulait dire en français.

CARTIER: Mais vous auriez dû, sans doute, avoir des maîtres qui étaient Franco-Américains comme vous pour vous aider.

BARMAN: They were the ones who said we couldn't talk right.

CARTIER: I don't understand!

TI-JEAN: Neither did we. So after a while, our two different people decided to go to public schools. There, the teachers spoke to us only in English . . . and they punished us if we spoke any French at all. That's where my English side really took a beating. Everybody said he couldn't talk very well either . . . and they decided that he was probably pretty dumb.

CARTIER: I think I'm starting to understand a bit, my good fellow, but shouldn't you have tried to perfect yourselves in both languages?

TI-JEAN: Exactly what I did. First, I decided to help my French person. I was determined to learn that goddamned language if it killed me.

CARTIER: I must ask you to speak of the most beautiful of tongues in more respectful terms, sir!

TI-JEAN: So I sign up for classes and they put me in French One. This guy named Mister O'Neil who speaks French with a English accent so thick you can cut it with a knife tells me that he knows I speak French with my parents. But my grammar and my pronunciation need soooo much work that it's better for me to start right from the beginning . . . as if I didn't know a damn word of French. Fine! I'll take French One. Just teach me things I can use . . . like how to say clothespin and second base and shortstop and clutch and windshield and bathing suit. Right! Fat chance! Instead they teach me stuff I've known for years: "J'entre dans la salle de classe. Je prends ma place. Le professeur entre. J'ouvre mon livre". . . and every time I see him, I want to shove it up . . . And they still tell me I can't speak right. Of course, I'm dumb enough to believe them. So, I'm always trying to speak THEIR way: "droit", not "dret," "froid," not "fret."

BARMAN: C'était eux-autres qui nous chantaient des bêtises.

CARTIER: Mais je ne comprends pas!

TI-JEAN: Nous-autres, non plus, on comprenait pas. Ça fait qu'après une secousse, on a décidé d'aller à l'école publique. Là, on parlait à mes deux personnes en anglais. Y nous punissaient même si on parlait français. Là, c'était mon côté anglais qui en mangeait une bonne. On y contait les mêmes niaiseries, pi a part de ça, on le trouvait pas mal épais.

CARTIER: Je crois que je comprends un peu la situation, Monsieur, mais il fallait essayer de se perfectionner dans les deux langues.

TI-JEAN: Quoi c'est que vous pensez que j'ai fait? D'abord, j'ai décidé d'aider mon côté français. J'étais têtu. J'allais l'apprendre, c't'a maudite langue-là.

CARTIER: Monsieur, c'est un peu fort, tout de même.

TI-JEAN: Bon, ben, j'va pour prendre des cours, pi on me met en pre-mière année. *(Avec un accent américain épais)* "Je sais que vous parlez déjà le français, mais votre entraînement grammatique et votre prononcia-tion laissent vraiment beaucoup à désirer." Bon, OK, j'les prends, vos maudits cours. Enseignez-moué comment dire clothes pin, pi second base, pi shortstop, pi clutch, pi windshield, pi bathing suit, pi wash cloth. Au lieu, y me montrent comment dire des choses que j'connais deja: "J'entre dans la salle de classe. Je prends ma place. Le professeur entre. J'ouvre mon livre". . . pi j'y fourre ça dans le . . . Pi en même temps, y me disent toujours que j'parle mal. Moué, j'envale tout ça. J'essaie de ben pratiquer mes leçons. Droit, pas dret. Froid, pas fret.

CARTIER: At least you seemed to be making progress.

TI-JEAN: That's what the teacher said. So I went home and tried to talk THEIR way to my folks. My father told me to stop talking like a god-damned grammar book . . . and my mother got down on her knees to ask God not to punish me for acting like I was better than the parents who brought me into this world and sacrificed for years so that I could be better off than them.

BARMAN: Well, it's true, Ti-Jean. That's not OUR French . . . and there's no way you can tell me that it's natural for us to talk like that.

TI-JEAN: (To CARTIER) See? Well, Mister Cartier, I may be stupid. But I'm not quite as stupid as I seem. After a while, I realized that if I spoke the French I learned at home—OUR French—teachers were going to laugh at me. And if I spoke the French I learned in school—THEIR French—my family and friends were going to laugh at me. But if I didn't speak French at all . . . So now, I almost never speak French any more. In fact, the French language can go straight to hell, for all I care! And my kids won't go through the same bunch of crap I did, you can be sure of that. In this country, the boss speaks English. So English is the only language my kids are gonna need . . . and it's the only one they're gonna learn.

JOSÉPHINE and LÉO enter right just in time to hear the last part of TI-JEAN's speech.

JOSÉPHINE: Well, Mister Cartier, I still care about the French language. I'm proud that I can still speak it . . . and I speak it as often as I can. You'll be happy to know that my younger brother Leo, here, feels exactly the same way. He doesn't act like he's better than everyone else like some people I know.

CARTIER: Ah, how wonderful, my dear lady. It does my heart good to hear you speak those words. I was beginning to sorely regret my decision to return to this land.

CARTIER: Mais du moins vous faisiez du progrès.

TI-JEAN: C'est ça que la maîtresse disait. Ça fait que j'va chez nous pi j'essaie de parler comme ça. On me dit de parler comme du monde. On m'accuse de parler en cul de poule, pi de péter plus haut que le trou.

BARMAN: Mais c'est vrai ça, Ti-Jean. C'est pas naturel pour nous-autres de parler comme ça. C'est comme une autre langue.

TI-JEAN: *(A* CARTIER*)* Voyez-vous? Ben moué, là, M. Cartier, tedben que chu épais. Mais chu pas si épais que ça. Après une secousse, j'ai réalisé que si j'parlais le français de chez nous, on allait me chanter des bêtises ... pi si j'parlais le français de l'école, on allait me chanter des bêtises. Mais si je l'parlais pas pantoute, le français ... Ça fait qu'asteur, je l'parle presque pu, le français. J'm'en sacre du français. Pi j'vous assure que mes enfants, y passeront pas par là. L'anglais, c'est la langue des bosses par icit, pi c'est c't'elle-là qui vont apprendre, pi rienque c't'elle-là.

JOSÉPHINE *et* LÉO *entrent de droite à temps pour entendre la dernière section du discours de* TI-JEAN.

JOSÉPHINE: Ben, moué, là, M. Cartier, j'm'en sacre pas du français. Chu fière de l'parler. Pi mon p'tit frère, Léo, icit, c'est la même chose. C'est pas un p'tit fantasse comme les autres.

CARTIER: Ah, excellent, Madame. Ça fait du bien d'entendre de telles paroles. Je pensais la situation sans espoir.

JOSÉPHINE: Thank you. Then I'm sure you'll be pleased to learn that I'm a member of the Friends of the French Language and Culture Ladies Auxiliary. Perhaps you've heard about our group and our work?

CARTIER: Euh . . . I'm dreadfully sorry, but I . . .

JOSÉPHINE: Oh, that's alright. Our goal is to protect and conserve the French language here in New England. Well, as the club's secretary, I'm in charge of finding people to speak at our meetings. And when I told Evelyn . . . oh, that's our club president, Evelyn Paradis. You may know her. Everybody does. She's judge Paradis' wife.

CARTIER: I can't say that I . . .

JOSÉPHINE: Oh, don't worry. You'll get to meet her soon enough. Anyway, when I told Evelyn that you were here, she insisted that I ask you to speak at our next club meeting. It's on Sunday, the twenty-eighth. You'll still be here, I hope?

CARTIER: Really, my dear woman, I don't know if . . .

JOSÉPHINE: Good. Naturally, we can't give you the entire hour. We've already committed time to two of our girls. But I'm sure I can find ten to twelve minutes for you somewhere in between. That should be plenty of time, don't you think?

CARTIER: For what, Madam?

JOSÉPHINE: To talk about your life as an explorer, of course! *(Doesn't let him answer)* Now, before I forget, Evelyn wanted me to make sure that you start off with a couple of jokes, or something light. The girls don't like it when our speakers get too serious, you know.

CARTIER: But my dear lady . . .

JOSÉPHINE: Merci. Ça vous intéresserait tedben de savoir que chu même membre de l'Union des Femmes Françaises. Vous en avez tedben entendu parler?

CARTIER: Euh . . . je regrette, mais . . .

JOSÉPHINE: Oh, ça fait rien. On travaille pour la conservation de la langue française ici en Nouvelle-Angleterre. Pi moué, là, comme secrétaire du groupe, j'suis en charge d'avoir du monde pour parler à nos assemblées. Ben, quand j'ai dit à Evelyn . . . oh, ça c'est notre présidente, Evelyn Paradis. Tedben que vous la connaissez? C'est la femme du juge Paradis.

CARTIER: Je ne crois pas . . .

JOSÉPHINE: Ah, ben c'est pas vraiment important. Mais quand j'ai dit à Evelyn que vous étiez icit, a voulait absolument que j'vous demande pour parler à notre prochaine assemblée. Ça sera dimanche, le 28. Vous serez encore icit?

CARTIER: Vraiment, Madame, je ne sais pas si . . .

JOSÉPHINE: Bon. Nautrellement, on pourra pas vous donner toute l'heure. On a déjà deux de nos membres qui font quèque chose. Mais j'pense qu'on pourra trouver une dizaine de minutes entre les deux. C'est assez de temps, vous pensez?

CARTIER: Pourquoi, Madame?

JOSÉPHINE: Mais pour parler de vos expériences, voyons. *(Sans attendre de réponse)* Oh, ça s'rait bon si vous pouvez mettre un couple de p'tites jokes, de p'tites farces, dans votre discours. On aime pas ça quand c'est trop sérieux, vos savez.

CARTIER: Mais, Madame . . .

JOSÉPHINE: Perfect! Then it's all set! You can speak right after Marie-Marthe does her lip syncing.

CARTIER: Lip syncing?

JOSÉPHINE: Oh, you'll love it. We play Maurice Chevalier tapes and Marie-Marthe makes it look like she's the one who's singing.

CARTIER: *(Completely lost)* Tapes??

JOSÉPHINE: I'll explain it all to you later. And after your speech, you can watch the slides that Hilda took on her trip to Disney World . . . and then we'll all play cards. It'll be the best meeting we've had in years. Just wait 'til I tell Evelyn. Ooooooh, she'll be so excited! *(She crosses to the door right. To herself)* Let's see now, we should have about sixty there for the meeting. Oh no, that's right. We've had at least twenty members die on us this month. So . . . that leaves about . . . *(She exits right.)*

CARTIER: *(Pointing to his empty glass. To the* BARMAN*)* My good man, if you please. *(The* BARMAN *fill the glass.* CARTIER *drinks it in one gulp. He grimaces at the taste.)* Thank God that women don't rule the world.

TI-JEAN: Yep. It would depress the hell out of us to watch them do a better job than us.

CARTIER: Surely, sir, you jest. Women are so flighty and unreliable. You simply cannot entrust any matter of importance to their care.

LÉO: I couldn't agree more.

BARMAN: Ah, the expert speaks! If you don't mind, Mister Cartier, I'll excuse myself for a while. I've heard this all before. In fact, I hear it over and over again night after night after night. Côté, watch the bar for a while, will you? *(*BARMAN *exits right.)*

LÉO: Mister Cartier, I'm proud to say that I'm a member of the Grand

JOSÉPHINE: Comme ça, c'est toute arrangé! Vous allez parler tout de suite après les pantomimes de Marie-Marthe.

CARTIER: Pantomimes?

JOSÉPHINE: Oui. On joue des tapes de Maurice Chevalier pi Marie-Marthe, elle, a fait comme si c'était elle qui chantait.

CARTIER: *(Perdu)* Tapes??

JOSÉPHINE: Ah, j'vous expliquerez toute ça plus tard. Après, vous pourrez watcher les slides qu'Hilda a pris pendant son voyage à Disney World, pi après ça, on pourra jouer aux cartes. Oh, que ça va-ti donc être le fun. Attends qu'Evelyn entende ces nouvelles-là! *(Elle se dirige vers la porte à droite. A elle-même)* Voyons, comme ça, y devrait n'avoir une soixantaine là dimanche. Ah, non, c'est vrai. Y en a une vingtaine qui sont mortes ce mois-cit. Ça fait que s'en reste . . . *(Elle sort à droite.)*

CARTIER: *(Il indique son verre. Au* BARMAN*)* Monsieur, s'il vous plaît. *(Il boit le vin d'un trait. Grimace)* Dieu merci que le monde n'est pas gouverné par les femmes.

TI-JEAN: Ouais. Ça nous blesserait de les voir faire mieux que nous-autres.

CARTIER: Mais vous plaisantez, Monsieur. Elles sont tellement frivoles . . . même dans les affaires les plus sérieuses.

LÉO: Oui, c'est vrai, ça.

BARMAN: Bon, v'là l'expert qui arrive. Vous allez m'excuser, eh, M. Cartier. Moué, j'me fais tanner par lui à toutes les soirs. Côté, prends soin du bar pour une escousse. *(Il sort à droite.)*

LÉO: Moué, M. Cartier, chu membre du Grand Conseil Unificateur

National Franco-American Culturo-Linguistic Council for Ethnic Unification and Facilitation. We call it the MNFACLCEUF for short. And when we get together, it's not like my sister and her women's club. WE know how to get things get done.

CARTIER: Ah, that's wonderful, my good man.

TI-JEAN: Is that so? I went to a GRAND meeting of your GRAND National Council once. Everybody made GRAND speeches that didn't make any sense, and then they started handing out GRAND medals and GRAND awards to people who had done absolutely nothing. Then, they passed GRAND and wonderful resolutions about the preservation and advancement of the glorious French language. Do you know what really came out of those three days of GRAND and intense meetings? A GRAND total of nothing. Is that how you get things done? Because if it is, I think I'd get more done by watching Hilda's Disney World slides and playing cards.

LÉO: Mind your own business, Côté. At least, it's helped bring Franco-Americans together.

TI-JEAN: Yeah. Like Jews and Arabs.

LÉO: That's not true. Everybody gets along at our meetings.

TI-JEAN: *(To* JACQUES CARTIER*)* Know why? Because they never talk to each other during these wonderful three-day meetings. First of all, they listen to speeches all day long. That doesn't leave much time for conversation. Then, at night, everybody gets together in these little groups to drink and sing and tell jokes and stories. They say they do that because we Franco-Americans just naturally like to have fun. Bull! It's really because they're afraid that if they don't drink and sing and tell stories, they won't have any excuse for not talking to each other. So they sing and they laugh and the young don't talk to the old and rich people don't talk to the middle class . . . and nobody talks to the poor because everyone made it very, very clear that they just weren't welcome.

des Franco-Américains. Pi quand on se met ensemble, nous-autres, c'est pas comme ces femmes-là. J'vous dis qu'on en fait des affaires.

CARTIER: Ah, c'est excellent, Monsieur.

TI-JEAN: Ah, oui? J't'allé à une GRANDE réunion du GRAND Conseil moué, une fois. On a prononcé des GRANDS discours qui voulaient rien dire, pi on a donné des GRANDES médailles pi des GRANDS certificats de mérite à du monde qui avait fait des GRANDS riens. Ensuite, on a faite des GRANDES résolutions sur la préservation et l'avancement de la GRANDE langue française. Après trois jours, savez-vous quoi c'est qui en est sorti? Un GRAND zéro! C'est-ti ça, les affaires que vous faites? Parce que si c'est ainque ça vos "affaires," j'pense que j'aimerais mieux aller voir les slides à Hilda pi jouer aux cartes.

LÉO: Mèle-toué de tes affaires, toué, Côté. Au moins, ça unit les Franco-Américains.

TI-JEAN: Oui. Comme les Juifs pi les Arabes.

LÉO: C'pas vrai, ça! Tout le monde s'accorde ensemble à nos meetings.

TI-JEAN: (A JACQUES CARTIER) Savez-vous pourquoi? Parce qu'ils passent le moins de temps possible à se parler. Pour commencer, y a des discours toute la journée. Ça donne pas beaucoup de temps à se parler, ça. Ensuite, le soir, tout le monde se met ensemble dans des p'tits groupes pour chanter des chansons pi raconter des histoires. Y disent que c'est parce qu'on aime ça avoir du fun, les Franco-Américains. Pantoute! C'est parce qu'on a peur que si on chante pas, y va falloir se parler. Ça fait qu'on chante, pi on rit, pi les jeunes parlent pas aux anciens, pi les riches parlent pas à la classe moyenne, pi les pauvres parlent pas pantoute, parce que personne a bâdré des inviter.

LÉO: Now that's going too far, Côté!

TI-JEAN: But after the meetings . . . when everyone's back home, then all hell breaks loose. Everyone starts stabbing everyone else in the back.

LÉO: And if I were you, I keep my mouth shut instead of talking about us like that in front of a stranger. Thanks to you, I don't think he's getting a very good impression of us at all.

TI-JEAN: What difference does it make what kind of impression he gets. In a few years, there won't be any Franco-Americans left. Let him think whatever he wants. So what?

LÉO: And whose goddamn fault will that be?

CARTIER: Gentlemen, please . . .

LÉO: I'll tell you whose fault it'll be. You and every other negative son of a bitch like you who'd rather criticize everything in sight rather than work for the cause.

CARTIER: Gentlemen, gentlemen, please. Perhaps if you could calm yourselves and speak rationally, you could arrive at an understanding on these crucial issues.

TI-JEAN: O.k., o.k, fine. Let's say I had the time, Léo . . .

LÉO: If you're truly committed, you MAKE time!

TI-JEAN: . . . and I wanted to work for your cause, what should I do?

LÉO: That's simple. You should become a member of the Grand National Council.

TI-JEAN: And just how does one go about becoming a member of your Grand National Council?

Léo: Ah, ben là, tu ambitionnes, Côté!

Ti-Jean: Mais après les meetings, quand tout le monde est rendu à la maison . . . là, ça sort!

Léo: Pi tu f'rais mieux de te taire plutôt que de parler de nous-autres comme ça en avant d'un étranger. Quelle sorte d'idée qui va se faire de nous-autres?

Ti-Jean: Quelle différence que ça peut ben faire quelle sorte d'idée qui se fait? Dans une couple d'années, y en aura pu de Franco-Américains. Qui pense c'qui veut. So what?

Léo: Pi ça va être la faute à qui, ça, si y en a pu de Franco-Américains?

Cartier: Messieurs, du calme, du calme.

Léo: J'va t'el dire à qui. A toué pi à toutes les maudits comme toué qui aiment mieux critiquer que de travailler pour la cause.

Cartier: Messieurs, Messieurs. Je crois que si on parlait sans emportement, on pourrait arriver à s'entendre sur cette question importante.

Ti-Jean: O.k., o.k. Disons que j'avais le temps, Léo, . . .

Léo: On trouve le temps!

Ti-Jean: . . . pi j'voulais travailler pour ta cause, quoi c'est que j'devrais faire?

Léo: Ben, ça c'est facile! Tu devrais devenir membre de notre Conseil.

Ti-Jean: Pi comment qu'on devient membre de votre Conseil?

Léo: You have to be nominated by an existing member.

Ti-Jean: Ah, I see.

Léo: Well, most of our members are lawyers and judges and doctors and teachers. We have to be selective . . . make sure that new members will fit right in.

Ti-Jean: Ah, I see. So, someone who works in the mill probably wouldn't not fit right in with that bunch, would he?

Léo: I know what you're trying to imply and I can tell you you're way off base. I've often thought of nominating you for membership myself. But now that you've shown your true colors and the defeatist ideas you have about our language and culture, there's no way in hell I'd nominate you now.

Ti-Jean: Ah, I see.

Léo: No way in hell! *(Pause)* Ah, what's the use. I shouldn't have even tried to have a rational conversation with YOU! *(To Jacques Cartier)* Mister Cartier, I have a major speech to prepare for our next meeting. Perhaps I'll show it to you when I'm done. I'm sure your input would really help. Anyway, I hope we can talk again later and discuss areas of mutual interest without these constant interruptions. *(Léo exits right, just as the Barman enters right and crosses to the bar.)*

Cartier: Euh, very well, Sir.

Barman: Ah, Léo seems to be in his usual fine mood.

Ti-Jean: Your brother-in-law just excommunicated me as a heretic and a blasphemer.

Barman: Congratulations.

Léo: Faut être invité par quèqu'un qui est déjà membre.

Ti-Jean: Ah, j'comprends.

Léo: Ben, les autres membres, c'est toutes des avocats pi des juges pi des docteurs pi des professeurs. On peut pas laisser entrer n'importe qui là-dedans.

Ti-Jean: Ah, j'comprends. Par exemple, un gars qui travaille au moulin, ça ferait pas de laisser entrer ça.

Léo: Je voué où c'est que tu veux en venir avec ça, toué, pi j'peux te dire que c'est pas vrai. J'ai souvent pensé à t'inviter moué-même à devenir membre, mais j'va t'l'dire franchement, là, asteur que j'voué ta façon de penser, y a pu une chance dans le monde que j't'invite.

Ti-Jean: Ah, j'comprends.

Léo: Pu une chance! *(Pause)* Ah, ça sert à rien d'essayer de t'parler, toué. *(A Jacques Cartier)* M. Cartier, j'ai un discours à préparer pour notre prochaine réunion. Tedben que vous pourriez m'en donner des commentaires. Anyway, j'vous reverrai plus tard et nous pourrons parler de la cause SANS INTERRUPTIONS! *(Léo sort à droite au même moment ou le Barman entre de nouveau et se dirige vers le bar.)*

Cartier: Euh, très bien, Monsieur.

Barman: Ben, Léo a d'l'air de bonne humeur, comme de coutume.

Ti-Jean: Ton beau-frère vient juste de m'excommunier.

Barman: Mes félicitations.

CARTIER: But gentlemen, you must admit that he makes some excellent points. It is your duty to act. I fully understand that you've had a few problems with the language, but that is certainly no sound reason for rejecting an entire culture.

TI-JEAN: Which culture?

BARMAN: Oooooh, I'd be careful, if I were you, Mister Cartier. Côté always prepares a little speech after he's been excommunicated . . . and it looks like he's just raring to give it.

CARTIER: Of course, I'm referring to the culture . . .

BARMAN: *(Makes a pained face)* Oooof!

CARTIER: *(Looks at the* BARMAN*)* The culture . . .

BARMAN: *(Makes a pained face)* Yeeesh!

CARTIER: *(Looks at the* BARMAN. *Makes up his mind)* The glorious culture of France!

BARMAN: *(Moans)* Well, that it! We'll be here for days. *(Pretends he's holding a microphone)* Mister Côté, could you say a few words to our listeners about the glorious culture of France here in New England?

TI-JEAN: No.

BARMAN: No?

TI-JEAN: No. I'll tell our honored guest a little story instead.

BARMAN: Phew! That was close. I was afraid that for once, you had nothing to say.

TI-JEAN: You see, Mister Cartier, in seventy-six . . .

CARTIER: Mais Messieurs, il faut admettre qu'il a un peu raison, tout de même. C'est votre devoir de faire quelque chose. Je comprends que vous ayez eu des ennuis avec la langue, mais ce n'est pas une raison pour rejeter toute une culture!

TI-JEAN: Quelle culture?

BARMAN: Attention à ce que vous disez, là, M. Cartier. Après qui se fait excommunier, Côté prépare toujours un sermon . . . pi ça l'air qui est prêt à le donner.

CARTIER: Mais la culture . . .

BARMAN: *(Fait une grimace)*

CARTIER: *(Regarde le* BARMAN *)* La culture . . .

BARMAN: *(Même jeu)*

CARTIER: *(Regarde le* BARMAN. *Se décide enfin)* La culture française!

BARMAN: *(Grand gémissement)* Bon, ça y est. On n'a pour une heure. *(Fait comme s'il tenait un microphone)* Monsieur Côté, pourriez-vous dire un couple de mots à nos chers auditeurs concernant la grande culture française ici dans la Nouvelle-Angleterre?

TI-JEAN: Non.

BARMAN: Non?

TI-JEAN: Non. J'va raconter une p'tite histoire plutôt.

BARMAN: Phew! Fais-moué pas peur comme ça, toué! J'pensais que t'avais rien à dire.

TI-JEAN: En soixante-et-seize, là . . .

CARTIER: Fifteen seventy-six?

TI-JEAN: No, no, no! In nineteen seventy-six. Well, in nineteen seventy-six, our country celebrated its bicentennial. Do you remember when we talked about a war?

CARTIER: The first one or the second one?

TI-JEAN: The second one.

CARTIER: Hmmm . . . let me see . . .

TI-JEAN: War, piece of paper, Zap! We're Americans!

CARTIER: Ah, yes. Now, I remember.

TI-JEAN: Well during that war, the Americans and the French were allies, fighting side by side against England.

CARTIER: Bravo!

BARMAN: I'd wait a bit before celebrating, if I were you. He's not done.

TI-JEAN: My ancestors were already in Cana . . . er . . . in New France that now belonged to England. Which means that my ancestors and those of most of the other Franco-Americans fought for England against the French and the Americans.

CARTIER: *(Shocked. Tries to find an excuse)* But . . . but . . . they must have done so against their will, because those English swine forced them to.

TI-JEAN: No. The Americans even invited our ancestors to join their cause. They refused.

CARTIER: In the name of God, why would they do such a thing?!?

CARTIER: Quinze cent soixante-seize?

TI-JEAN: Non, non, non! En dix-neuf cent soixante-et-seize, voyons. Ben, en dix-neuf cent soixante-et-seize, c'était le bicentennaire de notre pays. Vous vous rappelez quand j'ai parlé d'une guerre?

CARTIER: La première ou la deuxième?

TI-JEAN: La deuxième.

CARTIER: Euh . . . voyons . . .

TI-JEAN: Guerre, papier signé, bang! Américain.

CARTIER: Ah, oui, ça y est.

TI-JEAN: Ben dans c't'a guerre-là, les Américains pi les Français étaient alliés contre l'Angleterre.

CARTIER: Bravo!

BARMAN: Attendez un peu avant de célébrer. Y a pas fini.

TI-JEAN: Mes ancêtres, eux-autres, y étaient déjà rendu au Cana . . . euh . . . en Nouvelle-France que les Anglais avaient pris. Ça fait que mes ancêtres à moué, pi ceux de la plupart des autres Franco-Américains, y se battaient pour l'Angleterre contre les Français et les Américains.

CARTIER: (Assommé. Cherche une excuse) Mais . . . mais . . . ils devaient le faire à contre-coeur, parce que ces barbares d'Anglais les forçaient.

TI-JEAN: Non. Les Américains les ont même invités à se joindre à eux. Y ont refusé.

CARTIER: Mais pourquoi, nom de Dieu?!?

TI-JEAN: Ah, they had their reasons. But that's not the point. For one reason or another, we don't want to admit that our ancestors fought against the Americans during the War of Independence. So Francos go on and on about the huge contribution that France made to the American cause. Well, that's all true. The French sent armies and fleets and a whole bunch of other things to help out the Americans. But it might as well have been the Chinese as far as we're concerned, because our ancestors were out there fighting like hell for the other side.

CARTIER: And to think that my discovery of this country was instrumental in providing a steady supply of troops to the British army. My exploration of this savage land served only to help England expand its oppressive empire. Worst of all, it seems that my call for valiant settlers to colonize this wonderful land was instead heard only by a race of traitors and cowards!

BARMAN: Don't be too hard on them, Mister Cartier. They fought for England because they wanted to keep on being French and Catholic.

CARTIER: What?

BARMAN: While France was helping those who were famous for persecuting Catholics and didn't give a damn about French.

CARTIER: But, this is all so difficult to comprehend. I'm all at sea. *(To the* BARMAN*)* Tell me, my good fellow, which side was blessed and favored by God?

TI-JEAN: Neither one.

BARMAN: Or maybe both.

CARTIER: *(Indicates that he'd like another glass of wine. He drinks it in one gulp. Indicates he'd like still another glass. He drinks it in one gulp.   Pause. He crosses to the door stage left and exits.   Pause.   From off-stage)* AAAAAAAAAAHHHHHHHHHHHH! *(He enters and returns to the bar.)*

Ti-Jean: Ah, y avaient leurs raisons. Mais c'est pas ça qui est important. Pour une raison ou une autre, on veut pas admettre que nos ancêtres, y se sont battus contre les Américains. Ça fait qu'on parle de la grande contribution que les Français ont faite à la cause américaine. Ben, c'est toute vrai, ça. Les Français avaient tout une gang de soldats pi de bateaux de guerre pi toutes sortes d'autres choses icit. Mais tant qu'à nous-autres, ç'aurait pu aussi ben être des chinois . . . parce que nos arrières grand-pères, y étaient sur l'autre côté.

Cartier: Et à penser que c'est moi qui, en découvrant ce pays, a fourni des troupes à l'armée anglaise. C'est moi qui, en explorant ce terrain, donna une autre colonie à l'Angleterre. C'est moi qui, en encourageant des colons à venir s'établir ici, donna naissance à toute une race de lâches et de traîtres!

Barman: Soyez pas trop rough sur eux-autres, M. Cartier. Y ont aidé l'Angleterre parce qui voulaient rester Français et Catholiques.

Cartier: Comment?

Barman: Pi la France aidait ceux qui persécutaient les Catholiques pi qui s'en sacraient du français.

Cartier: Mais c'est absolument impossible à comprendre, ça. Je suis tout confus. *(Au* Barman*)* Dites-moi, Monsieur, quel côté avait raison?

Ti-Jean: Ni l'un, ni l'autre.

Barman: Ou ben, tous les deux.

Cartier: *(Indique qu'il veut encore du vin. Il le boit d'un trait. Indique qu'il veut un autre verre. Le boit d'un trait. Pause. Il se dirige vers la porte à gauche et sort. Des coulisses)* AAAAAAAAAAAHHHHHHHHHHH! *(Il entre et revient au bar.)*

TI-JEAN: I'm sorry, Mister Cartier. I didn't want to upset you. I only told you that story to show that Franco-Americans have to forget a lot about what really happened when they claim that we have a direct link to France and French culture.

BARMAN: Or they have to stretch the truth just a bit.

CARTIER: But you must admit that the link is there.

TI-JEAN: Yep, but it's there with Native American culture, English culture, American culture, and a whole bunch of others, too.

CARTIER: Fine. But the culture of France is clearly and demonstrably superior to any and all of those. Therefore, it is your links with French culture that you should strive to cherish and strengthen.

TI-JEAN: And that's exactly what we did. Now, we're so scared of French culture that we can't do a damn thing ourselves.

CARTIER: What nonsense. How can you possibly fear a culture of such splendor, glory, and beauty? A culture that brings joy to the entire civilized world . . . a culture that . . .

TI-JEAN: *(Doesn't let him finish)* Because it's suffocating us! If we want anything in French, we get it from France. Plays, books, music . . . everything comes from over there. Nothing from right here. It's a little different with television. We can't get French programming from France. So do we create our own? Not a chance! We bring it in from Canada.

CARTIER: Television??

BARMAN: That's something I can show you later, Mister Cartier. It's a lot of fun. Just like having movies right in your living room.

Ti-Jean: Ecoutez, là, M. Cartier. J'voulais pas vous décourager. C't'histoire-là, j'vous l'ai ainque racontée pour montrer que nous-autres, les Franco-Américains, quand on essaie de se rapprocher de la France ou de la culture française, faut souvent qu'on ignore pas mal de choses.

Barman: Ou ben y faut qu'on conte des p'tites menteries.

Cartier: Mais il est indéniable que le lien existe.

Ti-Jean: Oui, mais il existe étou avec la culture indienne, anglaise, américaine, pi tout un tas d'autres.

Cartier: Bon, d'accord. Mais c'est évidemment la culture française qui est supérieure à toutes les autres. C'est à celle-là qu'il faut s'identifier surtout.

Ti-Jean: Pi c'est ça qu'on a fait. Asteur, on a tellement peur de la culture française qu'on peut rien faire nous-autres-mêmes.

Cartier: Comment ça? Pourquoi avoir peur d'une culture si glorieuse, si resplendissante? Une culture qui fait la joie du monde entier . . . une culture qui . . .

Ti-Jean: *(Ne le laisse pas finir)* Parce qu'a nous étouffe! Si on veut quèque chose de français, on fait venir ça d'la France. Pièces, livres, musique . . . ça vient toute de là-bas. Rien d'icit. Asteur la télévision, ça, c'est différent. On peut pas avoir des programmes français de France. On les fait-ti nous-autres-mêmes? Pantoute! On les fait venir du Canada.

Cartier: Télévision??

Barman: J'va vous montrer ça tout à l'heure, M. Cartier. C'est ben le fun. C'est comme avoir des mouvins dans le salon.

CARTIER: Movies??

TI-JEAN: There are lots of Franco-Americans who could get out there and do some things in French. But they look at that grand and glorious French culture, and their knees start knocking together. They're afraid they'll never be able to talk in REAL French . . . or sing in REAL French . . . or write in REAL French, so they don't even try. Ooops, sorry. That's not true. Sometimes, they try to imitate the REAL French. Usually, that's even more pathetic. You see, Mister Cartier, our culture is a little like Marie-Marthe and her lip syncing. The song we seem to be singing isn't our own. It comes from somewhere else. Oh, we put on a good show when the tape is playing. We've got just the right gestures to go with the words. We can make you believe that we're happy or sad or angry or in love . . . whatever it calls for in the lyrics. For a few minutes, you'd swear that we're award-winning performers. But when the tape stops, so does the illusion. Sometimes, we'll try to keep performing without the tape. But nothing comes out because we've been so busy imitating the REAL French that we've never taken the time to develop a voice of our own. We stand there like idiots with absolutely nothing to say. *(Pause)* Until we find our own song to sing . . . and a real voice to sing it with, I'm afraid the grand and glorious culture of France will do us more harm than good.

BARMAN: Bravo! Bravo! Encore! *(He pretends he's an emcee.)* And now, the prize for the best sermon given outside of church. And this year's winner is . . . Ti-Jean Côté! *(TI-JEAN is deep in thought.)* Ti-Jean can't be here tonight to accept his prize. He's writing another sermon on rabid Volkswagens that he plans to give at the door of the neighborhood liquor store tomorrow afternoon. Therefore, in his absence, I'm happy to accept his prize: a glass of beer. I offer you his humble thanks . . . and my own! *(He drinks a glass of beer. Pause)*

CARTIER: So, you are fully prepared to abandon your native language and culture?

TI-JEAN: I don't see any alternatives. Do you?

CARTIER: Mouvins??

TI-JEAN: Y en a des Franco-Américains qui pourraient en faire, des bonnes choses. Mais y regardent la culture française pi y shakent dans leurs culottes. Y se disent qui pourront jamais parler comme les Français, jamais chanter comme les Français, jamais écrire comme les Français. Ça fait qui essaient même pas. Ah, excusez. Y essaient des fois des imiter. Dans c'temps-là, c'est encore pire. Voyez-vous, M. Cartier, notre culture, c'est un peu comme les pantomimes à Marie-Marthe. Notre chanson, c'est pas vraiment la nôtre. A vient d'en dehors. Oh, ça l'air beau quand le tape marche. On fait des beaux gestes, on s'émotionne, on se donne des élans. Mais quand le tape arrête, c'est fini. Des fois, on essaie de continuer sans le tape . . . mais y a rien qui sort, parce que notre voix, on a jamais eu la chance de la développer. On reste là à faire des simagrés. *(Pause)* Jusqu'à temps qu'on peut trouver notre chanson, pi la chanter nous-autres-même, la grande culture française va nous faire plus de mal que de bien.

BARMAN: Bravo! Bravo! Encore! *(Il fait comme un annonceur.)* Et maintenant, le prix pour le meilleur sermon donné en dehors de l'église. Et le gagnant c't'année, c'est Ti-Jean Côté. *(*TI-JEAN *reste perdu dans ses pensées.)* Ti-Jean y est pas icit à soir pour accepter son prix. Y est après préparé un sermon sur les Volkswagen enragées qu'il va donner demain à la commission de liqueur. Comme ça, moué, j'accepte son prix: un verre de bière. Merci! *(Il boit. Pause)*

CARTIER: Comme ça, vous allez rejeter la langue et toute la culture française?

TI-JEAN: Qu'est que vous voulez qu'on fasse?

CARTIER: But, of course I do. You simply have to . . . *(Pause)* . . . It's merely a matter of . . . *(Pause)* . . . All it would take would be . . . *(Pause)* I'm afraid you're right, my good man. After what you've told me today, I'm not sure I have any alternatives at all. Long ago, when I was alive, everything seemed so simple. France versus England, Catholic versus Protestant, Good versus Evil . . . everything was in its proper place. Choices seemed easy to make . . . and we made them. But today . . . *(Pause)* Tell me, don't you feel any sorrow, any pain, as you watch this once vibrant language and culture disappear completely?

TI-JEAN: I'm still two persons, Mister Cartier. Don't you think it tears me apart to have to kill off half of who I am? Something that's actually BEEN you for that long doesn't just lie down and die. Oh, no. It puts up a hell of struggle. It screams. It kicks. It punches. It tries to tear your own guts out. Every once in a while, I think I've done it. Great! It's finally dead. No more struggling, no more screaming, no more kicking. Nothing! But then it happens. Some night when it's perfectly still and I'm all alone . . . suddenly, I'll hear this annoying little voice. "You won't get rid of me as easy as that, you ungrateful son of a bitch." *(Pause)* It's weird, isn't it, Mister Cartier. Even after everything I've told you today, I'm glad that my little annoying voice is still around.

CARTIER: It's not over, then! Perhaps you retain a small glimmer of hope that this language and culture that you still seem to cherish can be saved.

TI-JEAN: Perhaps.

Pause

CARTIER: Gentlemen, I have come to a momentous decision. From this very moment onwards, you shall have Jacques Cartier at your side in your noble fight!

TI-JEAN: I don't know if . . .

CARTIER: Mais il faut que . . . *(Un temps)* . . . Vous n'avez qu'à . . . *(Un temps)* . . . C'est évident que . . . *(Un temps)* Je ne sais pas, Monsieur. Après ce que vous venez de me dire, je ne sais absolument pas. Autrefois, quand j'étais sur terre, tout parassait si simple. Français-Anglais, Catholique-Protestant, Bien-Mal . . . tout était à sa place. Les choix semblaient faciles à faire, et on les faisait. Mais aujourd'hui . . . *(Un temps. Il se tourne vers* TI-JEAN.) Dites-moi, Monsieur, ne sentez-vous aucune tristesse de voir disparaître d'ici cette langue et cette culture?

TI-JEAN: J't'encore deux personnes, moué, M. Cartier. Vous pensez pas que chu triste quand j't'obligé de tuer la moitié de moué-même. Ça meurt pas facilement, ça, la moitié d'une personne. Ça s'débat pour des années pi des années, ça crie, ça laisse des blessures. Des fois, j'pense que j'ai fini par la tuer. Bon! C't'à peu près l'temps. Pu de débattage, pu de criage, pu rien! Mais le soir, là, quand chu tout seul, des fois j'entends une p'tite maudite voix: "Tu t'débarrasseras pas d'moué si facilement que ça, mon p'tit fantasse." *(Pause)* Savez-vous, M. Cartier, même avec tout ce que j'vous ai dit c't'après-midi, chu content que c't'a p'tite voix, a est encore là.

CARTIER: Tout n'est pas fini, donc! Il y a peut-être chez vous encore de l'espoir que les choses peuvent s'arranger.

TI-JEAN: Peut-être.

Pause

CARTIER: Messieurs, j'ai pensé à mon affaire. Désormais, vous aurez l'aide de Jacques Cartier dans votre lutte!

TI-JEAN: J'sais pas si . . .

CARTIER: Of course I wish to become involved! But from everything I've heard this afternoon, the situation is extreme in its gravity. I fear you may need the help of one even more powerful than I.

BARMAN: That sounds about right.

CARTIER: Hmmmm . . . let me see . . . who among the many whom I know and trust could possibly . . . Why, of course! That's it! I should have thought of it instantly! *(To the* BARMAN *and* TI-JEAN*)* Gentlemen, I am ready to bring your desperate request for assistance directly to the throne of our lord.

BARMAN: Our Lord?!?

CARTIER: Yes, dear settlers, to the most powerful sovereign of them all.

BARMAN: You mean . . . ?

CARTIER: Yes, my friends, I will see to it that your sorry plight is brought forthwith to the attention of the King of France!!!

BARMAN: But, Mister Cartier . . .

CARTIER: I leave at once! Is there a port nearby?

BARMAN: Yes, Mister Cartier, but . . .

CARTIER: Please, my friends, do not try to dissuade me from my chosen path. I know that the voyage I face is long and perilous, but I will brook no opposition!

BARMAN: But . . .

CARTIER: The help you need will soon be on its way, my friends. I go . . . TO THE KING*!!! (He rushes to the door at left and exits. The* BARMAN *follows after him to the door.)*

CARTIER: Mais si, je veux! Mais d'après ce que j'ai entendu cet après-midi, la situation est extrêmement critique. Je crois qu'il vous faut un soutien même plus puissant que le mien.

BARMAN: Là, vous l'avez dit!

CARTIER: Voyons . . . qui de ma connaissance pourrait . . . Mais oui! C'est ça! Pourquoi n'y ai-je pas pensé auparavant?!? *(Au* BARMAN *et à* TI-JEAN*)* Messieurs, je suis prêt à intercéder pour vous auprès de notre seigneur!

BARMAN: Notre Seigneur?!?

CARTIER: Oui, auprès du plus puissant souverain de tous.

BARMAN: Vous voulez dire . . . ?

CARTIER: Oui, Messieurs, je vais plaider votre cause auprès du Roi de France!!

BARMAN: Mais, Monsieur . . .

CARTIER: Je pars immédiatement! Y a-t-il un port près d'ici?

BARMAN: Oui, Monsieur, mais . . .

CARTIER: Non! N'essayez pas de me détourner de mon but. Je sais que le voyage est long et dangereux, mais ma décision est prise!

BARMAN: Mais, Monsieur . . .

CARTIER: L'aide ne tardera pas à venir, Messieurs. Je vais voir LE ROI!!!! *(Il se précipite vers la porte à gauche et sort. Le* BARMAN *court après lui jusqu'à la porte.)*

BARMAN: *(To off)* Mister Cartier! I've got a bit of bad news for you!

Pause. TI-JEAN goes to the bar and pours himself another beer. The BARMAN crosses to the center table and sits.

BARMAN: Hey, Côté! Do you think the king will help us out?

LÉO enters right with papers in his hand. He looks around the room as if he were looking for someone. TI-JEAN notices him. They stare at each other for an instant. LÉO turns and exits right. TI-JEAN crosses to the center table and sits.

TI-JEAN: Right now, Joe, I'd say he's just about the only one who can.

Curtain

Ergo, no one can.

BARMAN: *(Aux coulisses)* M. Cartier! J'ai des p'tites nouvelles pour vous!

Pause. TI-JEAN *va au bar. Il prend une autre bière. Le* BARMAN *revient vers la table au centre et s'assoit.*

BARMAN: Hey, Côté! Penses-tu que le roi va nous aider?

LÉO *entre de droite avec des papiers à la main. Il regarde autour du bar comme s'il cherchait quelqu'un.* TI-JEAN *l'aperçoit. Ils se regardent pour un instant.* LÉO *se tourne et sort à droite.* TI-JEAN *va à la table au centre et s'assoit.*

TI-JEAN: A ce point-cit, Joseph, c't'a peu près le seul qui peut.

Rideau

CHÈRE MAMAN

Pièce en trois actes / A drama in three acts

CAST OF CHARACTERS

JEANNETTE DUFOUR, *58 year old Franco-American woman, unmarried*

ALICE DUFOUR, *Jeannette's sister. 62 years old and unmarried*

YVONNE DUFOUR, *Jeannette's sister. 59 years old and unmarried*

JOSEPH DUFOUR, *The three women's oldest brother. About 65 years old*

ANDRÉ DUFOUR, *A Dufour brother, about 52 years old*

NORMAND DUFOUR, *The three women's youngest brother. About 48 years old*

CONSTANCE LEDOUX, *One of the Dufours' nieces. 21 years old*

EVA LEDOUX, *Sister of the Dufours and Constance's mother. About 49 years old*

ROGER LEDOUX, *Eva's husband. Constance's father. About 51 years old*

ALMA DUFOUR, *Joseph's wife*

EMILIEN DUFOUR, *Another Dufour brother. About 57 years old*

CHARLOTTE DUFOUR, *Emilien's wife*

PERSONNAGES

JEANNETTE DUFOUR, *Vieille fille d'environ 58 ans*

ALICE DUFOUR, *Soeur de Jeannette. Vieille fille d'environ 62 ans*

YVONNE DUFOUR, *Soeur de Jeannette. Vieille fille d'environ 59 ans*

JOSEPH DUFOUR, *Frère aîné des trois femmes. Environ 65 ans*

ANDRÉ DUFOUR, *Frère des trois femmes. Environ 52 ans*

NORMAND DUFOUR, *Frère cadet des trois femmes. Environ 48 ans*

CONSTANCE LEDOUX, *Nièce des Dufour. 21 ans*

EVA LEDOUX, *Soeur des Dufour et mère de Constance. Environ 49 ans*

ROGER LEDOUX, *Epoux d'Eva et père de Constance. Environ 51 ans*

ALMA DUFOUR, *Epouse de Joseph*

EMILIEN DUFOUR, *Frère des Dufour. Environ 57 ans*

CHARLOTTE DUFOUR, *Epouse d'Emilien*

SETTING

The play takes place in the informal dining room of the DUFOUR *homestead, where the three unmarried sisters have continued to live since the death of their mother. The house is in a middle class, Franco-American section of a New England industrial city. The room betrays the taste of an ethnic middle class family of the late 1950s or early 60s. However, much of the furniture is from the '20s or '30s, left over from the* DUFOUR *parents.*

A round oak dining room table is downstage left. It is covered with a white tablecloth and could have a centerpiece, i.e. a bowl of fruit, and a smaller bowl filled with candy or mints. There are four chairs placed around the table. To the left of the table, also downstage, is a sideboard. A large picture of the late mother DUFOUR *hangs above the sideboard. Two straight chairs are upstage left. Upstage right is a rocking chair, with a small table covered with magazines, newspapers, cigarettes, ash trays, etc., between the rocking chair and the straight chairs.*

There is a window behind and slightly to the left of the rocking chair. On the wall above the small table are a crucifix with palms and a calendar. Two straight chairs are placed against the right hand wall downstage, with a clock on the wall above the chairs. A door upstage left leads to the outside. Another door down right leads to other rooms in the house, especially the kitchen.

MISE EN SCÈNE

L'action de la pièce se passe dans la salle à manger/salle à parler de la maison paternelle des DUFOUR où habitent les trois vieilles filles depuis la mort de leur mère. La maison est située dans le quartier bourgeois franco-américain d'une ville industrielle de la Nouvelle-Angleterre. Le décor est celui d'une salle dans une maison bourgeoise franco-américaine des années cinquante/début des années soixante.

A l'avant-scène, à gauche, il y a une table ronde en chêne, couverte d'une nappe blanche assez élégante sur laquelle se trouvent un bol de fruits et un plat de bonbons. Il y a quatre chaises autour de la table. A côté de la table, également à l'avant-scène, il y a un buffet au-dessus duquel se trouve un portrait assez large de la mère DUFOUR. A l'arrière-scène à gauche, contre le mur du fond, se trouvent deux chaises droites. Il y a une chaise berçante à droite et une petite table couverte de revues, journaux, cigarettes, et cendriers entre la chaise berçante et les chaises droites.

Derrière et légèrement à gauche de la chaise berçante se trouve une fenêtre. Au-dessus de la petite table, on retrouve un crucifix avec des rameaux, et un calendrier. Contre le mur à droite et à l'avant-scène se trouvent deux chaises droites. Une horloge est affixée au mur au-dessus des chaises. Une porte à l'arrière-scène à gauche mène à l'extérieur. Une porte à l'avant-scène à droite mène à l'intérieur, surtout à la cuisine.

ACT I

Early morning. Dim lighting. When the curtain opens, we can hear coughing from offstage right. Pause. More coughing. JEANNETTE, *dressed in a bathrobe and slippers enters right and crosses to center. She stops for a moment as if she were listening. She crosses to the sideboard, opens it, and takes out a bottle of vodka. She opens the bottle, takes a swig, and puts it back in the sideboard. Pause. She turns around, looks at the room, and sighs as though she were try-ing to gather strength for the coming day. She crosses to the rocking chair upstage right and sits. Pause. She starts rocking and looking out the window. She stops rocking. Pause. She takes a cigarette from the small table and lights it. Pause. She starts rocking again. Suddenly, she starts coughing violently.*

When she stops coughing, she takes a handkerchief from her sleeve and blows her nose. She puts the handkerchief back in her sleeve and starts rocking. She starts coughing once again. She gets up and exits right, coughing all the while. Pause. She returns with a glass of water and a plastic container of pills. She crosses to the rocking chair, places the pills and the water on the small table, sits, and keeps smoking her cigarette. Pause. She picks up the container of pills and reads the instructions printed on the label. Her lips form the words as she reads. She takes the cap off the container, takes out two pills, and puts the container back on the table. Pause. She starts coughing once again. She picks up the pill container, reads the directions once more, takes out two more pills, and puts the container back on the table. She takes the four pills with the glass of water. Pause. She starts rocking. Shortly after, she starts coughing once again. Pause.

*(*NOTE: JEANNETTE *is a true chain smoker. Throughout the play, she should always be smoking a cigarette. If possible, she should light her next cigarette with the butt of the cigarette she is currently smoking.)*

She takes a deck of cards from the table and begins a game of solitaire. She starts coughing. Pause. She tries to continue her game of solitaire but has an uncontrollable coughing fit. Pause. She gets up and crosses to the sideboard. She

ACTE I

Le matin. Eclairage sombre. On entend quelqu'un tousser des coulisses à droite. Pause. On tousse encore. Jeannette, *habillée en sortie de bain, entre de droite et se dirige vers le centre. Elle s'arrête un moment comme si elle écoutait. Elle se dirige vers le buffet à gauche. Elle l'ouvre, en sort une bouteille de vodka, la débouche, prend une gorgée, et remet la bouteille dans le buffet. Un temps. Elle se tourne, regarde la salle, pousse un soupir comme si elle prenait son courage, et se dirige vers la chaise berçante à droite. Elle s'assoit. Un temps. Elle commence à se bercer. En même temps, elle regarde par la fenêtre. Elle arrête de se bercer. Un temps. Elle prend une cigarette de la petite table et l'allume. Un temps. Elle commence de nouveau à se bercer. Tout à coup, elle se met à tousser. La toux doit être sévère et doit durer assez longtemps.*

Elle arrête de tousser. Elle prend un mouchoir de sa manche et se mouche. Elle remet le mouchoir et recommence à se bercer. Elle se remet à tousser. Elle se lève en toussant et sort à droite. Un temps. Elle revient avec un verre d'eau et une bouteille de pilules. Elle se dirige vers la chaise berçante, pose le verre et les pilules sur la petite table, s'assoit, et continue de fumer sa cigarette. Un temps. Elle prend la bouteille et lit l'ordonnance. Ses lèvres se remuent en lisant. Elle débouche la bouteille, prend deux pilules et remet la bouteille sur la table. Un temps. Elle commence à tousser. Elle reprend la bouteille, la contemple, en sort deux autres pilules, et remet la bouteille sur la table. Elle prend les quatre pilules avec le verre d'eau. Un temps. Elle recommence à se bercer. Elle se met à tousser. Un temps.

*(*NOTE: Jeannette *fume à la chaine. Donc elle doit toujours être en train de fumer une cigarette. Si possible, elle devrait allumer la nouvelle cigarette avec le bout de la cigarette qu'elle fume actuellement.)*

Elle prend un jeu de cartes de la table et commence un jeu de patience. Elle se met à tousser. Un temps. Elle recommence son jeu de patience et se met à tousser d'une façon incontrôlable. Un temps. Elle se lève et se dirige vers le buffet

opens the door, takes out the bottle of vodka, and takes a swig. She hears a noise from offstage right and looks in that direction. Quickly, she takes another swig of vodka and puts the bottle back in the sideboard. Noises from off right get louder. She crosses to the rocking chair, sits, and starts rocking. Pause.

ALICE enters right. She is dressed in her Sunday best, with a black dress and high heels. She is well (perhaps a little too well) made up. When she enters, she is trying to put on earrings that are clearly out of style. She crosses to the table down left and puts down her coat and handbag. She keeps trying to put on the clip-on earrings which keep falling off. Pause. JEANNETTE starts coughing. ALICE stops in her tracks and clenches her fists as if JEANNETTE's cough were physically painful to her. Pause. ALICE crosses to the sideboard. She takes out a prayer book and a huge rosary. She turns to JEANNETTE.

ALICE: Better hurry or we'll be late. You know how long it takes you to get dressed.

JEANNETTE: I'm not going.

ALICE: *(In disgust)* Ah! Here we go again!

JEANNETTE: What do you want me to do, Alice? The way I feel today, I don't think I could go anywhere . . . not even to mass.

ALICE: *(Sarcastic)* And where's the problem today? Your back? Your hips? Your little pinkie finger? Well, I think I know where it is. *(She indicates her head with her finger.)* It's right here . . . and it's getting worse every day.

JEANNETTE: You wouldn't say that if you felt the way I do. It's no fun living this way, you know.

ALICE: Well, I won't argue with that. And I can tell you that it's no fun living with someone who lives this way either.

JEANNETTE: What should I do? Tell me. Go ahead. Tell me! Do you really think I like spending every day like this . . . day in and day out? I'd

à gauche. Elle sort la bouteille de vodka et prend une gorgée. Elle entend un bruit de droite et regarde dans cette direction. Rapidement, elle prend une autre gorgée de vodka. Bruit plus fort des coulisses à droite. Elle retourne à la chaise berçante et s'assoit. Elle recommence à se bercer. Un temps.

Alice entre de droite bien habillée. Elle porte une robe "du dimanche" et des talons hauts. Elle est bien (peut-être un peu trop) maquillée. Quand elle entre, elle est en train de mettre des boucles d'oreilles énormes et démodées. Elle se dirige vers la table à gauche, y dépose son manteau et son sac à main. Elle essaie toujours de mettre ses boucles d'oreilles qui tombent sans cesse. Un temps. Jeannette se met à tousser. Alice arrête ce qu'elle fait et se crispe les mains comme si la toux de Jeannette lui faisait mal. Un temps. Alice va au buffet. Elle en sort un missel et un chapelet énorme. Alice se tourne vers Jeannette.

Alice: T'es aussi ben de t'dépêcher. On va être en retard. Tu sais comment longtemps ça t'prend pour t'habiller.

Jeannette: J'y va pas.

Alice: Bon! Ça y est. Tu vas encore commencer ça.

Jeannette: Quoi c'est que tu veux, Alice. D'la façon que j'file aujourd'hui, là, j'ai pas envie de sortir pantoute . . . même pour aller à messe.

Alice: *(Ironique)* Pi quoi c'est que c'est aujourd'hui, hein? Ton dos? Tes reins? Tes orteils? Ben moué, j'pense que j'sais quoi c'est que c'est. *(Elle se tappe la tête du doigt.)* C'est icit. Dret ben icit, ta maladie. Pi ça rempire.

Jeannette: Ti dirais pas ça si tu filais comme j'file, moué. C'est pas drôle de vivre comme ça, t'sais.

Alice: Ben ça, là, j'te donne ça. Pi j'te dis que c'est pas drôle de vivre avec quèqu'un qui vit comme ça non plus.

Jeannnette: Quoi c'est que tu veux que j'fasse? Dis-moué, hein! Dis-moué! Penses-tu que j'aime ça, moué, filer comme ça tous les jours?

love to be healthy and happy like everybody else. I'd like to have fun every once in a while. I'd like to go out and sing and dance like I used to.

ALICE: Well then, do it! No one's stopping you.

JEANNETTE: I can't, Alice.

ALICE: Why not?

JEANNETTE: I'm sick. (ALICE *turns her back on her.*) It's true! I hope you never end up feeling the way I do. Then, you'd see what I have to deal with every day.

ALICE: *(Turns back to* JEANNETTE*)* And just exactly what kind of sickness do you have? It must be pretty darn rare because there isn't a doctor in this town who can tell you what you've got. Amazing, isn't it. Here's a bunch of really smart people who spent years in college and who read these biiiig books, and not one of them can tell you the name of what you've got. Ever think that maybe it's because you aren't really sick that no one can figure out what you've got? And maybe that's why you go from doctor to doctor to doctor without ever feeling any better?

JEANNETTE: If I'm not sick, why do they keep giving me pills, then? You said it yourself. Doctors are smart. And they'd be pretty stupid to hand out pills to people who aren't sick.

ALICE: *(Sarcastic)* Ah, right. Your wonderful pills. I'd forgotten how much they help you, your wonderful pills. How long have you been taking them? Twenty years? Thirty years? (JEANNETTE *starts to protest.*) Oh, I know. It's not always the same pills. You get different ones every other week. And the new ones always work sooo much better than the old ones. Oh, yes. That's for sure. Even I've noticed a change in your condition over the years. When you started taking them, you were young and sick. But, after thirty years, that's all changed. Now, you're old and sick. That's what I call change!

J'aimerais ben pouvoir filer comme les autres. J'aimerais ça avoir du fun, des fois. J'aimerais ça sortir pi chanter pi danser comme j'faisais avant.

ALICE: Ben fais-le, tapince! Y personne qui t'arrête.

JEANNETTE: J'peux pas, Alice.

ALICE: Pourquoi pas?

JEANNETTE: Chu malade. (ALICE *se tourne le dos.*) C'est vrai! J'te souhaite de jamais filer comme j'file, moué. Tu verrais que c'est pas le fun.

ALICE: *(Se retourne)* Pi quoi c'est que c'est, c't'a maladie que t'as? Ça doit être rare en mautadit, parce qui a pas un sacré docteur dans toute la ville qui peut trouver quoi c'est que c'est. Pourtant, c'est pas des niaiseux ça, ces docteurs-là. C'est allé au collège. Ça lit des grands livres. Pi y n'a pas un qui peut te dire le nom de ta maladie. As-tu pensé que c'est tedben parce que tu n'as pas de maladie, que c'est pour ça que personne peut te dire quoi c'est que tu as? Que c'est pour ça que tu passes d'un docteur à un autre sans jamais prendre du mieux?

JEANNETTE: Si chu pas malade, pourquoi c'est qui me donnent des pilules comme ça, hein? Tu l'as ben dit. C'est pas des niaiseux, ça, les docteurs. Y donnent pas des pilules à n'importe qui.

ALICE: *(Ironique)* Ah, oui. Tes pilules. J'avais presqu'oublié le bien qui te font, tes belles pilules. Ça fait comment longtemps que t'es prends, ces pilules-là? Vingt ans? Trente ans? (JEANNETTE *commence à protester.*) Ah, j'l'sais. C'est pas toujours les mêmes pilules. Ça change à toutes les deux semaines. Pi les nouvelles, y marchent toujours mieux que les vieilles. Ah, oui, ça, c'est certain. J'ai remarqué le progrès que tu fais. Quand t'a commencé à les prendre, t'étais jeune pi malade. Asteur, après trente ans, ça tout changé. Ouais. Là, t'es vieille pi malade. Tu me parles d'un beau change!

JEANNETTE: Alice!

ALICE: It's true! If I were you, I'd throw every damn pill of yours out the window.

JEANNETTE: And what good would that do? Would it make me feel better?

ALICE: I think it would, Jeannette. Listen, in the morning, you say you just don't have any pep, that you can't seem to get anything done . . . so you take a pill. You work for a while and then you get a few aches and pains . . . so you take another pill for that. But that pill makes you a little drowsy, so you take another pill to wake you up. It's one pill after another all day long. And you wonder why you can't get to sleep at night. Ooops. Sorry. You don't even wonder any more. You just take another pill to make you sleep. Do you want to know why you don't have any pep, why you always feel run down and depressed and can't do anything? Well I'm no doctor, but this is so obvious that even I can see what's wrong. You're sick because you're always on some damn drug.

JEANNETTE: There's only one thing that's true in everything you just said. You're no doctor, so don't start lecturing me about something you don't know anything about. You don't know how awful I feel and how much I'd like to feel better. *(She starts crying.)* I get down on my knees and pray for that every day. I'd give everything I own to have my health back. *(She takes out a handkerchief from her sleeve.)* It's just awful. Since mama died, there are times when . . . *(They hear a noise from off right. JEANNETTE wipes her eyes.)* Ah, her highness has decided to get up.

ALICE: *(Looking at the clock)* She keeps pushing her luck.

JEANNETTE: She was supposed to make breakfast for us this morning. It was her turn.

ALICE: Good thing I didn't wait for her. It would have been instant coffee and burned toast again.

JEANNETTE: Alice!

ALICE: C'est vrai! Si j'serais toué, j'jetterais toutes ces maudites pilules-là par le chassis.

JEANNETTE: Pi quoi c'est que ça me donnerait, ça? J'serais-ti mieux?

ALICE: J'pense que oui, Jeannette. Ecoute, là. Le matin, tu dis que t'as pas de pep, que tu peux rien faire . . . ça fait que tu prends des pilules. Tu travailles un secousse pi y a des p'tites affaires qui commencent à te faire mal . . . ça fait que tu prends d'autres pilules pour ça. Mais ces pilules-là, y t'endorment un p'tit peu, ça fait que tu prends d'autres pilules pour te réveiller. Pi ça continue comme ça toute la journée. Pi après ça, tu te demandes pourquoi tu peux pas dormir le soir. Non, excuse. Tu demandes même pu asteur. Au lieu, tu prends d'autres pilules pour t'aider à dormir. Tu veux savoir pourquoi que t'as pas de pep, pourquoi que tu files toujours de même? Ben chu pas un docteur, moué, mais y a des affaires qu'on peut voir sans être ben instruit. T'es malade parce que t'est toujours assommée par tes maudites pilules.

JEANNETTE: Y a une chose de vrai dans tout ce que t'as dit. T'es pas un docteur. Ça fait que commence pas à me parler des affaires que tu connais pas. Tu connais pas comment j'file pi comment j'aimerais filer mieux. *(Elle se met à pleurnicher.)* J'prie pour ça à genoux à tous les jours. J'donnerais tout ce que j'ai pour pouvoir filer comme du monde. *(Elle sort un mouchoir de sa manche.)* C'pas drôle. Depuis que maman est morte, là, y a des fois . . . *(On entend un bruit des coulisses à droite.* JEANNETTE *s'essuie les yeux.)* Bon! V'la "la princesse" qui se lève.

ALICE: *(En regardant l'horloge)* Elle ambitionne!

JEANNETTE: A était supposée de faire à déjeuner, à matin, t'sais. C'était son tour.

ALICE: Une chance que j'ai pas attendu. Une cup de Nescafé, ça me remplit pas diable, ça.

JEANNETTE: You'd think that after almost sixty years, she'd have learned how to do a little house work, too. I'm sick and tired of having to do her work for her.

ALICE: And what about me? You're not the only one who works around here.

JEANNETTE: Yeah, but at least you feel halfway decent.

ALICE: Here we go again!

YVONNE *enters right. She is dressed much like* ALICE. *As she enters, she notices* JEANNETTE.

YVONNE: You're not even dressed yet?!?

ALICE: *(Sarcastic)* Madame needs a little coaxing.

YVONNE: Well, hurry up! We're going to be late.

JEANNETTE: I'm not going to church today.

YVONNE: *(Shocked)* You're not going to church?!? Today?!?

JEANNETTE: That's what I said. (YVONNE *looks at* ALICE *who shrugs her shoulders.)* What's wrong with that? It's not a mortal sin to miss mass on Saturday. Only on Sunday. It might surprise you, Yvonne, but lots of people never go to mass during the week.

YVONNE: Yes, but we're not like "lots of people." That's what mama used to tell us, anyway. Have you forgotten all of that. Have you forgotten the vow we all made to mama—the whole family—on her deathbed? That we'd go to mass every day? *(Pause)* Especially today, Jeannette.

JEANNETTE: Today's no different from any other day. I'm sick, Yvonne. I

JEANNETTE: Tu penserais qu'après une soixantaine d'années, a aurait appris à faire le ménage un peu. J't'l dis que chu ben tannée de faire toute son ouvrage.

ALICE: Pi quoi c'est que tu penses que j'fais, moué? T'es pas la seule qui travaille icit, ma fille.

JEANNETTE: Oui, mais au moins tu files comme du monde, toué.

ALICE: Bon, ça recommence!

YVONNE *rentre de droite. Elle est habillée comme* ALICE. *En rentrant, elle aperçoit* JEANNETTE.

YVONNE: Dis-moué pas que t'es pas habillée encore, toué!

ALICE: Mademoiselle veut se faire prier.

YVONNE: Dépêche-toué donc! On va être en retard.

JEANNETTE: J'y va pas à messe aujourd'hui.

YVONNE: *(Scandalisée)* Tu vas pas à messe?!? Aujourd'hui?!?

JEANNETTE: C'est ça que j'ai dit. (YVONNE *regarde* ALICE *qui se hausse les épaules.)* Quoi c'est qui a, donc? C'est pas péché mortel de manquer la messe le samedi. Rienque le dimanche. Ça te surprendrait tedben mais y a en masse du monde qui vont jamais à messe pendant la semaine.

YVONNE: Mais nous-autres, là, on est pas comme "en masse du monde." C'est ça que maman nous disait, au moins. As-tu oublié ça? As-tu oublié la promesse qu'on a fait à maman, toute la famille, quand a était sur son lit de mort? Qu'on irait à messe à toutes les jours? *(Pause)* Surtout aujourd'hui, Jeannette.

JEANNETTE: Aujourd'hui, c'est pas différent d'une autre journée. Chu

don't feel good at all, so I'm not going to mass. There's nothing wrong with that.

YVONNE: *(To* ALICE*)* You mean she doesn't remember? And you didn't tell her?

ALICE: What could I do? She started in on her aches and pains and sick this and pill that . . . and I didn't stand a chance. *(Still trying to put her earrings on)* These earrings aren't worth a damn. *(To* YVONNE*)* Listen, if you want to try to talk some sense into your sister, go right ahead. I've got to find earrings that won't keep falling off. *(She exits right.)*

YVONNE: *(Sighs)* I don't know, Jeannette. *(Pause)* I really don't know.

JEANNETTE: Well I do know! I'm sick. I'd say that's pretty easy to understand.

YVONNE: I never thought you'd forget.

JEANNETTE: What are you talking about?

YVONNE: Oh, I know you're sick, Jeannette. I don't understand what the doctors say, and all the things they give you, but I can tell that you're sick. When you live with a person practically all of your life, you don't have to be a brain surgeon to see what's going on. Sometimes, I don't even recognize you any more. Sometimes, I think you died with mama. That's why I never thought you'd forget her anniversary mass. *(Pause.* JEANNETTE *seems incredulous.)* That's right. Don't you even know what the date is?

JEANNETTE: *(Gets up and goes to the calendar.)* May thirteenth.

YVONNE: Right. May thirteenth. Mama died ten years ago today.

malade, Yvonne. J'file pas ben pantoute, ça fait que j'va pas à messe. Y a rien de mal là-dedans.

YVONNE: *(A* ALICE*)* Dis-moué pas qu'a s'en souvient pas? Tu y a pas dis?

ALICE: Quoi c'est qu'tu voulais que j'fasse? A commencé sur ses maladies, pi j'ai pas eu la chance. *(Elle essaie toujours de mettre ses boucles d'oreilles.)* Ces mautadits pendants d'oreilles-là, ça vaut pas d'la colle! *(A* YVONNE*)* Ecoute, si tu veux essayer de parler à ta soeur, là, j'te souhaite d'la chance. Moué, j'va aller chercher des pendants d'oreilles qui ont du bon sens. *(Elle sort à droite.)*

YVONNE: *(En poussant un soupir)* J'sais pas, Jeannette. *(Un temps)* J'sais pas pantoute.

JEANNETTE: Quoi c'est que tu sais pas? Chu malade. C'est ben simple, ça.

YVONNE: J'pensais jamais que tu oublierais.

JEANNETTE: Quoi c'est que tu veux dire?

YVONNE: J'l'sais que t'es malade, Jeannette. Oh, j'comprends pas toute ce que ces docteurs-là disent, pi j'comprends pas toutes les affaires qui te donnent, mais j'sais que t'es malade. Quand on vit pour trente ans avec une personne, on a pas besoin d'être ben smarte pour voir quoi c'est qui se passe. Des fois, j'te r'connais même pu. Des fois, j'pense même que t'es morte avec maman. C'est pour ça que j'penserais jamais que tu oublierais son service anniversaire. *(Un temps.* JEANNETTE *paraît incrédule.)* Ben oui. Sais-tu même pas quelle date que c'est, aujourd'hui?

JEANNETTE*: (Se lève et va au calendrier. Murmurant)* Le treize de mai.

YVONNE: Oui, le treize de mai. Ça fait dix ans aujourd'hui que maman est morte.

JEANNETTE: *(Goes back to the rocking chair and slumps into the chair. Ashamed)* I forgot.

YVONNE: That's what happens when you care more about yourself than about other people. You end up forgetting a mother who never had a selfish thought even once in her entire life. Everything she did, she did for others . . . especially for us. She scrimped and saved and sacrificed to send the boys to college. And she scrimped and saved and sacrificed to take care of us after papa died. And if other people asked her to do things, she never said no. She was always the one who did the most for people's birthdays or anniversaries. It's a good thing she watched out for you when you were going out with Bernie.

JEANNETTE: *(*YVONNE *hit a nerve.)* Yvonne!

YVONNE: It's true! You would have married that worthless son of a . . . gun if mama hadn't told you not to.

JEANNETTE: I don't want to talk about it!

YVONNE: Why not? Well, I think I know why not. Because it bothers you to know that you'll never be like mama.

JEANNETTE: *(Angry)* And I suppose you think you're her spit and image. Well, think again. If mama did everything for everybody, you do nothing for nobody. You can't cook. You can't pick up after yourself. You can't even get up in the morning.

YVONNE: Maybe you've forgotten, but while you were busy learning how to make your fancy cakes, I was working in the mill. Forty-two years on the same machine in the same mill. Yep! Nonstop fun, that was. But we needed the money, and it sure wasn't going to come from you. I only wish I had a chance to learn to make cakes and tourtières and all those other things like you did.

Jeannette: *(Elle retourne à la chaise berçante et s'asscoit lourdement. Murmurant. Avec honte)* J'avais oublié.

Yvonne: C'est ça qui arrive quand on pense plus à nous-autres-même qu'aux autres. On oublie une mère qui a jamais pensé à elle-même une fois pendant sa vie. C'qu'a faisait, c'tait toujours pour les autres. Parle de sacrifices! A n'a fait, elle, pour ses enfants. Comment ce que tu penses qu'a pu envoyer les gars au collège? Comment ce que tu penses qu'a pu prendre soin de nous-autres après que papa est mort? J'te dis que ça n'a pris, des sacrifices, ça. Pi quand les autres lui demandaient de faire quèque chose, a disait jamais non. C'tait toujours elle qui faisait le plus quand c'était la fête à quèqu'un ou l'anniversaire à quèqu'un. Une chance qu'a pensait à toué quand tu sortais avec ton p'tit Bernard.

Jeannette: *(*Yvonne *a frappé un point sensible.)* Yvonne!

Yvonne: C'est vrai! Tu l'aurais marié, c'vaurien-là, si maman te l'avait pas défendu.

Jeannette: J'veux pas que tu parles de ça!

Yvonne: Pourquoi pas, hein? J'l'sais pourquoi. Parce que ça t'bâdre de voir que tu seras jamais comme maman.

Jeannette: *(En colère)* Pi toué, là, penses-tu que tu y ressembles? Ben j'va t'l'dire. Si maman faisait toute pour tout le monde, toué, tu fais rien pour personne. Tu peux pas faire à manger, tu peux pas faire le ménage. Tu peux même pas t'elver, le matin.

Yvonne: Tu oublies tedben que pendant que t'apprenais à faire tes beaux gâteaux, moué, j'travaillais au moulin. Quarante-deux ans sur la même mautadite machine dans le même mautadit moulin. C'tait ben le fun, ça, hein? Mais on avait besoin de l'argent, pi ç'avait pas l'air que ç'allait venir de toué. J'te dis que j'aurais ben mieux aimé apprendre comment faire des tourtières.

JEANNETTE: I worked in the mills, too.

YVONNE: Ah, yes. But suddenly, after Bernie the old boyfriend got married, Madame started feeling sick and said she couldn't work anymore. Of course, it didn't matter to her if we needed money. It made no difference to her if she was in everybody's way at home. No. As usual, Madame cared only about herself. She was the only one who counted. And after all that . . . after everything that mama did for you, you have the nerve to say that you're too sick to go to her anniversary mass?!?

JEANNETTE: *(Pitifully)* I forgot.

YVONNE: And I suppose you forgot that today is Connie's birthday. Any plans to make her a cake or are you too sick for that too, Madame?

JEANNETTE: I forgot.

Pause

YVONNE: *(More softly)* Listen, Jeannette, the rest of the family will be here anytime to go to mass. You'd better go get dressed. *(Pause)* I'll get your things ready. *(Pause)* You'll see, you'll feel better once you're dressed. I'll get the black dress you bought last year for Frank's funeral. You know how good you look in black. *(She exits right. JEANNETTE stays seated for a moment. Then she gets up slowly and painfully. Once up, she sways noticeably and uses the small table to steady herself. YVONNE enters again.)* Don't worry about Connie's birthday cake. I'll help you with it. Even if I can't make tourtières, I can at least break a couple of eggs or sift some flour. Now come on.

YVONNE *exits.* JEANNETTE *slowly stands straight. Pause. She crosses to the sideboard, gets out the bottle of vodka and takes a swig. Pause. She stares at her mother's portrait, takes another swig, and stares again at the portrait. She closes her eyes and lowers her head. Pause. She crosses to the door down right and exits. Pause. Someone knocks on the door up left and enters right away. It's* JOSEPH. *He is short and somewhat stocky. He wears a black suit, white shirt and*

Jeannette: J'ai travaillé là, moué étou.

Yvonne: Ah, oui. Mais tout d'un coup, après que Bernard s'est marié, Mademoiselle a commencé à avoir ses maladies pi a pouvait pu travailler. Ça faisait rien si on avait besoin de l'argent. Ça faisait rien si a était dans les jambes à maison. Mademoiselle pensait rienqu'à elle-même, pas aux autres. C'tait ainque elle qui comptait. Pi après tout ça, tu oses nous dire que t'es trop malade pour aller au service anniversaire de maman?

Jeannette: *(Piteuse)* J'avais oublié.

Yvonne: Ouais. J'suppose que t'as oublié que c'est la fête à Connie aujourd'hui étou. As-tu commencé le gâteau?

Jeannette: J'avais oublié.

Pause

Yvonne: *(Plus douce)* Ecoute, là, Jeannette, les autres vont être icit ben vite pour aller à messe. T'es aussi ben d'aller t'habiller. *(Un temps)* J'va aller préparer tes affaires. *(Un temps)* Tu vas voir, une fois que t'es habillée, là, tu vas filer mieux. J'va sortir la robe noire que t'as achetée l'année passée pour le service à François. Tu sais comment le noir te fait ben. *(Elle sort à droite. Jeannette reste assise pour un moment. Lentement et péniblement, elle commence à se lever. Une fois debout, elle chancelle et se retient sur la petite table. Yvonne revient.)* Occupe-toué pas du gâteau à Connie. Même si j'sais pas comment faire des tourtières, j'peux au moins t'aider à l'faire. Asteur, viens.

Yvonne sort. Jeannette se redresse péniblement. Un temps. Elle se dirige vers le buffet à gauche. Elle sort la bouteille de vodka, la débouche et prend une gorgée. Un temps. Elle contemple le portrait de la mère. Elle prend une autre gorgée. Contemple de nouveau le portrait. Elle ferme les yeux et baisse la tête. Un temps. Elle se dirige vers la porte à droite et sort. Un temps. Quelqu'un frappe à la porte à gauche et entre immédiatement. On aperçoit Joseph, court,

dark tie. He crosses to the small table up left, takes a newspaper, and crosses to sit in a chair around the table down left.

JOSEPH: *(Loud. To offstage)* Get a move on! We're all going to be late!

ALICE *enters right and crosses quickly to the table.*

JOSEPH: Where are the others?

ALICE: Madame the invalid, played a little trick on us this morning.

JOSEPH: What's her problem today?

ALICE: *(Looking through her handbag)* Oh, nothing big. She just decided she wasn't going to church.

JOSEPH: *(Shocked)* Not go to her own mother's anniversary mass? I don't believe it!

ALICE: She said she forgot.

JOSEPH: *(Hard)* Forgot, my ass! You don't forget a day like this. You don't forget your own mother. Especially one like ours.

ALICE: It's not really her fault, Joe. With all the pills she takes, I'm surprised she can remember her name. Anyway, Yvonne is helping her get ready. It shouldn't take too long. *(She takes a necklace from her handbag, closes the bag, and puts it back on the table.)* Let the others in when they get here, o.k.? *(She exits right.)*

Pause. There's a knock at the door up left. ANDRÉ, dressed in a black suit, enters and crosses to the chairs down right. He seems nervous. He remains standing throughout the scene.

habillé en noir. Il se dirige vers la petite table à droite, prend un journal, retourne à gauche et s'assoit sur une chaise près de la grande table.

Joseph: *(Assez fort. Aux coulisses)* Dépêchez-vous, vous-autres. On va être en retard.

Alice *entre de droite et marche rapidement vers la table.*

Joseph: Où ce que les autres?

Alice: Mademoiselle, la malade, nous a joué un p'tit tour à matin.

Joseph: Quoi c'est que c'est aujourd'hui?

Alice: *(Se met à fouiller dans son sac à main)* Ah, pas grand'chose. Elle avait décidé de pas aller à messe.

Joseph: *(Scandalisé)* Pas aller au service anniversaire de maman? Ça pas de bon sens, ça.

Alice: A dit qu'avait oublié.

Joseph: *(Dur)* Parle d'une maudite affaire! Ça s'oublie pas, ça, une journée comme ça. Des mères, on oublie pas ça. Surtout des mères comme maman.

Alice: C'est pas vraiment de sa faute, Joe. Avec toutes les pilules qu'a prend, ça me surprend qu'a se souvient de son nom des fois. Anyway, Yvonne est après y aider à se préparer. Ça s'ra pas long. *(Elle sort un collier de son sac à main. Elle ferme le sac et le remet sur la table.)* Laisse rentrer les autres mèque qu'ils arrivent, hein? *(Elle sort à droite.)*

Pause. On frappe à la porte. André, *habillé en noir, entre et se dirige vers une des chaises à droite. Il est nerveux. Il n'arrivera pas à s'asseoir.*

ANDRÉ: Hello, Joe. *(He looks around the room.)* They aren't ready yet?!? *(He looks at his watch.)* I wouldn't want to be late today. We've got the first ten pews reserved for the family. We're supposed to all come in together. It sure as hell wouldn't look good if we were all late.

JOSEPH: You can thank Jeannette . . . again!

ANDRÉ: *(Sarcastic)* What a surprise. Every holiday, it's always the same routine. Christmas, Easter, Thanksgiving, Mothers' Day . . . Jeannette always says she can't come with us. She's too tired, she's too sick, she's too depressed. I'm really getting fed up with her. *(Pause)* Maybe you can talk some sense into her, Joe. After all, you're the oldest.

JOSEPH: Talking wouldn't help your sister. Not one damn bit. I even think it'd make things worse. Think about it. Does she end up by coming along on all the holidays? *(Doesn't let him answer)* Every damn time! She wouldn't miss the chance to have an audience of fifty people to complain to for all the money in the world.

ANDRÉ: But why does she keep on . . .

JOSEPH: *(Doesn't let him finish)* Because she wants attention, that's all. She wants everybody to get down on their knees and plead with her to come. And that's exactly what everybody does. Well, not me. If she wants attention, she ain't getting it from me. And if I had my way, she wouldn't get it from anybody else, either. That's the best way to deal with her.

ANDRÉ: I don't know, Joe. Sometimes, when I see her, I think she's really sick.

JOSEPH: Yeah! And it's the kind of sickness that gets cured with a good, swift kick in the rear.

ALICE *enters right and sits on a straight chair stage right.*

ANDRÉ: Allô, Joe. *(Il regarde autour de la chambre.)* Y sont pas prêtes encore?!? *(Il regarde sa montre.)* J'voudrais pas être en retard aujourd'hui. On a les dix premiers bancs de l'église réservés pour la famille. On est supposé de tout rentrer ensemble. On aurait d'l'air ben niaiseux si on était tout en retard.

JOSEPH: C'est Jeannette encore.

ANDRÉ: J'aurais dû l'savoir. A toutes les fêtes, c'est toujours la même affaire. Noël, Pâques, Thanksgiving, Mothers' Day . . . Jeannette dit toujours qu'a vient pas avec nous-autres. A est trop fatiguée, a est trop malade, a file pas ben. J'te dis que ça commence à être platte. *(Un temps)* Tu devrais y parler, Joe. Ça pas de bon sens, c'qu'a fait là. Après tout, c'est toué le plus vieux.

JOSEPH: Penses-tu que ça aiderait, ça, y parler? Pas une sacrée miette! Ça l'encouragerait à faire pire. Tu t'en souviens à toutes les fêtes, a finit-ti par venir? *(Ne le laisse pas repondre)* Toujours! A manquerait pas la chance d'avoir une cinquantaine de personnes à qui a peut raconter toutes ses maladies pour tout l'argent du monde.

ANDRÉ: Mais comment ça se fait que . . .

JOSEPH: *(Ne le laisse pas finir)* Parce qu'a veut de l'attention, c'est tout. A veut que tout le monde se mette à genoux pour l'implorer de venir. Pi c'est ça que tout le monde fait. Ben, pas moué. Si a veut de l'attention, a n'aura pas de moué. Pi si j'avais les affaires de ma façon, a n'aurait pas des autres, non plus. C'est la seule façon d'la traiter, ça.

ANDRÉ: J'l'sais pas, Joe. Des fois, là, quand j'la voué, a d'l'air vraiment malade.

JOSEPH: Ouais, pi c'est la sorte de maladie qui se guérit ainque avec des bons coups de pieds dans le derrière.

ALICE *entre de droite et s'assoit sur une chaise à droite.*

ALICE: Phew! I tell you, things are hoppin' upstairs. I haven't seen those two move that fast in thirty years. *(Yelling to off)* Step on it! That mass is today, you know! *(To* ANDRÉ*)* Have a seat, André. Standing up won't help them get ready any faster.

ANDRÉ: I don't understand how you can joke about this. You know how Father Paquette hates it when people come in late. Last week, during ten-thirty mass, he stopped right in the middle of the "Gloria" because Clem Sirois was late. It's true. He stopped everything . . . and he even watched every step Clem took until he got to his seat.

JOSEPH: He should do that more often. There's no excuse for being late for church. I'd even go a step farther and stand in front of the church doors before communion.

ALICE: What for?

JOSEPH: To keep people from leaving before mass is over.

ANDRÉ: That's right. At communion, half of the people head for the altar and the rest head for the hills.

JOSEPH: Mass starts at the beginning and ends only after the Last Gospel. It's a priest's duty to make sure his parishioners stay for it all.

ALICE: Well, if you were the parish priest, you'd send the cops to everybody's house on Sunday morning to make sure they went to church.

JOSEPH: There's nothing wrong with that.

ALICE: Yep! Catholics, Protestants, Jews, Chinese . . . whoever. To mass or to jail!

ANDRÉ: That's what it takes, sometimes.

ALICE: Phew! J'te dis que ça brasse en haut. Ça fait trente ans que j'ai pas vu ces deux-là se dépêcher comme ça. *(Elle crie par la porte.)* Grouillez-vous! C'pour aujourd'hui! *(A* ANDRÉ*)* Assis-toué donc, André. Y arriveront pas plus vite parce que t'es debout.

ANDRÉ: J'sais pas comment tu peux rester si calme. Tu sais comment le Père Paquette hait ça, le monde qui sont en retard. La semaine passée, à messe de dix heures et demie, y a arrêté au beau milieu du "Gloria" parce que Clem Sirois est rentré en retard. C'est vrai. Y a tout arrêté ... pi y a même watché Sirois jusqu'à temps qui arrive à son banc.

JOSEPH: Y devrait faire ça plus souvent. Y pas d'excuse pour être en retard pour la messe. Pi si j'tais lui, j'me mettrais en avant d'la porte en arrière de l'église avant la communion.

ALICE: Pi quoi c'est que ça f'rait, ça?

JOSEPH: Ça empêcherait le monde de partir avant que la messe est finie.

ANDRÉ: C'est vrai, ça. A communion, là, la moitié du monde qui se lève va à l'autel pi le reste sacre son camp.

JOSEPH: La messe, ça commence au commencement pi ça finit rienque après le dernier évangile. Le prêtre devrait être certain que le monde reste pour tout.

ALICE: Ben toué, là, si t'étais curé, tu enverrais la police à chaque maison le dimanche matin pour être certain que le monde alle à messe.

JOSEPH: J'voué rien de mal là-dedans.

ALICE: Ouais. Catholiques, protestants, Juifs, Chinois ... n'importe qui. Bang! envoie à messe! Bon pour eux-autres!

ANDRÉ: C'est ça que ça prend, des fois.

There's a knock at the door. NORMAND, *dressed in a black suit, enters without waiting for someone to open the door.*

JOSEPH: At least, it would keep them from committing a mortal sin and spending all of eternity in hell.

NORMAND: *(Looking at his watch. Teasing)* Isn't it a little early to damn people to hell, Joe? *(He crosses right and sits next to* ALICE.*)* Maybe you could let them stay over in purgatory until noon to make sure they're awake. Then, you can send them into the eternal flames.

ALICE: From what I hear, the food's a lot better in purgatory, You wouldn't want them to die of hunger before the devil got his hands on them. *(To* NORMAND*)* Hello, dear.

JOSEPH: *(Hard and sarcastic)* Mama would certainly be proud of both of you of she were alive today. Making fun of the Church like that! Well go ahead and laugh! But it's because of people like you that nobody goes to church any more.

ANDRÉ: *(Nervous)* That's true, you know. I remember when the whole church used to be full for ten thirty mass. Now, it's not even half full.

JOSEPH: *(He ignores* ANDRÉ's *comment.)* In a way, you can't blame them. With all the changes they've made, it might as well be a Protestant church.

NORMAND: Oh, come on, Joe. It's not that bad. Most of the kids even like it better this way.

JOSEPH: Oh, yeah! The damned kids. There's nothing we won't do for kids, these days. If we think they might not like something, we change it . . . and it's always a change for the worst. Bunch of damned juvenile delinquents. Let them stay home if they don't church the way it is. I can get along just fine without them.

On frappe à la porte. NORMAND, *habillé en noir, entre sans attendre qu'on lui ouvre.*

JOSEPH: Au moins, ça les empêcherait de commettre un péché mortel, pi de passer une éternité en enfer.

NORMAND: *(Il regarde sa montre. Taquineur)* Tu penses pas que c'est un peu de bonne heure pour envoyer du monde en enfer, Joe? *(Il va s'asseoir à côté d'*ALICE.*)* Tedben que tu pourrais les faire passer au purgatoire jusqu'à midi pour être certain qui sont réveillés. Après ça, tu pourrais les condamner.

ALICE: J'ai entendu dire que les lunchs sont meilleurs au purgatoire. Tu voudrais pas qui meurent de faim avant qui se rendent chez le diable. *(A* NORMAND*)* Allô, chéri.

JOSEPH: *(Dur)* Maman s'rait ben fière de vous-autres si a était encore en vie. Rire de l'Eglise comme ça! Ben, vous pouvez rire si vous voulez, mais c't'à cause du monde comme vous-autres qui a pu personne à l'église.

ANDRÉ: *(Nerveux)* C'est vrai, ça. J'm'en souviens quand l'église était pleine pour la messe de dix heures et demie. Là, a est même pas la moitié remplie.

JOSEPH: *(Il ignore la remarque de son frère.)* D'une façon, j'les blâme pas. Depuis toutes les changes, ça ressemble plutôt à un service protestant.

NORMAND: Voyons, Joe, c'est pas si pire que ça. Les jeunes aiment mieux ça, même.

JOSEPH: Ouais. Les mautadits jeunes. On fait tout pour eux-autres, asteur. Si y pensent que les jeunes aimeront pas ça, on le change. Pi ça change toujours pour le pire. Bande de maudits excités! Qui restent à maison si y aiment pas ça! Moué, j'peux ben m'en passer d'eux-autres.

ALICE: It might come as a surprise to you, Joe, but I think that most kids could get along just fine without you. *(To off)* Move it! *(She looks at* ANDRÉ *who is still just as nervous. To off)* The reverend Andrew here is getting nervous.

NORMAND: It's true that most of the rest of the family is already there.

ANDRÉ: What did I tell you? I knew it. Father Paquette will have a fit.

ALICE: Was Connie there?

NORMAND: I didn't see her. She'll probably stop here first, like she always does.

JOSEPH: *(With his mind still on kids)* Now that one's different. She's quiet, reserved, polite. Not jumping up and down and screaming all the time like most kids today.

ALICE: She's always been like that.

ANDRÉ: She'd better hurry up, too, before Father Paquette . . .

ALICE: *(Interrupting)* Would you keep quiet with your Father Paquette. I'm sick of Father Paquette. After all, it's not like he's Saint Peter and we're late for Judgment Day

JEANNETTE *and* YVONNE *enter right, dressed in black and wearing high heels. They have their make up on and are carrying fur jackets.* JEANNETTE *crosses to the rocking chair and sits.* YVONNE *crosses left and sits on one of the straight chairs up left. Everyone exchanges greetings.*

ALICE: *(To* ANDRÉ*)* See? I told you not to worry. They're ready . . . and with fifteen minutes to spare.

JOSEPH: It's a good thing we're right next to the church.

ALICE: J'veux pas t'faire trop d'peine, Joseph, mais j'ai l'impression que la plupart des jeunes, là, y peuvent ben se passer de toué, étou. *(Aux coulisses)* Dépêchez-vous donc! *(Elle regarde* ANDRÉ *qui est toujours nerveux. De nouveau aux coulisses)* Le curé commence à être nerveux!

NORMAND: C'est vrai que la plupart des autres sont déjà à l'église.

ANDRÉ: Voués-tu? J'l'savais. Le Père Paquette va être enragé noir.

ALICE: Connie était-ti là?

NORMAND: J'l'ai pas vue. Pour moué, a va arrêter icit avant, comme de coutume.

JOSEPH: *(Qui pense toujours aux jeunes)* Ça, c't'une bonne p'tite fille. Ben raisonnable. C'est pas une énervée comme les autres jeunes.

ALICE: A toujours été comme ça. Fine, polie, raisonnable . . .

ANDRÉ: A est aussi ben de s'dépêcher, elle étou. Le Père Paquette . . .

ALICE: *(Ne le laisse pas finir)* Veux-tu ben te taire avec ton Père Paquette, toué! A t'entendre parler, on dirait qui était Saint Pierre, pi nous-autres, on était en retard pour le Dernier Jugement.

JEANNETTE *et* YVONNE *entrent de droite, vêtues en noir, talons hauts, bien maquillées, avec des vestes en fourrure.* JEANNETTE *se dirige vers la chaise berçante et s'assoit.* YVONNE *se dirige à gauche et s'assoit sur une chaise du fond. Bonjours à tous.*

ALICE: *(A* ANDRÉ*)* Voués-tu? J'te l'ai dit de pas te tracasser. On a encore quinze minutes.

JOSEPH: Une chance qu'on est juste à côté de l'église.

JEANNETTE: *(Gazing out the window)* Ten years. *(Pause)* I can't believe it's been that long. Poor mama. *(She starts to cry. Takes a handkerchief from her sleeve and wipes her nose)* Our dear, sweet mama.

YVONNE: "Poor mama," alright. I wonder what she'd say of she knew that her daughter didn't even remember the day she died.

JEANNETTE: *(Quickly, trying to defend herself)* That's not true, Yvonne!

YVONNE: Lying's not going to help anything, Jeannette. You know very well you forgot. Poor mama. She certainly doesn't deserve that kind of treatment. *(She also starts to cry. Takes a handkerchief from her sleeve and wipes her eyes)*

JOSEPH: We couldn't have asked for a better mother, that's for sure.

ANDRÉ: That's very true. Mama was an angel, a saint.

YVONNE: That woman never thought of herself.

JOSEPH: I can tell you that mothers today aren't like that. They certainly won't do without things for the sake of their children. No. They want everything for themselves. I know. My son married a woman like that.

NORMAND: *(Lost in a dream)* I remember, the day she died . . . I went to the hospital straight from work. Do you know the first thing she said to me when I got there? She rattled off a list of everything there was to eat here and she told me to come right home and have supper. Not a word about her illness. Not a word about the pain she must have felt. Her only concern was about me.

ALICE: She took good care of us . . . all of us.

JEANNETTE: It's strange how things work out, isn't it. She died on Connie's birthday.

JEANNETTE: *(En regardant par la fenêtre. Rêveuse)* Dix ans. *(Un temps)* Ça presque pas de bon sens. Pauvre maman. *(Elle commence à pleurer. Sort son mouchoir de sa manche et se mouche)* Chère maman.

YVONNE: Oui, pauvre maman. J'me demande quoi c'est qu'a dirait si a savait que sa fille avait oublié l'anniversaire de sa mort.

JEANNETTE: *(Rapidement. Elle essaie de se défendre.)* C'pas vrai, ça, Yvonne!

YVONNE: Ah, ben commence pas à conter des menteries, asteur. Tu sais ben que tu avais oublié. Pauvre maman. A méritait certainement pas ça, elle. *(Elle commence à pleurer, elle aussi. Sort un mouchoir de sa manche et s'essuie les yeux)*

JOSEPH: On aurait pas pu demander pour une meilleure mère que ça, j't'l dis.

ANDRÉ: Ah, oui, c'est vrai, ça. Maman, c'tait un ange, une sainte.

YVONNE: Ç'a jamais pensé à elle-même, ça, c't'a femme-là.

JOSEPH: J'te dis que les mères aujourd'hui, c'est pas comme ça. Y veulent pu sacrifier pour leurs enfants. Non, y veulent tout pour eux-autres-mêmes. Je l'sais, moué. Mon gars en a marié une, une femme comme ça.

NORMAND: *(Rêveur)* J'm'en souviens, sur son lit de mort. Moué, j'venais juste d'arriver de l'ouvrage, pi savez-vous la première chose qu'a m'a dit? A m'a raconté tout quoi c'est qui avait à manger icit pi a m'a dit d'aller souper. Rien de sa maladie. Rien du mal qu'a sentait. A pensait rienque à moué.

ALICE: A n'a pris ben soin de nous-autres.

JEANNETTE: C'est drôle comment les affaires arrivent, hein? A est morte la journée de la fête à Constance.

YVONNE: The granddaughter she loved so much.

ALICE: And the granddaughter who loved her so much, too. You could see it, even when she was a little girl.

NORMAND: Connie was always right here at grandma's house.

JEANNETTE: *(Lost in the past)* Cards. That was her favorite thing to do, especially if we let her play with us. I remember the first time she got a chance to play cards with the grownups. It was on her birthday, like today. She couldn't have been much more than nine. She was so happy. We couldn't have given her a better gift.

YVONNE: You're all coming tonight, right?

NORMAND: I wouldn't miss it for the world. Twenty-one years old! What do you think she'd like for a present, Jeannette?

JOSEPH: *(Doesn't let her answer)* I'm going to give her money. That's always a sure bet. The way kids spend the stuff nowadays, they always need more.

JEANNETTE: I wouldn't worry too much, Normand. You know she likes everything we give her. She's easy to please. As for money, Joe, she's one of the few who doesn't really need any more, now that she's working and living at home with Eva and Roger.

JOSEPH: Well, if I were her father, I'd at least make her pay room and board. If kids can work and earn money, they sure as hell can contribute a few bucks to their keep every week.

ALICE: That's probably why both of your kids took off real fast after college.

ANDRÉ: I've got to go to the parish hall at seven tonight, so I might be a little late.

Yvonne: Celle qu'a aimait tant.

Alice: Pi qui l'aimait tant, étou. On pouvait le voir, même quand a était ben petite.

Normand: A était toujours chez sa mémère, Connie.

Jeannette: *(Rêveuse)* Jouer aux cartes. A aimait-ti ça, jouer aux cartes avec nous-autres, c't'a p'tite fille-là. J'm'en souviens la première fois qu'on l'a laissée jouer aux cartes avec le grand monde. C'tait sa fête, comme aujourd'hui. A devait pas avoir plus que neuf ans. A était assez contente, c't'a fille-là. On aurait pas pu y donner un meilleur cadeau.

Yvonne: Vous allez venir à soir, hein, vous-autres?

Normand: Moué, j'manquerais pas ça. Vingt-et-un ans! Quelle sorte de cadeau qu'a aimerait, penses-tu, Jeannette?

Joseph: *(Ne la laisse pas répondre)* Moué, j'va y donner d'l'argent. On peut toujours être certain avec de l'argent. Les jeunes n'ont toujours besoin, d'la façon qui la dépensent.

Jeannette: Ça fait pas grand différence, Normand. Tu sais qu'a aime tout ce qu'on y donne. A est pas difficile à plaire. Quand à l'argent, Joe, à n'a pas vraiment de besoin asteur qu'a travaille. Ça coûte pas cher, rester à maison avec Eva pi Roger, t'sais.

Joseph: Si j'tais son père, moué, a payerait pension. Des enfants qui travaillent, on devrait pas nourrir ça pi loger ça pour rien.

Alice: Ça doit être pour ça que tes enfants ont décollé aussi vite que possible après le collège.

André: Moué, faut que j'alle à la salle paroissiale à sept heures à soir, ça fait que j'va être en retard un peu.

NORMAND: Are you making that world famous cake in the shape of a lamb, Jeannette?

YVONNE: If she doesn't forget all about it.

NORMAND: I remember that when Connie was young, she loved that cake so much that she wouldn't let anybody eat it.

There's a knock at the door. CONSTANCE *enters up left. She is attractive, but her whole outfit is somewhat out of style, just like those of her aunts.*

NORMAND: Well, speak of the devil. Happy birthday, Connie! Let me be the first to give you a big birthday hug. *(He gets up, crosses to* CONSTANCE, *gives her a big hug, and returns to his seat.)* How are you, my darling . . . and aging niece?

CONSTANCE: Fine, Uncle Normand, fine. Hi, Uncle Joe . . . Uncle Andy. *(She goes to each relative and gives them a kiss. The aunts and uncles all greet her with a "Hello, dear" "Happy Birthday, Connie," etc.)*

ANDRÉ: Great! Now if everybody's here, let's get going.

ALICE: Don't be in such a hurry, André.

NORMAND: Yeah, slow down. I'd like to hear how it feels to be twenty-one. It's been such a long time that I've completely forgotten.

YVONNE: Come on, now. You're not that old, Normand.

NORMAND: Yeah, but I forget fast. You know, about the only thing I remember is that the beer I drank when I was twenty-one was never quite as good as the beer I drank at eighteen. Maybe that's because the beer I had at eighteen was illegal.

NORMAND: Fais-tu ton fameux gâteau-lapin, c't'année, Jeannette?

YVONNE: Si a l'oublie pas.

NORMAND: J'm'en souviens, quand a était jeune, Connie l'aimait tant, ce gâteau-là, qu'a voulait même pas qu'on le mange.

On frappe à la porte. CONSTANCE entre. Elle est jolie, mais habillée d'une façon démodée, un peu comme ses tantes.

NORMAND: Tiens, en parlant de la bête, on y voué la tête! Bonne fête, Connie! Laisse-moué être le premier à t'embrasser. (NORMAND *se lève et se dirige vers* CONSTANCE. *Il lui donne un gros baiser et retourne à sa chaise.*) Comment ça va, ma fille?

CONSTANCE: Pas pire, mon oncle, pas pire. Allô, mon oncle Joe . . . mon oncle André. (*Elle va à chaque personne et lui donne un baiser. Les oncles et tantes répondent avec des "Allô, chérie," "Bonne fête," "Allô, Connie," etc.*)

ANDRÉ: Bon, ben si on est tout icit, on est aussi ben de décoller.

ALICE: Presse-toué pas tant, André.

NORMAND: Ouais. Moué, j'aimerais ben entendre comment ça file d'avoir vingt-et-un ans. Ça fait si longtemps que chu passé par là que j'm'en souviens pu.

YVONNE: Voyons, t'es pas si vieux que ça, Normand.

NORMAND: Ça prend pas d'temps d'oublier ça. Sais-tu, la seule chose que j'me souviens c'est que la bière de vingt-et-un ans a jamais goûté aussi bonne que la bière de dix-huit ans. Tedben c'est parce qu'on avait le droit de la boire, à vingt-et-un ans.

JOSEPH: It's a good thing that mama never knew you were drinking beer at eighteen. It would have killed her to know that her youngest wasn't the good little boy she thought you were.

ALICE: Don't exaggerate, Joe. Your mother was a lot tougher than you think. It would have taken a lot worse than that to knock her off.

JOSEPH: Well, she wouldn't have liked it, that I'm sure of.

NORMAND: Relax, Joe. We all had our first sips of beer when we were pretty young.

JOSEPH: Not me!

ALICE: *(Sarcastic)* You've always been just a bit different from everybody else, Joe.

ANDRÉ: Enough with the drinking. We should have been at church ten minutes ago. We'd all better get moving.

NORMAND: *(Getting up. To* CONSTANCE*)* Ready for your party tonight? After all, you're only twenty-one once in your life. How many people are you going to invite, Jeannette? Two hundred? Maybe three hundred?

JEANNETTE: *(Getting up)* Only the immediate family.

NORMAND: Ah, four hundred, then.

ALICE: If you don't count the children.

All the characters except for CONSTANCE *get up and head for the door up left.*

NORMAND: *(To* CONSTANCE*)* We'll have a great time, you'll see.

YVONNE: *(Sighs)* It will do all of us some good to have a little fun after this morning. That's what mama would have wanted. *(To* CONSTANCE*)* She loved you a lot, you know.

JOSEPH: Une chance que maman a jamais su que tu buvais à c't'âge-là, toué. Ça l'aurait tué de savoir que son plus jeune se débauchait.

ALICE: Commence pas à exagérer, toué. A était pas mal tough, ta mère. Ça aurait pris plus que ça pour la tuer.

JOSEPH: Ben, a l'aurait pas aimé ça. Ça, j'l'sais.

NORMAND: Voyons, Joe, on a tout pris notre première p'tite bière quand on était pas mal jeune.

JOSEPH: Pas moué!

ALICE: *(Ironique)* T'as toujours été rienque un p'tit peu différent, toué.

ANDRÉ: Voulez-vous arrêter ces histoires de buvage. Ça fait dix minutes qu'on aurait dû être à l'église. On est aussi ben de s'grouiller.

NORMAND: *(En se levant. A* CONSTANCE*)* As-tu hâte pour ton party, à soir? Après tout, vingt-et-un ans, ça arrive pas souvent, ça. Combien de monde que tu vas inviter, Jeannette? Deux cents? Trois cents?

JEANNETTE: *(Se levant aussi)* Rienque la famille.

NORMAND: Ça, ça veut dire quatre cents.

ALICE: Ça, c'est ainque si tu comptes pas les enfants.

Les autres personnages, sauf CONSTANCE*, se lèvent et se préparent à sortir.*

NORMAND: *(A* CONSTANCE*)* On va avoir du fun, tu vas voir!

YVONNE: *(Pousse un soupir)* Ça va nous faire du bien de célébrer un peu après à matin. C'est ça que maman aurait voulu. *(A* CONSTANCE*)* A t'aimait gros, tu sais, ma p'tite fille.

CONSTANCE *nods. She stares at the floor.*

JEANNETTE: What's wrong, Connie?

NORMAND: If you think turning twenty-one is sad, wait till you get to my age. That's when birthdays become disasters.

CONSTANCE: *(Still staring at the floor. Very softly)* It's not that.

ANDRÉ: Well, I'm not going to wait another minute. You can hang around and be late if you want, but I'm taking off. *(To* JOSEPH *and* NORMAND*)* Are you two coming?

JOSEPH: Sure.

NORMAND: O.k. Lets go.

ALICE: This won't take long. We'll be there in just a minute.

During the next scene, the three aunts should form a semicircle around CONSTANCE *and gradually move in closer with practically each line.*

JEANNETTE: What is it, Connie?

Pause

YVONNE: You can tell your old aunts.

ALICE: We can tell that something's bothering you.

Pause

JEANNETTE: Come on, my little Connie. Tell us.

Pause

CONSTANCE *fait signe de tête que oui. Elle regarde le plancher.*

JEANNETTE: Quoi c'est qui a, donc, chérie?

NORMAND: Si tu penses que c'est triste à vingt-et-un ans, attends que tu arrives à mon âge. Là, une fête, c'est un vrai désastre.

CONSTANCE: *(Elle regarde toujours le plancher. Très doucement)* C'est pas ça.

ANDRÉ: Ben moué, chu tanné d'attendre. Vous pouvez être en retard si vous voulez, mais moué, j'décolle. *(A* JOSEPH *et* NORMAND*)* V'nez-vous, vous-autres?

JOSEPH: Oui.

NORMAND: O.k. Allons-y.

ALICE: Ça s'ra pas long. On va être là dans une minute.

Pendant la scène suivante, les trois tantes devraient se rapprocher de CONSTANCE *presqu'à chaque réplique.*

JEANNETTE: Quoi c'est qui a, donc, Connie?

Pause.

YVONNE: Tu peux nous le dire.

ALICE: On peut voir qui a quèque chose qui te bâdre.

Pause

JEANNETTE: Dis-nous donc, chérie.

Pause

CONSTANCE: Well, . . . *(she raises her eyes, looks at her aunts, and lowers them once more)* . . . I might not be able to come tonight.

The three aunts react almost in unison.

JEANNETTE: What?

YVONNE: How come?

ALICE: Why not, Connie?!?

CONSTANCE: *(Still staring at the floor)* Well, Jerry wants us to go out to eat and then to a rock concert.

YVONNE: Who's Jerry?

JEANNETTE: Where have you been? Jerry's her new boyfriend.

YVONNE: Well, I didn't think it was getting this serious.

ALICE: It doesn't have to be serious for a boy to ask a girl out for dinner and a concert. This isn't 1920, you know. *(Pause)* And I think it's a great idea. It's fun to go out for your birthday.

YVONNE: But the party? The whole family is looking forward to it.

JEANNETTE: *(To CONSTANCE)* Listen, sweetheart, we'd better go if we don't want to be late for church. We can work this all out later, o.k.? *(CONSTANCE looks at her aunts and nods.)* O.k. Let's go!

The women take their handbags and their rosary beads. ALICE and CONSTANCE take their prayer books. All four cross to the door up left and exits while talking. Pause.

Curtain

CONSTANCE: Ben, . . . *(elle se lève la tête, regarde les tantes, et la baisse de nouveau)* . . . j'pense pas que j'va pouvoir venir à soir.

Les trois tantes réagissent presque tous ensemble.

JEANNETTE: Quoi?

YVONNE: Voyons!

ALICE: Pourquoi pas, donc?!?

CONSTANCE: *(Toujours la tête baissée)* Ben, Jerry veut qu'on alle manger à un restaurant, pi après ça au concert à soir.

YVONNE: Qui c'est ça, Jerry?

JEANNETTE: C'est son nouveau boyfriend, voyons!

YVONNE: Ah, ben j'savais pas que c'tait si sérieux que ça.

ALICE: Pas besoin que ça soit sérieux pour qu'un gars invite une fille pour sortir manger pi aller à un concert. On est pas en 1920, t'sais. *(Un temps)* Ben moué, j'trouve que c'est une bonne idée. C'est le fun de sortir, surtout quand c'est sa fête.

YVONNE: Mais le party. Toute la famille est prête à venir.

JEANNETTE: *(A* CONSTANCE*)* Ecoute, chérie. On est aussi ben de partir si on veut pas manquer la messe. On parlera de ça plus tard, o.k.? *(*CONSTANCE *regarde les tantes et fait signe de tête que oui.)* O.K. Allons-y.

Les femmes prennent leurs sacs à main et leurs chapelets. ALICE *et* CONSTANCE *prennent leurs missels. Les quatre se dirigent vers la porte à gauche en parlant. Un temps.*

Rideau

ACT II

Same room as in Act I. It's just after lunch. JOSEPH is sitting on one of the straight chairs up left. YVONNE is sitting at the table on a chair stage left. ALICE is clearing the table. All three sisters are now wearing everyday dresses with aprons. JOSEPH is wearing a sport shirt and pants. As the curtain opens, we hear coughing coming from off right.

JOSEPH: *(Loud. To off right)* If you ask me, it's a total waste of time to bake a cake for nothing.

JEANNETTE: *(From off right)* It won't be for nothing, you'll see.

JOSEPH: *(To off)* She said she wasn't coming. Sounds pretty definite to me. She's not coming. That's it.

ALICE: *(Loud, so that JEANNETTE can hear)* Let her be, Joe. She's got to learn that when most people say no, they're not doing it just to get attention. They really mean no!

YVONNE: Well I think it's sad. Connie's birthday parties were always so much fun with all the food and everybody singing and laughing. You can't tell me she's not going to miss all that. *(She takes a deck of cards from her apron pocket and starts a game of solitaire.)*

ALICE: I think that's all up to Jerry. Could very well be she won't miss it at all.

JOSEPH: Who the hell is this Jerry? I've never heard a thing about him before this morning.

YVONNE: I guess she's been going out with him for a while.

ACTE II

L'heure du midi, juste après le déjeuner. JOSEPH *est assis sur une chaise au fond à gauche.* YVONNE *est assise à table sur la chaise à gauche. Après un temps, elle commence à jouer à un jeu de patience.* ALICE *dessert la table. Les femmes portent maintenant des robes de tous les jours.* JOSEPH *porte un pantalon et une chemise ouverte au cou. On entend du toussage des coulisses à droite.*

JOSEPH: *(Fort. Aux coulisses)* Ben moué, j'trouve que c'est bête, faire un gâteau pour rien.

JEANNETTE: *(Des coulisses)* Ça s'ra pas pour rien, tu vas voir.

JOSEPH: *(Même jeu)* A dit qu'a venait pas. Ça m'a d'l'air ben simple, ça. A vient pas, c'est tout!

ALICE: *(Fort, pour que* JEANNETTE *entende)* Laisse-la faire, Joe. Faut qu'apprenne que quand la plupart du monde disent "non," c'est pas parce qui veulent se faire prier. C'est parce qui veulent dire "non."

YVONNE: Ben moué, j'trouve que c'est ben de valeur, anyway. C'tait toujours des si beaux parties qu'on avait pour Connie. Tu peux pas me dire qu'à manquera pas ça.

ALICE: Ça, ça dépend pas mal de Jerry. Ça se peut qu'a manque pas ça une sacrée miette.

JOSEPH: Qui c'est que c'est ça, ce Jerry-là? C'est la première fois que j'n'entends parler.

YVONNE: Ça d'l'air que ça fait une secousse qu'a sort avec.

JOSEPH: Is it serious?

ALICE: Could be.

YVONNE: She didn't even tell us about him. That's what bothers me. With her other boyfriends, we were the first to know all about them.

JEANNETTE: *(From off)* Yep. The first thing she'd do was bring 'em over here for us to meet them.

ALICE: Maybe that's why none of them lasted very long. We scared them off.

YVONNE: Be serious, Alice. Anyway, I've only seen this one once, and it wasn't close up. Last week . . . *(to off right)* . . . was it Friday or Saturday, Jeannette?

JEANNETTE: *(From off right)* Saturday.

YVONNE: Well last Saturday, I just happened to be going by the window in the living room . . .

ALICE: *(Interrupting her)* Don't believe it! She'd been waiting at that window all afternoon to try to catch a glimpse of him. She's lucky that Connie lives right across the street.

YVONNE: *(Continuing)* . . . and I see him get out of his car to pick her up .

JEANNETTE: *(From off right)* He's tall and really good looking.

ALICE: She just happened to be going by the very same window at the very same time.

JOSEPH: But that doesn't tell us much. What does Eva think about all this?

JOSEPH: C'est sérieux, comme ça?

ALICE: Ça d'l'air.

YVONNE: A nous en a même pas parlé. C'est ça qui me tracasse. Avec ses autres boyfriends, a nous racontait tout.

JEANNETTE: Oui, la première chose qu'a faisait c'était des amener icit pour qu'on les rencontre.

ALICE: C'est tedben pour ça que toutes ses autres boyfriends l'ont laissée. On les épeurait.

YVONNE: Voyons, Alice. Anyway, celui-là, on l'a ainque vu une fois, pi c'tait pas de proche. La semaine dernière . . . *(aux coulisses)* . . . c'tait-ti vendredi ou samedi, Jeannette?

JEANNETTE: *(Des coulisses)* Samedi.

YVONNE: Ben samedi passé, j'passais par le châssis d'en avant . . .

ALICE: *(Interrompant)* Cré-la pas! Ça faisait toute l'après-midi qu'a était plantée là pour essayer d'l'voir. Une chance que Connie reste juste à côté.

YVONNE: *(Continuant)* . . . pi je l'aperçois qui sort de sa machine pour aller chercher Connie.

JEANNETTE: *(Des coulisses)* C't'un beau, grand gars.

ALICE: A s'adonnait à passer par le même châssis en même temps.

JOSEPH: Mais ça nous dit pas grand'chose, ça. Quoi c'est qu'Eva pense de ça?

JEANNETTE: *(From off right)* Well, from what I've heard . . .

ALICE: *(Interrupting)* If you wait a minute, you can ask her yourself. Here she is.

EVA *enters from up left, crosses to the straight chair next to* JOSEPH *and sits. She is attractive and wears slacks, a blouse, and a cardigan sweater. Everyone exchanges greetings.*

EVA: Hello. That was really beautiful this morning. *(Everyone nods.)* I think it was the best anniversary mass we've ever had for mama.

YVONNE: Poor mama. She certainly deserves the best.

EVA: And Father Paquette spoke so well. I thought it was really nice of him to say all those wonderful things about her.

JOSEPH: They were all true.

JEANNETTE: *(From off right)* From what I could see, there wasn't a dry eye in the place.

YVONNE: Poor Connie. I've never seen anyone cry so much. She really loved her grandma, didn't she?

JEANNETTE: *(Appears at the door down right)* I remember when she was little. She used to come over here and Yvonne and I would try to get her to go out with us. We'd promise her everything . . . toys, candy, ice cream, whatever she wanted. "No!" she'd say. "I gonna stay grammy house!" *(She exits right.)*

EVA: *(To* JEANNETTE*)* What are you doing in there?

ALICE: She's making the birthday cake.

EVA: A birthday cake for who?

JEANNETTE: *(Des coulisses)* Ben, j'te dis que . . . .

ALICE: *(Ne la laisse pas finir)* Si tu attends une minute, tu pourras y demander en personne. La v'là qui arrive.

EVA *entre, se dirige vers la chaise à côté de* JOSEPH, *et s'assoit. Elle est assez jolie. Elle porte des slacks, une chemise, et un gilet. Bonjours de tous.*

EVA: Allô. C'tait beau, à matin, hein? *(Tout le monde fait signe de tête que oui.)* J'pense que c'était le plus beau service anniversaire qu'on a pas eu.

YVONNE: Pauvre maman. A méritait tout ce qui a de plus beau.

EVA: Y a ben parler, hein, le Père Paquette? J'ai trouvé qui était ben fin de dire ces belles affaires-là à propos de maman.

JOSEPH: C'tait tout vrai.

JEANNETTE: *(Des coulisses)* J'te dis qui avait pas grand monde qui avait pas les larmes aux yeux.

YVONNE: Pauvre Connie. J'ai jamais vu une fille pleurer tant. A l'aimait sa mémère, c't'a fille-là.

JEANNETTE: *(Se montre à la porte à droite)* J'm'en souviens quand a était p'tite pi a venait icit. On essayait d'la faire sortir avec nous autres, Yvonne pi moué. On promettait d'y acheter toutes sortes d'affaires . . . du candé, d'l'ice cream, des bébelles. "Non!" a disait. "Moué, veux rester avec mémère!" *(Elle sort de nouveau.)*

EVA: *(A* JEANNETTE*)* Quoi c'est que tu fais là-dedans, toué?

ALICE: A est après faire le birthday cake.

EVA: Mais pour qui, donc?

YVONNE: Come on, Eva. Don't tell me you're starting to forget everything like your sister. It's your own daughter's birthday today.

EVA: *(Taken aback a little)* I know, but . . . *(Pause)* . . . Didn't she talk to you about that this morning?

ALICE: Of course she did, but your sister's stubborn as a mule. She still thinks that Connie's coming.

JEANNETTE: *(Enters right carrying a covered platter. She crosses to the large table and puts the platter down.)* Of course, she's coming. Do you think she'd miss a cake like this?!? *(She lifts the cover to reveal a beautiful cake in the shape of a lamb. "Oohs" from everyone. She puts the cover back on, crosses to the rocking chair and sits.)*

YVONNE: Besides, Connie likes to spend her birthdays with us. She's said it often enough.

EVA: I think things might be starting to change.

ALICE: It's about time. Connie's not a little girl any more.

EVA: Since she met Jerry, things are starting to change a lot.

YVONNE: Strange. She doesn't seem all that different to me.

JEANNETTE: Well I've noticed that she's changed.

YVONNE: With all the time you spend complaining about your own life, I'm surprised you still find time to notice what's happening in other people's.

JEANNETTE: *(Pays no attention to her)* And it's not the types of changes you're all thinking of. You don't see it right away, but I think she's more serious.

YVONNE: Voyons donc, Eva. Dis-moué pas que tu commences à oublier, toué étou. C'est la fête à ta fille aujourd'hui, t'sais.

EVA: *(Un peu pris au dépourvu)* Oui, j'l'sais, mais . . . *(Un temps)* . . . a vous en a pas parlé à matin, comme ça?

ALICE: Ben sûr qu'a nous en a parlé, mais ta soeur a la tête dure. A pense encore qu'a va venir.

JEANNETTE: *(Entre de droite avec un gâteau magnifique en forme de lapin. Se dirige vers la table à gauche et y dépose le gâteau. Elle retourne à droite et s'assoit sur la chaise berçante.)* Ben sûr qu'a va venir. Penses-tu qu'a manquerait un beau gâteau comme ça?!?

YVONNE: A part de ça, c't'avec nous autres que Connie aime passer sa fête. A nous l'a dit assez souvent.

EVA: Ben, j'pense que les choses commencent à changer.

ALICE: C't'a peu près l'temps. A pu onze ans, asteur, Connie.

EVA: Depuis qu'a rencontré Jerry, j'vous dis que ça change pas mal.

YVONNE: C'est drôle. A me paraît pas ben différente.

JEANNETTE: Ben moué, j'ai remarqué qu'a changé.

YVONNE: Avec le temps que tu passes à te plaindre, j'pensais pas que t'avais la chance de remarquer c'qui s'passait chez les autres.

JEANNETTE: *(L'ignorant)* Pi c'est pas d'la façon que vous pensez, vous autres. Ça se voit pas tout de suite, mais j'trouve qu'a est plus sérieuse qu'avant.

YVONNE: She's always been serious.

JEANNETTE: And sadder, too.

ALICE: A true sign of love.

EVA: I'm afraid so.

YVONNE: What do you think about all this, Eva?

EVA: Well, Jerry's real nice. He's polite, well-dressed . . . *(Pause)* And he seems to have a good head on his shoulders.

JEANNETTE: Where did she meet him?

EVA: That's a little complicated. Do you know Debbie Beaulieu who went to college with Connie?

JEANNETTE: I don't think so.

JOSEPH: Sure you do. She lives on Sixth Street. Her father's Alfred Beaulieu who runs that little grocery store on the corner of Broad and Park.

JEANNETTE *(She remembers.)* Oh, right!

EVA: Well, Jerry's a friend of one of her friends. They all went out together one night and it seems that Jerry and Connie hit it off pretty well.

YVONNE: So how long have they been going out?

EVA: About two months, I guess. But in the past few weeks, they've started seeing each other more often . . .

ALICE: Hmmm.

YVONNE: A toujours été sérieuse.

JEANNETTE: Pi plus triste, étou.

ALICE: Ça, c'est l'amour, certain.

EVA: Ça ben d'l'air à ça.

YVONNE: Quoi c'est que tu penses de ça, toué, Eva?

EVA: Ah, ben y est ben fin, Jerry. Poli, ben habillé . . . *(Un temps)* Pi y a pas d'l'air excité.

JEANNETTE: Où c'est qu'a l'a rencontré, donc?

EVA: Ça, c'est un peu compliqué. Connais-tu la p'tite Beaulieu qui est allée au collège avec Connie?

JEANNETTE: Ah, j'pense pas.

JOSEPH: Ben oui, tu la connais. A reste sur la Sixième. Son père, c'est Alfred Beaulieu qui a le p'tit magasin au coin d'la Broad pi la Park.

JEANNETTE: *(Qui se souvient)* Ah oui!

EVA: Ben, Jerry, c'est le frère d'un de ses chums. Y ont tout sorti ensemble un soir, pi ça d'l'air que Jerry a trouvé Connie pas mal de son goût.

YVONNE: Pi ça fait comment longtemps qui sortent ensemble?

EVA: Oh, à peu près deux mois. Mais depuis une couple de semaines, y se voient plus souvent . . .

ALICE: Hmmm.

EVA: . . .. almost every day. He picks her up at work. Then, they go out for a while and he drives her home.

ALICE: And where does he work?

EVA: He doesn't right now. He graduated from college last year, but he hasn't been able to find a job. I guess teaching jobs are hard to find these days.

JOSEPH: Why doesn't he get another job while he's waiting?

EVA: He tried, but it didn't work out.

YVONNE: What do you mean?

EVA: I don't know, really. He just said it didn't work out.

JOSEPH: Yeah, well I know. When I was young, I was happy just to have a job . . . any job. Kids today, they just don't . . .

ALICE: Will you stop it! I know I wouldn't like to spend four years in college just to end up picking up garbage for a living.

JOSEPH: *(Loud)* There are other things he could do. And even collecting garbage is better than being on welfare and taking money from the government.

ALICE: Well if that's the way you feel, why don't you turn down your Social Security and Medicaid next year when you retire and get a job at the town dump.

JOSEPH: That's not the same thing at all!

EVA: . . . . même presque tous les jours. Y va la chercher à l'ouvrage. Y sortent pour une secousse, pi y vient la reconduire.

ALICE: Où c'est qui travaille, lui?

EVA: Y travaille pas, comme c'est là. Y a gradué du collège l'année passée, mais y a pas pu trouver de job. C'est tough de trouver, des jobs à enseigner l'école asteur.

JOSEPH: Me semble que ça l'empêcherait pas de trouver une autre job en attendant.

EVA: Y a essayé, mais ça pas marché.

YVONNE: Quoi c'est que tu veux dire?

EVA: J'l'sais pas trop. Y a ainque dit que ça pas marché.

JOSEPH: Ben moué, j'l'sais. Moué, quand j'tais jeune, j'tais content d'avoir une job . . . n'importe quelle job. Les jeunes aujourd'hui, j'vous dis que . . . .

ALICE: Veux-tu arrêter, toué. J'l'sais que j'aimerais pas passer quatre ans au collège pi passer ma vie à ramasser d'la rubbish.

JOSEPH: *(Fort)* Y a pas ainque ça à faire. Pi même ramasser la rubbish, c'est mieux que de prendre d'l'argent d'l'état.

ALICE: Ben si tu files comme ça, j'veux que tu refuses ton Social Security pi ton Medicaid l'année prochaine, mèque tu t'retires, pi que tu alles t'engager à dompe.

JOSEPH: C'est pas la même chose pantoute, ça!

ALICE: Of course, it's not the same. One situation deals with somebody else . . . and the other applies to you. That seems to change everything, as far as you're concerned.

JEANNETTE: *(Still thinking of* CONSTANCE. *To* EVA*)* If they're together so often, I'm surprised I haven't seen them in church.

EVA: Well . . . he's Irish. His last name is Kelley.

JOSEPH: So he wouldn't belong to our parish.

YVONNE: He must go to Sacred Heart.

EVA: No . . . no. *(She hesitates.)* Actually, Jerry's Protestant.

Everybody reacts almost in unison.

JEANNETTE: What?!?

YVONNE: Oh, no!

JOSEPH: Damn!

EVA: At least he was raised Protestant. Now, he doesn't seem to believe in much of anything.

YVONNE: Ah!

JOSEPH: And you're still letting her go out with him?!?

EVA: What should I do, Joe? At twenty-one, she's old enough . . . and I hope smart enough . . . to decide for herself.

JOSEPH: From what you've just said, she could've fooled me.

ALICE: Ben non, c'est pas la même chose. Dans un cas, c'est quèqu'un d'autre . . . pi dans l'autre cas, c'est toué. Ça change ben des affaires, ça.

JEANNETTE: *(Qui pense toujours à* Constance. *A* Eva*)* Si y sont ensembles si souvent, ça me surprend que j'l'ai pas vu à messe avec elle.

EVA: Ben . . . c't'un anglais. Son nom de famille, c'est Kelley.

JOSEPH: Ah, ben ça s'rait pas d'la paroisse, ça.

YVONNE: Y doivent aller au Sacré-Coeur.

EVA: Non . . . non. *(Elle hésite.)* Si vous voulez savoir la franche vérité, Jerry, c't'un protestant.

Tout le monde réagit presque ensemble.

JEANNETTE: Dis-moué pas?!?

YVONNE: Ah, non!

JOSEPH: Y manquait ainque ça!

EVA: Au moins, y a été élevé protestant. Asteur, y cré pu dans grand chose d'la façon qui parle.

YVONNE: Ah!

JOSEPH: Pi tu la laisses encore sortir avec lui?!?

EVA: Quoi c'est que tu veux que j'fasse, Joe? A vingt-et-un ans, t'sais, a est capable de décider pour elle-même.

JOSEPH: Ça se voit pas, de ce que tu viens d'nous dire.

YVONNE: Have you talked to her, at least?

EVA: Of course, I've talked to her. But it's not like she's going to marry him. They're dating, that's all.

JOSEPH: All the more reason to put a stop to it now, before it gets even more serious.

EVA: I don't know.

JOSEPH: That's what your mother would have done. And she did it often. She didn't forget her duties as a mother. If we went out with someone she didn't like, she sure let us know. And you can be sure we didn't go out with that one again. Mama wasn't going to let us marry just anybody who came along.

Silence. We can tell that the women are not comfortable with this particular topic. JEANNETTE *rocks furiously and takes one drag after another from her cigarette.* YVONNE *forgets about her game of solitaire.* EVA *stares at the portrait of their mother. Pause*

ALICE: Congratulations, Joe. You single-handedly managed to stop your fours sisters from saying a word. Who wants a drink? *(She gets up and crosses to the sideboard.)* There's no rule against starting the party a little early. Besides, it looks like everybody could use one.

ALICE *takes out the bottle of vodka and stares at it for a moment.* JEANNETTE *stops rocking and watches* ALICE. ALICE *notices* JEANNETTE, *who quickly turns her head and looks out the window.* ALICE *crosses to the door down right and exits.*

JOSEPH: But it's all true. If I remember right, it happened to you a couple of times, Yvonne. You went out with two losers and mama put a stop to it but fast.

ALICE: *(Appears at the door)* It's a good thing, too, because neither one of them amounted to anything. One bought a hardware store in Connecticut

YVONNE: Y as-tu parlé, au moins?

EVA: Ben oui, j'y ai parlé. Mais voyons, c'est pas comme si a allait le marier, Jerry. Y sortent ensemble, c'est tout.

JOSEPH: Bonne raison d'arrêter ça tout de suite, avant que ça vienne plus sérieux.

EVA: J'l'sais pas.

JOSEPH: C'est ça que ta mère aurait fait, elle. Pi a l'a fait souvent. C'était pas une pour oublier ses devoirs de mère, elle, maman. Si on sortait avec quèqu'un qui était pas de son goût, a nous l'disait. Pi j'te dis qu'on sortait pu avec après ça. A était pas pour nous laisser marier n'importe qui, elle, maman.

Silence. On voit que les femmes ne sont pas du tout comfortables. JEANNETTE *se berce rapidement et prend plusieurs bouffées de sa cigarette.* YVONNE *devient distraite et oublie son jeu de patience.* EVA *regarde fixement le portrait de sa mère. Un temps*

ALICE: Bonne façon de tuer la conversation, Joe. Qui c'est qui veut une drink, là? *(Elle se lève et se dirige vers le buffet à gauche.)* On est aussi ben de commencer le party de bonne heure . . . pi ça d'l'air qu'on en a tout besoin.

ALICE *sort la bouteille de vodka et la contemple pour un instant.* JEANNETTE *arrête de se bercer et guette* ALICE. ALICE *aperçoit* JEANNETTE, *qui se tourne et regarde par la fenêtre.* ALICE *se dirige vers la porte à droite et sort.*

JOSEPH: Mais c'est vrai, voyons. Toué, Yvonne, ça t'es arrivé un couple de fois, si j'm'en souviens. Tu sortais avec deux escogriffes, pi maman a arrêté ça, hein?

ALICE: *(Elle se montre à la porte à droite.)* Une chance, parce que c'taient des vauriens. Un a acheté une besogne au Connecticut, pi y a fait en

and made loads of money. The other one became a lawyer in Worcester. That's not the kind of people you want to marry, that's for sure. *(She exits again.)*

JOSEPH: *(To off)* Well at least she kept Jeannette from wasting her life with Bernie. *(To* JEANNETTE. *Sarcastic)* You were in for a wonderful life with him, huh, Jeannette? *(Pause)* He was running around on you all the time you were going out with him *(Pause)* Yep, you would have lived "happily ever after" with him.

Silence. ALICE *enters down right with a tray and five full glasses. She serves* JOSEPH, *then* EVA, YVONNE *and* JEANNETTE. ALICE *crosses right, places the tray on one of the straight chairs and sits on the other.* JEANNETTE *downs her drink in one gulp the moment she gets it.*

JOSEPH: You know, it takes guts for a mother to do that. *(*JEANNETTE *gets up and exits down right.)* Yep, you would have been real happy with him, Jeannette.

ALICE *stares at* JOSEPH *and puts her finger up to her lips to try to get him to shut up.*

JOSEPH: What's wrong with all of you. Everything I said is true. Every word of it. Mama was right to be strict with us about who we liked and who we went out with. Her plan was to make sure we married just the right person . . . and the way I see it, it worked.

ANDRÉ *enters from up left. He stays at the door for a moment, somewhat surprised by the tone of the discussion.*

ALICE: *(Hard)* You're right, Joe. It worked so well that she ended up with a bunch of old maids.

JEANNETTE *enters down right with a full glass. She notices* ANDRÉ.

masse d'l'argent. Pi l'autre est devenu avocat à Worcester. C'est pas du monde à marier, ça, j'te l'dis. *(Elle sort de nouveau.)*

JOSEPH: *(Aux coulisses)* Ben au moins elle a empêché Jeannette de gaspiller sa vie avec Bernard. Parle d'un grément. *(A* JEANNETTE. *Ironique)* T'aurais fait une belle vie avec lui, hein, Jeannette? *(Silence)* Y couraillait même quand tu sortais avec. *(Silence)* Tu peux pas m'dire qui aurait arrêté ça après qui t'aurait mariée. *(Silence)* Ouais, t'aurais été ben amanchée avec lui, j'te l'dis.

Silence. ALICE *entre de droite avec cinq verres sur un tabouret. Elle traverse et sert Joseph d'abord, et ensuite* EVA, Yvonne, *et* JEANNETTE. *"Mercis" de chacun. Elle se dirige à droite, dépose le tabouret sur la chaise à côté d'elle et s'assoit avec son verre.* JEANNETTE *boit tout d'un trait le moment qu'elle reçoit son verre.*

JOSEPH: Tu sais, ça prend du courage pour une mère de faire ça. *(*JEANNETTE *se lève et sort à droite.)* Ouais, j'te l'dis que t'aurais été ben malheureuse avec lui, ma fille.

ALICE *regarde* JOSEPH *fixement. Elle met le doigt à la bouche pour lui indiquer de se taire.*

JOSEPH: Mais quoi c'est que vous avez, vous-autres?!? C'est tout vrai, quoi c'est que j'ai dit. Maman, a ben faite d'être sévère avec nous autres sur ces affaires-là. A voulait pas qu'on marie n'importe qui . . . pi tant qu'à moué, a ben réussi.

ANDRÉ *entre par la porte à gauche. Il reste à la porte pour un instant, un peu surpris par la discussion.*

ALICE: *(Dure)* A si ben réussi qu'a restée avec une bande de vieilles filles.

JEANNETTE *revient de droite avec un verre plein. Elle aperçoit* ANDRÉ.

JEANNETTE: Hi, André. Want a drink?

ANDRÉ *nods. He then crosses right and goes to sit next to* ALICE.

JEANNETTE: *(Indicating the tray)* Can you hand me that tray, Alice. *(She takes the tray and exits down right.* ANDRÉ *sits next to* ALICE.*)*

JOSEPH: That's not true! Take Eva, here, Mama never stopped her from getting married.

ALICE: No, but it was a pretty close call. Maybe you don't remember, Joe, but Eva was the only one of us who didn't listen to mama. Maybe it's because she was the youngest girl. Anyway, mama did everything she could to keep her from marrying Roger. Eva married him just the same and I think she did the right thing. Look at her today. Four great kids, a nice apartment, always food on the table. Does she look unhappy to you, Joe?

NORMAND *enters up left.* JEANNETTE *enters down right with a drink for* ANDRÉ.

NORMAND: Hello, everyone!

No one pays attention to NORMAND. *Somewhat taken aback by this reaction, he sits at a chair behind the large table down left.*

JOSEPH: *(Still arguing with* ALICE*)* No, she doesn't. But that's no reason for you to show a lack of respect for a mother who wanted nothing but the best for you and for all of us.

JEANNETTE: *('To* NORMAND*)* I suppose you want a drink, too?

NORMAND: I've been told it's unlucky to refuse a drink.

JEANNETTE *exits down right.*

JEANNETTE: Allô, André. Veux-tu une drink?

ANDRÉ *indique que oui. Ensuite, il se dirige à droite et s'assoit à côté d'* ALICE.

JEANNETTE: *(Indiquant le tabouret)* Donne-moué donc ça, Alice. *(Elle prend le tabouret et sort à droite.)*

JOSEPH: Ben, ça, c'est pas vrai. R'garde Eva. Maman l'a pas empêchée de s'marier, elle.

ALICE: Ah, non, mais ça passé proche. Tedben que tu t'rappelles pas, mais Eva, c'est la seule qui a pas écouté sa mère. Tedben que c'tait parce qu'a était la plus jeune. Mais maman a fait toutes sortes d'affaires pour pas qu'a marie Roger. A l'a marié pareil . . . pi moué, j'trouve qu'a ben fait. Regarde-là, Eva. Quatre enfants ben fins pi ben smartes . . . un beau loyer . . . en masse à manger. Trouves-tu qu'a d'l'air malheureuse?

NORMAND *entre de gauche.* JEANNETTE *entre de droite avec un verre pour* ANDRÉ.

NORMAND: Allô, tout le monde!

On ignore NORMAND. *Celui-ci, un peu surpris par cette réception, s'assoit sur une chaise derrière la table.*

JOSEPH: *(Toujours en train de discuter avec* ALICE*)* Non, mais j'trouve que tu commences à manquer de respect pour une mère qui voulait rienque le mieux pour toué.

JEANNETTE: *(A* NORMAND*)* J'suppose que tu veux une drink, toué étou?

NORMAND: On m'a dit que c'est malchanceux de refuser quèque chose à boire.

JEANNETTE *sort à droite.*

ALICE: Oh, come on, Joe. Mama was a wonderful mother, but she wasn't the Pope . . . and only the Pope is infallible.

JOSEPH: Well I'm sure of one thing. I'd never have found a good woman like Alma if mama hadn't been there . . . if she hadn't given me her advice . . . and especially if she hadn't said I couldn't go out with a couple of other girls that I was infatuated with for a while. And I'm proud that I was able to do the same thing for my sons.

JEANNETTE *enters down right with a drink for* NORMAND. *She crosses to the table and hands it to him. Her glass seems to stay eternally full, even though she takes sips frequently.*

JEANNETTE: How come you're all so late today? *(She crosses to the rocking chair and sits. To* ANDRÉ*)* You're usually the first one to visit after lunch.

ANDRÉ: Well, I had to stop by the rectory to ask Father Paquette if we could use the church parking lot for our Knights of Columbus barbecue. What a nice man he is. Even though he's a priest, he talks to us as if we're just as good as he is.

YVONNE: And what's your excuse, Normand?

NORMAND: I didn't know I needed one . . . and on top of that, I'm almost sorry I came. What are you two arguing about? You sound like those boring political talk shows on television on Sunday morning.

JEANNETTE: It's about Connie.

NORMAND: Is she coming tonight?

JEANNETTE: We don't know yet.

EVA: It's not just Connie. It's Jerry, too.

ALICE: Voyons, Joe. Maman, c'tait une ben bonne mère, mais y ainque le Pape qui est infaillible.

JOSEPH: Ben moué, j'sais une affaire. J'aurais jamais trouvé une femme comme Alma si maman avait pas été là . . . . si a m'avait pas donné des conseils . . . pi, oui, si a m'avait pas défendu de sortir avec des filles que j'trouvais ben de mon goût. Pi chu ben fier que j'ai fait la même chose pour mes enfants à moué.

JEANNETTE *entre de droite avec un verre pour* NORMAND. *Elle se dirige vers la table et lui donne son verre. Le sien semble rester plein éternellement, bien qu'elle boive assez souvent.*

JEANNETTE: Comment ça se fait que vous êtes si en retard, aujourd'hui, vous autres? *(Elle retourne à la chaise berçante et s'assoit. A* ANDRÉ*)* De coutume, t'es l'premier arrivé, toué.

ANDRÉ: Ben, j't'arrêté au presbytère pour demander au Père Paquette si on pouvait user la cour de l'école pour le barbecue des Chevaliers de Colomb de la paroisse. Y est assez fin, c'gars-là, que c'est pas drôle. Pas de cérémonie. Y me parlait comme si j'tais aussi bon que lui.

YVONNE: Pi toué, Normand, quoi c'est que ton excuse?

NORMAND: J'en ai pas . . . pi j'regrette presque d'être venu. Quoi c'est que vous discutez qui est si sérieux, donc? Ça me fait penser aux programmes tannants qui a sur la TV le dimanche matin après la messe.

JEANNETTE: C'est Connie.

NORMAND: A vient-ti à soir?

JEANNETTE: On l'sais pas encore.

EVA: C'est pas ainque Connie, c'est Jerry, étou.

NORMAND: What's the matter? Is he sick?

JOSEPH: Worse! He's a Protestant!

ANDRÉ: A Protestant!?!

JOSEPH: Sorry. Not even a Protestant. He doesn't believe in anything at all. At least if he were a Protestant, we might be able to get him to convert. But atheists don't . . .

NORMAND: It's no surprise to me. I've known Jerry's family for years and they've always been Protestants . . . Congregationalists, if I remember right.

JOSEPH: So why didn't you tell us when you found out that Connie was going out with him?

NORMAND: Because I don't think that Connie's boyfriends are any of my business.

JOSEPH: None of your business!?! It's not your business if your niece ends up marrying a damned Protestant or even a damned pagan?

NORMAND: Marrying? That's the first I've heard about marriage. Eva, did you forget to send out invitations?

ALICE: Your brother is still living in the past. He thinks that the person you go out with is the person you have to marry.

JOSEPH: *(Almost sermonizing)* Better to marry than to wallow in sins of sexuality!

ANDRÉ: Beside, Father Paquette said that even going out with a Protestant puts you in a dangerous occasion of sin.

ALICE: I see it's time for catechism class.

NORMAND: Quoi c'est qui a? Y est-ti malade?

JOSEPH: Pire que ça! Y est protestant!

ANDRÉ: Protestant!?!

JOSEPH: Non. Même pas protestant. Y cré pas à rien. Au moins, si y était protestant, y aurait d'l'espoir pour une conversion. Mais les athées . . .

NORMAND: Vous saviez pas ça, vous autres? Moué, ça fait longtemps que j'connais sa famille, pi ça toujours été protestant, ça.

JOSEPH: Mais pourquoi que tu nous l'as pas dit quand t'as appris que Connie sortait avec?

NORMAND: Ben, hey, c'est pas vraiment de mes affaires, ça, les boy-friends à Connie.

JOSEPH: Pas de tes affaires!?! Veux-tu que ta nièce marie un maudit protestant, un maudit païen?

NORMAND: Marie? C'est la première fois que j'entends parler de mariage, moué. As-tu oublié de nous envoyer les invitations, Eva?

ALICE: Ton frère vit encore au bon vieux temps. Y pense que si du monde sortent ensemble, c'est rienque parce qui veulent se marier.

JOSEPH: (Sermonisant presque) Mieux se marier que de tomber dans des péchés de sexualité!

ANDRÉ: Pi à part de ça, le Père Paquette dit que même sortir avec un protestant, ça cré une occasion de pécher.

ALICE: Bon, la classe de catéchisme qui commence.

JEANNETTE: That's not all, Alice. Jerry doesn't have a job, either. *(To* EVA*)* That's what you said, right, Eva? *(*EVA *nods.)*

YVONNE: A couple can't get far without a job these days, that's for sure.

EVA: I don't know why you're all in such a hurry to marry them off. Neither one of them has even mentioned the word marriage.

JOSEPH: Which is the best reason to put a stop to this whole thing now . . . before they do mention the word, or worse.

ALICE: I say it's none of our business! Connie is smart enough and old enough to know what she wants.

JOSEPH: And I say I wouldn't let her marry a Protestant even if she were turning seventy-five instead of twenty-one.

ANDRÉ: I agree!

ALICE: *(Losing her patience)* They're not getting marri . . . Ah, what's the use. I should know better than to try having an intelligent discussion with a blockhead like you, Joe. You remind me of someone walking around in a zoot suit from the thirties, that's how outdated your ideas are. Think about that before you start messing up everybody else's life. I'm going to make myself another drink. *(She gets up and exits down right.)*

JOSEPH: *(Ignoring* ALICE*)* Listen, Eva. I know it's hard. I know you don't want to hurt your own daughter. But you have to do something to put a stop to this. *(Pause)* Do you want me to talk to her?

EVA: I don't know, Joe. I don't know.

ANDRÉ: Well, I think that's a great idea. Kids take things better when it doesn't come from their mother or father.

JEANNETTE: Y a pas rienque ça, Alice. Y a pas de job, non plus, Jerry. *(A* EVA*)* C'est ben ça que tu disais, hein, Eva? *(*EVA *fait signe que oui.)*

YVONNE: Aujourd'hui, on va pas loin sans job, j'te l'dis.

EVA: J'l'sais pas pourquoi vous avez si hâte des marier, vous autres. Y ont pas dit un mot de mariage, ni l'un, ni l'autre.

JOSEPH: C'est pour ça que tu devrais arrêter ça tout de suite, avant que ça ait la chance d'aller plus loin.

ALICE: Pi moué, j'trouve que c'est pas d'nos affaires pantoute! Connie est assez smarte pi assez vieille pour choisir quoi c'est qu'a veut faire par elle-même.

JOSEPH: Ben, j'te dis que j'la laisserais pas marier un protestant, même si avait soixante-et-quinze!

ANDRÉ: Pi moué, non plus!

ALICE: *(Qui perd patience)* On parle pas de maria . . . . Ah, ça sert à rien, ça sert à rien de me casser la tête avec une tête de pioche comme toué, Joe. Mais laisse moué te dire une affaire. Y a rien qui paraît plus bête qu'un homme en zoot suit, comme aux années trente. Pense à ça une escousse avant que tu t'mèles des affaires des autres. Moué, j'va aller m'faire une autre drink. *(Elle se lève et sort à droite.)*

JOSEPH: *(Comme s'il n'avait pas entendu* ALICE*)* Écoute, Eva. J'sais que c'est tough. J'sais que tu veux pas faire d'la peine à ta fille. Mais faut que tu fasses quèque chose pour arrêter ça. *(Un temps)* Veux-tu que j'y parle, moué?

EVA: J'l'sais pas, Joe. J'sais pas.

ANDRÉ: Ben moué, j'trouve que c'est un ben bonne idée. Pour les jeunes, ça sonne ben plus raisonnable quand ça vient pas de leur père ou d'leur mère.

JOSEPH: What time does she get home from work?

EVA: Well, they gave her the afternoon off today, because it's her birthday, so she should be home pretty soon. She may even be there already.

JOSEPH: *(He looks at the clock.)* Then it's settled. I'll take care of everything in no time. *(To* JEANNETTE*)* Maybe you won't have made that cake for nothing after all, Jeannette. *(He gets up and exits up left.)*

Pause

ANDRÉ: Don't worry, Eva. Joe will straighten things out, you'll see.

ALICE: *(Enters down right)* Like he straightened out his kids' lives?

ANDRÉ: What do mean by that?

ALICE: You know darn well what I mean.

ANDRÉ: Louis and Albert?

ALICE: Yes, Louis and Albert.

ANDRÉ: What about them?

NORMAND: You don't think it's a bit strange that we haven't seen Albert since the day he got married fifteen years ago?

ANDRÉ: No, I don't. If I had broken my father's heart like he did, I'd be ashamed to show my face around here, too.

YVONNE: Well, it's all very sad. Albert was such a good little boy.

ANDRÉ: All he had to do was listen to his father, if he wanted to stick around here.

JOSEPH: Quand est-ce qu'a arrive de l'ouvrage?

EVA: Ben, c'est sa fête aujourd'hui, ça fait qui ont donné l'après-midi off. A devrait arriver ben vite, si a est pas déjà là.

JOSEPH: *(Il regarde l'horloge.)* Bon, ben, c'est décidé. J'va t'arranger ça, ça s'ra pas long. *(A* JEANNETTE*)* Tedben que t'auras pas fait ton gâteau pour rien après tout, Jeannette. *(Il se lève et sort à gauche.)*

Un temps

ANDRÉ: Occupe-toué pas, Eva. Joe va tout arranger ça, tu vas voir.

ALICE: *(Qui entre de droite)* Comme y a arrangé la vie à ses enfants?

ANDRÉ: Quoi c'est que tu veux dire?

ALICE: Tu sais ben quoi c'est que j'veux dire.

ANDRÉ: Louis pi Albert?

ALICE: Oui, Louis pi Albert.

ANDRÉ: Quoi c'est qui ont?

NORMAND: Tu trouves pas ça curieux qu'on a pas vu Albert depuis qui s'est marié, y a quinze ans?

ANDRÉ: Non, pantoute. Si j'avais fait d'la peine comme ça à mon père, j'me s'rais pu montré la face par icit non plus.

YVONNE: C'est ben de valeur, anyway. C'tait un bon p'tit gars, ça, Albert.

ANDRÉ: Si y avait voulu rester icit, y avait ainque à pas désobéir à son père.

JEANNETTE: I think Joe's talked to him. I can't believe he let all these Christmases and Father's Days go by without saying a word to Albert and his family.

ANDRÉ: No. He hasn't spoken to him in fifteen years. But it's not his fault. He's more than ready to forgive and forget. All Albert has to do is ask.

NORMAND: Forgive him? For what?!? Come on, André. The only thing Albert did was get married. Where's the crime in that?

ANDRÉ: He got married after his father refused his permission. That's the crime . . . and it's a serious one. I don't blame Joe one bit. I wouldn't want my son to marry a girl like that either.

YVONNE: What's wrong with her? She seemed to be real nice when Albert was going out with her. And I heard that she takes good care of the kids and the house.

ANDRÉ: You're his godmother. That's why you're making excuses for him.

EVA: Well, they seem to be happy . . . and that's good enough for me.

ALICE: If you ask me, Joe's the one who should apologize. He's kept that little family from being happy for too long.

ANDRÉ: That's too bad, but there's no Commandment that says "Thou shalt be happy." On the other hand, there is one that says "Honor thy father and thy mother." Father Paquette says that any marriage that starts off by breaking one of God's Commandments won't last long at all.

ALICE: Great. Catechism class, part two.

NORMAND: It's a good thing that Albert's been married for only fifteen years. Otherwise, we might be tempted to think that Father Paquette was wrong.

JEANNETTE: Pour moué, Joe y a parlé. Tu peux pas me dire qui a passé des Noëls pi des Father's Day sans un mot pour Albert pi sa famille.

ANDRÉ: Non. Y a pas dit un mot depuis quinze ans. Mais c'est pas d'sa faute. Pi y est ben prêt à le pardonner. Albert a rienque à y demander.

NORMAND: Le pardonner pourquoi? Voyons, André. Albert s'est marié. C'est tout c'qui a fait. Y a pas de crime là-dedans.

ANDRÉ: Après que son père l'a défendu d'l'faire! C'est grave, ça. Pi j'l'blâme pas. J'voudrais pas que mon garçon marie une fille comme ça.

YVONNE: A est pas si pire que ça. Moué, j'la trouvais ben fine quand Albert sortait avec. Pi j'ai entendu dire que leurs enfants sont ben élevés pi propres.

ANDRÉ: C'est rienque parce que t'es sa marraine que tu fais des excuses pour lui.

EVA: Y a d'l'air content. C'est tout ce que j'sais.

ALICE: Pour moué, c'est Joe qui devrais demandé pardon. Y a empêché c't'a p'tite famille-là d'être heureuse pour ben des années.

ANDRÉ: C'est ben d'valeur, mais y a pas de commandement qui dit "Heureux seras." Mais y en a un qui dit "Père et mère honoreras." Le Père Paquette dit qu'un mariage qui commence en brisant un des commandements, c'est un mariage qui durera pas longtemps.

ALICE: Bon, le catéchisme qui recommence.

NORMAND: Une chance que ça fait ainque quinze ans qu'Albert est marié, parce qu'autrement, on pourrait traiter le Père Paquette de menteur.

ANDRÉ: That's not funny!

JEANNETTE: Anyway, no one can say that Joe isn't a good father. Look at all he's done for Louis.

ANDRÉ: *(To* ALICE*)* You can't argue with that.

EVA: Yep. He gave him everything. A car, a house . . . and he'll probably get the business too when Joe retires.

ANDRÉ: He could have given him the sun and the moon.

YVONNE: Too bad Louis doesn't appreciate it.

JEANNETTE: *(To* YVONNE*)* He's just like you. He doesn't know how to do anything.

YVONNE: Don't start.

ALICE: Louis isn't that bad, if only people gave him a chance.

ANDRÉ: *(Indicating* ALICE*)* There she goes, making excuses for everybody's faults. Too bad she's not as forgiving with her own brother.

EVA: Those two boys were so cute when they were little. And they were polite and well-behaved too.

JEANNETTE: Sometimes, I think it's too bad that kids have to grow up.

NORMAND: Come on. It's not too bad. It's perfectly normal.

ALICE: Your sisters have this idea that no one should be allowed to grow up. They even kept you in short pants until you were ten. I think they would have kept you in diapers forever if mama hadn't put her foot down.

ANDRÉ: J'trouve rien de drôle, là-dedans, moué!

JEANNETTE: Anyway, vous pouvez pas dire que Joe, c'est pas un bon père. Regarde tout c'qui a fait pour Louis.

ANDRÉ: *(A* ALICE*)* Ça, c'est vrai.

EVA: Oui. Y a tout donné à ce gars-là. Une machine, une maison . . . Pi ça d'l'air que c'est lui qui va prendre la business mèque Joe se retire.

ANDRÉ: Y aurait pu lui donner la terre pi la lune.

YVONNE: C'est de valeur que Louis sait pas comment apprécier ça.

JEANNETTE: *(A* YVONNE*)* Y te ressemble. Y sait rien faire.

YVONNE: Commence pas, toué.

ALICE: Y est pas si pire que ça, Louis, si quèqu'un y donnait la chance.

ANDRÉ: *(Indiquant* ALICE*)* La v'là pris à défendre toutes les fautes des autres, elle. C'est de valeur qu'a est pas si charitable pour son frère.

EVA: Y étaient assez cute quand y étaient jeunes, ces gars-là. Fins, polis, raisonnables.

JEANNETTE: Ouais. Des fois j'pense que c'est d'valeur que ça grandit, ça, des enfants.

NORMAND: Voyons, vous autres. C'est pas de valeur. C'est naturel.

ALICE: Tes soeurs ont toujours voulu que les p'tits restent p'tits. Y t'ont gardé en culottes courtes jusqu'à l'âge de dix ans. J'pense qui t'auraient gardé en couches si maman les avait pas arrêtées.

JEANNETTE: That doesn't mean we didn't love you, Normand.

YVONNE: Not at all. It's no sin to want kids to enjoy being young as long as they can. You were cute, too, Normand. And we all loved you to pieces.

NORMAND: I think it's time to leave before you all realize that I have faults, too. *(He stands and crosses to door up left.)*

ANDRÉ: *(Getting up. To* NORMAND*)* Well, all I can say is I hope you do as well with your own kids as Joe did with his. It's not easy being a father, you know. Father Paquette says that sometimes, it's even harder than being a priest.

NORMAND: *(Making fun of* ANDRÉ*)* Father Paquette said that? Well, then, it certainly must be true.

NORMAND *and* ANDRÉ *exit up left.*

EVA: *(Looks at the clock)* I might as well get going, too. I've got to get a few things at the store and . . . *(she hesitates)* . . . I'm a little afraid of what Joe's going to say to Connie.

YVONNE: Don't worry, Eva.

JEANNETTE: After all, he is her uncle. He won't do anything to upset her.

ALICE: You can't be talking about the same Joe I know.

EVA: *(Getting up)* Anyway, I'll see you all later.

JEANNETTE: Don't forget the party.

EVA: I don't know, Jeannette.

JEANNETTE: You'll see. She'll be there.

JEANNETTE: Ça veut pas dire qu'on t'aimait pas, ça, Normand.

YVONNE: Non. C'est pas péché de vouloir que les jeunes restent jeunes aussi longtemps que possible. Toué aussi, t'étais cute, Normand. On t'a aimé en masse.

NORMAND: Ben moué, là, j'va décoller avant qu'on commence sur mes défauts. *(Il se lève et se dirige vers la porte à gauche.)*

ANDRÉ: *(Se levant)* Moué, j'souhaite ainque une affaire. *(A NORMAND)* Que tu fasses aussi ben avec tes enfants que Joe a fait avec les siens. C'est pas facile d'être un bon père de famille, t'sais. Le Père Paquette dit que des fois, c'est même plus difficile que d'être prêtre.

NORMAND: *(Se moquant un peu d'ANDRÉ)* Le Père Paquette a dit ça? Ben, ça doit être vrai, comme ça.

NORMAND *et* ANDRÉ *sortent à gauche.*

EVA: *(Elle regarde l'horloge.)* J'pense que j't'aussi ben de partir, moué étou. Faut que j'alle au magasin pi . . . *(elle hésite)* . . . j'ai un peu peur de c'que Joe va dire à Connie.

YVONNE: Occupe-toué pas, Eva.

JEANNETTE: Après tout, c'est son oncle. Y va pas y faire d'la peine.

ALICE: J'pense pas que vous parlez du même Joe que j'connais.

EVA: *(En se levant)* Anyway, j'vous verrai plus tard.

JEANNETTE: Oublie pas le party.

EVA: J'l'sais pas, Jeannette.

JEANNETTE: Tu vas voir. A va venir.

EVA: *(Upset)* I don't even know if I want her to be there any more.

YVONNE: Come on, Eva. Everything will work itself out for the best, you'll see.

JEANNETTE: And we'll all have fun.

EVA *crosses to up left door and exits.*

YVONNE: *(To* JEANNETTE*)* What do you think Joe will say to Connie?

JEANNETTE: *(Gets up and starts to pick up the empty glasses)* I'm not sure, but I think it will do some good. Your brother knows what to say.

ALICE: *(Gets up and picks up other glasses)* Yeah. He knows how to say exactly the wrong thing at exactly the wrong time.

ALICE *and* JEANNETTE *exit down right with glasses. Pause.* YVONNE *takes up her game of solitaire again. Pause.* CONSTANCE *enters up left. She has a handkerchief in her hand, but we do not see any tears. She seems upset, but smiles a little at* YVONNE *when she sees her.*

YVONNE: *(Surprised)* Oh, Connie! What are you doing here?

CONSTANCE: Is mama here, auntie?

YVONNE: She just left not more than two minutes ago.

JEANNETTE: *(From off right)* Is that Connie I hear?

JEANNETTE *and* ALICE *enter quickly from down right.* JEANNETTE *crosses to the rocking chair and sits.* ALICE *sits on a straight chair at right.*

JEANNETTE: How are you, sweetheart?

Eva: *(Troublée)* J'sais même pas si j'veux qu'a vienne, à c'point-cit.

Yvonne: Voyons, Eva. Tout va s'arranger pour le mieux, tu vas voir.

Jeannette: Pi on va avoir du fun.

Eva *se dirige vers la porte à gauche et sort.*

Yvonne: *(A Jeannette)* Quoi c'est que tu penses que Joe va y dire?

Jeannette: *(Se lève et se met à ramasser les verres vides)* J'l'sais pas, mais j'pense que ça va faire du bien. Tu peux avoir confiance dans ton frère.

Alice: *(Se lève et ramasse d'autres verres)* Ouais. On peut toujours être certain qui va dire la méchante affaire, juste au méchant moment.

Alice *se dirige vers la porte à droite et sort avec des verres. Pause.* Yvonne *reprend les cartes et se met à jouer à un jeu de patience. Pause.* Constance *entre par la porte à gauche. Elle a un mouchoir à la main, mais on n'aperçoit pas de larmes. Elle paraît agitée, mais elle donne un p'tit sourire à* Yvonne *en l'apercevant.*

Yvonne: *(Surprise)* Ah, Connie! Quoi c'est que tu fais icit?

Constance: Maman est-ti icit, ma tante?

Yvonne: A vient juste de partir y a pas deux minutes.

Jeannette: *(Des coulisses)* C'est-ti Constance, ça?

Jeannette *et* Alice *entrent rapidement à droite.* Jeannette *se dirige vers la chaise berçante et s'assoit.* Alice *s'assoit sur une chaise à droite.*

Jeannette: Comment ça va, chérie?

ALICE: Sit down for a minute.

CONSTANCE: Well, I was looking for mama.

JEANNETTE: She had to pick up a couple of things at the store before going back to your house. Why don't you wait for her here?

YVONNE: Sure. Come and sit down, dear.

CONSTANCE *sits in one of the straight chairs up left. She must seem uncomfortable. Pause.*

JEANNETTE: Quite a service, this morning, huh?

CONSTANCE *nods.*

JEANNETTE: I think it was the nicest anniversary mass we've ever had.

Pause

ALICE: Did you have a talk with your uncle Joe?

CONSTANCE *looks at* ALICE. *She has tears in her eyes. She nods.*

YVONNE: What's wrong, sweetheart?

Pause

JEANNETTE: We're not blind, you know. We can all see that something's wrong.

Pause

ALICE: Tell us all about it. It'll make you feel better.

ALICE: Tu veux pas t'assir une minute?

CONSTANCE: Ben, j'cherchais maman.

JEANNETTE: A dit qu'a allait au magasin avant de retourner chez vous. T'es t'aussi ben de l'attendre icit.

YVONNE: Oui, viens t'assir, chérie.

CONSTANCE *se dirige vers le centre et s'assoit dans une des chaises du fond. Elle doit paraître mal à l'aise. Pause.*

JEANNETTE: C'tait beau à matin, hein?

CONSTANCE *fait signe que oui.*

JEANNETTE: Moué, j'ai trouvé que c'tait le plus beau service anniversaire qu'on a pas eu jusqu'asteur.

Pause

ALICE: Mon oncle Joseph t'a-ti parlé?

CONSTANCE *regarde* ALICE. *Elle a les larmes aux yeux. Elle fait signe que oui.*

YVONNE: Quoi c'est qui t'a dit, chérie?

Pause

JEANNETTE: On est pas des sans-coeurs, nous autres, t'sais. On voit que t'as d'la peine.

Pause

ALICE: Parle-nous-en. Ça va aider, tu vas voir.

YVONNE: Yes, tell us.

Pause

JEANNETTE: Tell your old aunt.

CONSTANCE: *(After a pause)* Well . . . he told me not to go out with Jerry ever again.

JEANNETTE: That's it?

CONSTANCE: No.

ALICE: That would have been too good to be true.

CONSTANCE: *(Still hesitating)* He said that I was putting myself in danger by going out with someone who doesn't believe in God . . . and that it doesn't take much to lose your faith. He said that I was hurting everyone in the family by going out with him. And he said . . . *(she starts to cry)* . . . that if grammy is in heaven . . . and if she can see us all . . . that her heart must be breaking to see me going out with an atheist. *(She starts sobbing.)*

JEANNETTE: *(Gets up and goes to CONSTANCE. Trying to console her)* Poor little girl. Growing up is tough, isn't it?

ALICE: Especially when you've got an uncle who talks to you that way.

YVONNE: Don't cry, Connie. Everything's going to be o.k., you'll see.

JEANNETTE: *(Trying to change the subject)* Hey, remember when you were little . . . you couldn't have been more than four . . . you were the smartest little thing. One day, I took you to the store and I bought some apples. And when I went to pay, the man said "A dozen apples. Fifty cents." But right away, you said *(imitating a child's way of talking)* "Not dozen. Ten!" You had counted every one as I picked them out.

YVONNE: Raconte-nous ça.

Pause

JEANNETTE: Dis-le à ma tante, là.

CONSTANCE: *(Après un petit temps)* Ben . . . y m'a dit de pu sortir avec Jerry.

JEANNETTE: C'est-ti tout?

CONSTANCE: Non.

ALICE: Ça m'aurait surpris.

CONSTANCE: *(Elle hésite toujours.)* Y a dit que j'me mettais en danger en sortant avec un gars qui créyait pas au Bon Dieu . . . que ça prend pas grand chose pour perdre sa foi. Y a dit que j'f'rais ben d'la peine à ben du monde si j'continuais de sortir avec lui. Pi y a dit . . . *(elle commence à pleurnicher)* . . . que si mémère est au ciel . . . . *(elle pleure plus fort)* . . . pi si a peut nous voir . . . . qu'a doit pleurer en masse de voir quoi c'est que j'fais. *(Elle éclate en sanglots.)*

JEANNETTE: *(Se lève et traverse jusqu'à* CONSTANCE. *Elle essaie de la consoler.)* Pauvre p'tite fille, va. C'est tough de grandir, hein?

ALICE: Surtout quand on se fait dire des affaires comme ça.

YVONNE: Pleure pas, Connie. Ça va être o.k., tu vas voir.

JEANNETTE: *(Essaie de changer le sujet)* Hey, t'en souviens-ti quand t'étais p'tite, là . . . ah, tu d'vais pas avoir plus que quatre ans . . . t'étais smarte, t'sais. On est allé au magasin une fois pi j'avais acheté des pommes. Ben, quand on est allé pour payer, l'homme a dit: "Une douzaine de pommes, cinquante cennes." Pi toué, t'as dit *(imitant une voix d'enfant)* "Non, n'a dix!" T'es avais comptées quand j'les avait choisies. "Non,

"Not dozen. Ten!" I guess you wanted to make sure I didn't pay too much. You were the smartest little thing. *(Pause)* Don't cry, Connie. We'll work this out, o.k?

CONSTANCE: *(She nods.)* Jerry's really nice.

JEANNETTE: I know, I know.

CONSTANCE: And he's polite and smart . . . I know that uncle Joe would like him if he met him.

YVONNE: You really like him a lot, don't you, dear?

ALICE: Of course, she likes him. She so sweet and nice. She doesn't want to hurt anybody.

JEANNETTE: But you know that some of the things Uncle Joe said were true.

ALICE: Don't start!

JEANNETTE: It's true. Marriage is tough. It's not easy for two strangers to live together. And it's even tougher when the two are from different religions.

YVONNE: Plus he doesn't have a job. How will you make ends meet?

ALICE: Great! Another state heard from.

CONSTANCE: But we're not getting married, auntie. It's the furthest thing from our minds.

JEANNETTE: Maybe it is now . . . but it doesn't take much for things to change. It's never too early to think about things like that.

CONSTANCE: But . . .

n'a dix!" t'as dit. Tu voulais être certaine qui me charge pas pour douze, j'suppose. T'étais assez smarte. *(Pause)* Pleure pu, là, hein, Connie? On va arranger ça, o.k.?

CONSTANCE: *(Elle fait signe de tête que oui.)* C't'un bon gars, Jerry.

JEANNETTE: J'l'sais, j'l'sais.

CONSTANCE: Y est ben fin. J'sais que mon oncle Joe l'aimerait s'il rencontrait.

YVONNE: Tu l'aimes à plein, hein, ma p'tite fille?

ALICE: Ben sur, qu'a l'aime. Ça assez le coeur tendre, ça, c't'a fille-là. Ça veut pas faire de peine à personne.

JEANNETTE: Mais tu sais que quoi c'est que mon oncle Joe t'as dit, ça a du bon sens, quand même.

ALICE: Commence pas, toué.

JEANNETTE: Mais c'est vrai! Le mariage, c'est tough. C'est pas facile quand deux étrangers essaient de vivre ensemble. Pi c'est même plus difficile si les deux ont pas la même religion.

YVONNE: Pi un gars qui a pas de job . . . . quoi c'est que vous allez faire?

ALICE: Bon, l'autre qui met ses deux cennes.

CONSTANCE: Mais on va pas se marier, ma tante. On y pense même pas.

JEANNETTE: Pas asteur . . . mais ça prend pas grand chose pour changer les affaires. C'est jamais trop de bonne heure pour penser à ces affaires-là.

CONSTANCE: Mais . . .

JEANNETTE: Listen, sweetheart, if we met Jerry, I'm sure we'd all like him a lot.

YVONNE: Yeah. What if you brought him over to meet the whole family, like you did with your other boyfriends . . . You know . . . celebrate the holidays with us, visit all the aunts and uncles, go to church when . . .

ALICE: Aha, the missionaries have landed!

YVONNE: You never can tell, Alice.

JEANNETTE: Why don't you bring him over tonight . . . for your own birthday party? He could meet the whole family. Besides, I think he'd have a lot of fun with all of us.

YVONNE: And we'd enjoy getting to know him, too.

CONSTANCE: I don't know, auntie.

JEANNETTE: Why not?

CONSTANCE: Well, Jerry wanted us to spend a quiet evening together. Besides, Uncle Joe said that if he ever saw us together, he'd never speak to me again, and that he'd never have anything more to do with me.

JEANNETTE: Oh, don't worry about that. Your uncle's bark is always worse than his bite.

YVONNE: You might be surprised to know that he's real sensitive, too.

JEANNETTE: I know he always seems grouchy, but that's just way he is.

YVONNE: When Albert got married, he cried for days. I've never seen a man cry so much. *(Pause)* So I know he didn't want to hurt you. Whatever he said, he said out of love.

JEANNETTE: Écoute, là. Si on rencontrait Jerry, chu certaine qu'on l'trouverait de notre goût.

YVONNE: Oui. Si y v'nait avec toué rencontrer toute la famille comme tes autres boyfriends . . . T'sais, venir aux parties, aller chez tes oncles pi tes tantes, aller à messe . . .

ALICE: Tiens, les missionnaires qui arrivent.

YVONNE: Ben, on sait jamais, Alice.

JEANNETTE: Pourquoi que tu l'amènes pas à ton party, icit à soir? Y pourrait rencontrer tout le monde, pi j'pense qui aurait du fun à part de ça.

YVONNE: Nous autres, ça nous f'rait ben plaisir de l'rencontrer, étou.

CONSTANCE: J'l'sais pas, ma tante.

JEANNETTE: Mais pourquoi pas?

CONSTANCE: Ben, Jerry voulait qu'on passe la soirée tout seuls, rienque nous deux . . . pi mon oncle Joseph a dit que si nous voyait ensemble, qui me parlerait pu, pi qui aurait pu rien à faire avec moué.

JEANNETTE: Ah, occupe-toué pas de ça. Ton oncle, y est pas si farouche qui paraît. Y exagérait, chu certaine.

YVONNE: Ça te surprendrait tedben, Connie, mais y a le coeur tendre, lui aussi.

JEANNETTE: J'l'sais qui a toujours l'air marabout, mais c'est ainque sa façon, ça.

YVONNE: Oui. Quand Albert s'est marié, y a assez pleuré que c'tait pas drôle. J'ai jamais vu un homme pleurer comme ça. *(Pause)* Ça fait que, quoi c'est qui t'a dit, là, y te l'a dit parce qui t'aimait.

ALICE: Strange way to show someone you love them.

JEANNETTE: It's true, Alice. *(To* CONSTANCE*)* He wouldn't have said a thing to you if he didn't love you. He only wants to make sure you don't do anything you'll regret later on.

JOSEPH *enters up left. He looks at the scene being played out before him and hesitates.* JEANNETTE *notices him.*

JEANNETTE: That's right, isn't it, Joe? You love our little Connie, don't you?

JOSEPH *nods. He looks a little sheepish.*

JOSEPH: Listen, Constance, I didn't want to hurt you. *(*CONSTANCE *stares at the floor.)* You know I love you . . . and I only want the best for you . . . right?

CONSTANCE *nods. She keeps staring at the floor.*

JOSEPH*: (Doesn't know what to say or do. Finally, he takes out his wallet, pulls out a fifty dollar bill, and tries to hand it to* CONSTANCE*.)* Here. Here's something for your birthday.

CONSTANCE: Oh, no Uncle Joe. That's too much.

JOSEPH: *(Trying to tease her)* You're twenty-one. That only happens once in a lifetime. Go ahead, take it.

CONSTANCE: I really can't . . .

JOSEPH: *(Almost begging)* Do it for me, Connie . . . please.

CONSTANCE: *(Takes the money)* Thank you, Uncle Joe.

YVONNE: You see? You see? Your Uncle Joe loves you a lot, doesn't he?

ALICE: Drôle de façon de montrer qu'on aime quèqu'un, ça, . . . y chanter des bêtises.

JEANNETTE: C'est vrai, ça, Alice. *(A CONSTANCE)* Y t'aurait jamais parlé si y t'aimait pas. Y voulait rienque être certain que tu fasses rien que tu regrettes plus tard.

JOSEPH *entre par la porte à gauche. Il regarde la scène qui se présente devant lui et hésite un peu.* JEANNETTE *l'aperçoit.*

JEANNETTE: C'est vrai, hein, Joe? Tu l'aimes, notre p'tite Connie.

JOSEPH *fait signe de tête que oui. Il doit paraître un peu honteux de lui-même.*

JOSEPH: Écoute, Constance, j'voulais pas te faire d'la peine, hein. *(CONSTANCE commence à pleurer doucement.)* Tu sais que j't'aime, hein . . . pi que j'veux tout ce qui a de mieux pour toué?

CONSTANCE *fait signe que oui. Elle pleure toujours.*

JOSEPH: *(Ne sait pas quoi faire. Il sort enfin son porte-feuille de sa poche et en sort un billet de cinquante dollars. Il l'offre à CONSTANCE.)* Tiens, prend ça pour ta fête.

CONSTANCE: *(Elle pleure toujours.)* Non, non, mon oncle. C'est trop.

JOSEPH: *(Essayant de la taquiner)* T'as vingt-et-un ans. Ça arrive ainque une fois, ça. Voyons, prends-le.

CONSTANCE: Non, mon oncle, j'peux pas . . .

JOSEPH: *(La suppliant presque)* Pour moué, Connie . . . s'il vous plaît.

CONSTANCE: *(Qui prend l'argent)* Merci, mon oncle.

YVONNE: Voué-tu, chérie? Y t'aime à plein, ton oncle Joe, hein?

JEANNETTE: Connie was afraid you'd get mad if we invited Jerry to the party tonight.

JOSEPH: *(Suddenly harder)* He can come if he wants to.

JEANNETTE: *(To* CONSTANCE*)* There! You see?!?

JOSEPH: Well, I'd better get back to the store. A business doesn't look after itself, you know. *(To* CONSTANCE*)* I'll see you at the party tonight, right? *(Pointing to the fifty dollar bill)* And don't spend that all in one place. *(He exits up left.)*

JEANNETTE: Didn't I tell you that everything would turn out fine?

YVONNE: Now all you have to do is invite Jerry.

JEANNETTE *crosses to the table down left and takes the cover off the cake without* CONSTANCE *noticing.*

JEANNETTE: And take a look at the surprise I've got for you both!

CONSTANCE *appears surprised. We see a little smile that disappears almost instantly.*

JEANNETTE: You didn't think we'd let your birthday go by without making your favorite cake? Maybe if Jerry wants a piece, this might finally be the year where you let us cut it.

The three aunts laugh heartily. CONSTANCE *looks at the cake and gives a little smile.*

Curtain

JENNETTE: Connie avait peur que tu t'fâcherais si on invitait Jerry à venir à soir.

JOSEPH: *(Soudain plus dur)* Y peut venir si y veut.

JEANNETTE: *(A CONSTANCE)* Bon! Tu voués?!?

JOSEPH: *(Plus doux)* Ben, j't'aussi ben de retourner au magasin. Des besognes, ça, ça marche pas tout seul. *(A CONSTANCE)* J'te verrai à soir, hein? *(Indiquant le billet de cinquante dollars)* Dépense pas tout ça à même place, là. *(Il sort à gauche.)*

JEANNETTE: J'te l'ai dit que ça allait s'arranger, hein?

YVONNE: Là, y te reste pu ainque à inviter Jerry.

JEANNETTE *se dirige vers la table à gauche et enlève le couvert du gâteau sans être aperçue de* CONSTANCE.

JEANNETTE: Pi regarde quoi c'est qui vous attend!

CONSTANCE *paraît surprise. On voit un petit sourire qui disparaît presqu'aussitôt.*

JEANNETTE: Tu penses pas que j'laisserais passer ta fête sans faire ton gâteau favori, hein? Tedben c't'année, si Jerry en veut un morceau, tu nous laisseras le couper.

Rire des trois tantes qui sont debout autour de CONSTANCE. CONSTANCE *regarde le gâteau et donne un petit sourire.*

Rideau

ACT III

Evening of the same day. It's CONSTANCE'*s party. To successfully convey the experience of a Franco-American party with all the relatives, it is essential to involve the audience in the first scene of this act. The easiest way to do this is to place four characters—*ROGER, ALMA, CHARLOTTE, *and* EMILIEN—*in the audience. If there is room, they could sit among audience members. Directors might prefer to place them on straight chairs in the aisles to make it easier for them to move around.*

When the curtain goes up, these characters should immediately start talking to the audience members around them. Some possible topics of conversation include:

1. ROGER *is a sports fan. He can talk about baseball, hockey, basketball, golf, etc.*

2. ALMA *has just been discharged from the hospital. She talks about her illness and her operation.*

3. CHARLOTTE *has just had her house done over. She's changed every room and talks about those changes.*

4. EMILIEN *owns a furniture store. He talks about the current state of business.*

These are only suggestions. The actors should choose a subject that they know well to make sure the conversations are as natural as possible. Also, the actors should treat the audience members like members of the family . . . and as if all of them know about CHARLOTTE'*s house,* EMILIEN'*s store, and* ALMA'*s illness.*

This improvisation should last a maximum of five to seven minutes. If a certain actor is having trouble sustaining a conversation in the audience, I suggest three options:

ACTE III

Le soir du même jour. C'est la soirée pour CONSTANCE. *Pour donner l'impression d'une soirée franco-américaine avec toute la parentée, il est essentiel que l'assistance devienne partie de la scène au début de l'acte. La façon la plus facile d'accomplir ceci, c'est de placer quatre personnages—*ROGER, ALMA, CHARLOTTE, *et* EMILIEN—*parmi l'assistance. S'il y a de la place, ils pourraient s'asseoir sur des fauteuils libres dans l'assistance. Autrement, ils pourraient s'asseoir sur les chaises droites qu'on mettrait dans les allées pendant l'entr'acte.*

Au lever du rideau, ces personnages devraient immédiatement entamer une conversation avec les membres de l'assistance autour d'eux. J'offre ici quelques suggestions de sujets:

1. ROGER *est amateur de sport. Il peut donc parler du baseball, football, hockey, etc.*

2. ALMA *vient de sortir de l'hôpital. Elle parle de sa maladie et de son opération.*

3. CHARLOTTE *vient de faire décorer sa maison. Elle a tout changé. Elle parle de ces changements.*

4. EMILIEN *est propriétaire d'un magasin de meubles. Il parle de la "besogne."*

Ce ne sont que des suggestions. Les comédiens devraient choisir un sujet qu'ils connaissent très bien pour que ces conversations soient aussi naturelles que possible. On devrait traîter les membres de l'assistance comme des cousins, frères, soeurs, etc. Les comédiens doivent parler comme si tout le monde connaissait très bien la maison de CHARLOTTE, *le magasin d'*EMILIEN, *et la maladie d'*ALMA.

Cette improvisation devrait durer cinq à sept minutes, au maximum. S'il est difficile de soutenir certaines conversations parmi l'assistance, je suggère trois possibilités:

1. Ask to be excused to go get something to eat or drink. Be sure to offer to get some for the audience members near you, too.

2. Excuse yourself to go talk to another section of the audience. ("Oh, I've got to go say hi to Josephine over there.")

3. Excuse yourself to return to the stage to observe the card game or to talk to ALICE.

The other characters are on the stage.

EVA, ANDRÉ, YVONNE, JOSEPH, JEANNETTE, *and* NORMAND *are seated around the table down left. They are playing cards.* JOSEPH *is his usual, grouchy self and gets angry often during the game.* NORMAND *is in a good mood and often teases* ANDRÉ. EVA *is nervous and distracted, which only makes* JOSEPH *even grouchier.* YVONNE, *who does not play the game well but wins fairly often anyway, always complains about the cards she is dealt.* JEANNETTE *chain smokes. She looks at the clock frequently and drinks quickly and often. If necessary, she can get up to get herself other drinks.*

This improvisation should also last from five to seven minutes. Unfortunately, I can't even suggest appropriate dialog, since much depends on how the "game" is going. However, it should follow the well-established ritual and include the time-worn comments that are common to every card game played by Franco-Americans (and others). The best way (perhaps the only way) to determine these comments is to actually observe a card game in progress.

ALICE *is seated in a straight chair up left, next to the small table. She is playing a game of solitaire on the table.* CONSTANCE's *birthday cake is also on the table.*

The director and the actors should strive to make the audience feel as though it's part of the family. This includes acting and reacting with them; offering them a drink; passing them bowls of potato chips, peanuts, candy, etc. They could also ask an audience member for a match, or to sign CONSTANCE's *birthday card, etc.*

1. S'excuser pour aller chercher quelque chose à boire ou à manger. Soyez certain d'en offrir aux gens de l'assistance près de vous.

2. S'excuser pour aller parler à un autre groupe. ("J'va aller dire hi à Joséphine, là")

3. S'excuser et revenir à la scène principale pour observer les joueurs de cartes ou pour parler avec Alice.

Les autres personnages se trouvent sur la scène principale.

Eva, André, Yvonne, Joseph, Jeannette, *et* Normand *sont autour de la table à gauche. Ils sont en train de jouer aux cartes.* Joseph *est marabout comme toujours et se fâche souvent en jouant.* Normand *est de bonne humeur et taquine* André *assez souvent.* Eva *est nerveuse et paraît distraite, ce qui rempire la mauvaise humeur de* Joseph. Yvonne, *qui ne joue pas bien mais qui gagne souvent, se plaint toujours des cartes qu'elle reçoit.* Jeannette *fume à la chaîne. Elle regarde souvent l'horloge et boit rapidement et souvent. Si nécessaire, elle peut se lever pour remplir son verre.*

Cette improvisation doit aussi durer cinq à sept minutes. Quand à la conversation des comédiens à propos du jeu de cartes, elle devrait suivre le rite bien connu. Il y a toute une série de commentaires qui sont de rigueur au cours d'un jeu de cartes. Mais beaucoup dépend du jeu. Il serait donc impossible de créer des conversations vraisemblables hors du jeu. Je suggère que les comédiens observent une partie de cartes franco-américaine s'ils ont des difficultés avec cette improvisation.

Alice *est assise sur une chaise à gauche de la petite table du fond. Elle joue à un jeu de patience sur la table, sur laquelle se trouve aussi le gâteau-lapin.*

Le metteur-en-scène et les comédiens doivent tout faire pour que l'assistance se sente membre de la famille. Par exemple, les personnages sur la scène devraient agir et réagir avec les membres de l'assistance autant que possible, eux aussi. Ils/elles pourraient descendre pour leur demander si certains veulent quelque chose à boire, pour leur passer des plats de croustillantes ou de bonbons, pour leur demander une allumette, pour leur demander de signer la carte de vœux pour Constance, *etc.*

One of the characters (I suggest ROGER) could even start a Franco "sing along" song, such as Chevaliers de la Table Ronde, Alouette, Son Voile qui Volait, and encourage the audience to join in. Use your creativity if there are no Francos or French speakers in the audience.

JOSEPH *signals the end of the improvisation. It will be after a hand that* NORMAND *should win.*

JOSEPH: *(Angry)* That's it! I quit! I haven't won a damned game all night.

ROGER: *(Coming back from the audience)* Who's got all the luck tonight?

ANDRÉ: *(Annoyed. Pointing to* NORMAND*)* Your dear brother-in-law.

YVONNE: You're always lucky at cards, Normand.

NORMAND: Now, if I could just make it work for women and money . . .

JEANNETTE: Anyway, it's no fun when the same people win all the time.

YVONNE: You won a couple of games, Jeannette.

JEANNETTE: *(Ignoring her. To the others)* And it's always those who don't know how to play who win the most.

YVONNE: Great. She's off!

JEANNETTE: It's true, you know. I'd be ashamed to play like you.

YVONNE: Well how come I win so often, if I don't know how to play.

JEANNETTE: God must protect the feeble minded.

Un personnage (je suggère ROGER*) pourrait même commencer une chanson à répondre, e.g., Chevaliers de la Table Ronde, Alouette, Son Voile qui Volait, et encourager l'assistance à y participer. Pendant la chanson, les joueurs de cartes peuvent chanter mais ils ne doivent pas interrompre la partie.*

C'est JOSEPH *qui donne le signal pour la fin de l'improvisation. Ce sera à la fin d'un jeu que* NORMAND *devrait gagner.*

JOSEPH: *(En colère)* Ben moué, joue pu! J'ai pas gagné une maudite main d'la soirée.

ROGER: *(Il revient de l'assistance.)* Qui c'est qui a la "luck" à soir?

ANDRÉ: *(Un peu irrité. Indiquant* NORMAND*)* C'est ton beau-frère, icit.

YVONNE: T'es toujours chanceux aux cartes, toué, Normand.

NORMAND: C'est de valeur que c'est pas la même chose avec les femmes pi l'argent.

JEANNETTE: En tout cas, c'est pas l'fun quand c'est toujours les mêmes qui gagnent.

YVONNE: T'as gagné, toué aussi, Jeannette.

JEANNETTE: *(Aux autres)* Pi c'est toujours ceux qui savent pas jouer qui gagnent le plus.

YVONNE: Bon, ça commence.

JEANNETTE: Ben, c'est vrai. J'aurais honte de jouer comme toué.

YVONNE: Si j'joue si mal que ça, comment ça se fait que j'gagne?

JEANNETTE: Dieu doit protéger les simples d'esprit.

JOSEPH: *(To* YVONNE*)* I think we should make it a rule that people play right, or they don't play at all. There's no way you should have raised me with the cards you had.

NORMAND: Come on, Joe. We're only playing for fun.

JOSEPH: *(Ignores him. To* YVONNE*)* You didn't even have a pair showing and I had two eights. You had no right to raise me.

NORMAND: What difference does it make, Joe? What did it cost you? A couple of pennies?

JOSEPH: That's not the point. I'm sick and tired of losing money to people who can't play worth shit. So I quit! *(Gets up, crosses to a straight chair up left and sits)*

EVA: Roger, do you want sit in?

ROGER: No, thanks. If I really need someone to yell at me, I'll re-enlist in the army.

EVA: *(To* ALMA *who is coming back from the audience)* How about you, Alma? Want to play?

ALMA: No. It's getting late . . . and I'm still a little weak from the operation, I think we'd better go, Joe.

JEANNETTE: *(Quickly)* So soon? It's still early, you know.

JOSEPH: Still think she'll show up, Jeannette?

JEANNETTE: Yes!

JOSEPH: It's already nine thirty. We've been waiting for three hours. If you ask me, they would have been here long ago if they were coming.

Joseph: *(A* Yvonne*)* Ben moué, là, j'trouve que t'as pas le droit d'entrer icit si tu vas pas jouer comme du monde. T'avais pas le droit de "m'raiser" avec la main que t'avais.

Normand: Voyons, Joe. On joue ainque pour le fun.

Joseph: *(Ne l'écoute pas. A* Yvonne*)* T'avais même pas une paire qui montrait, pi moué, j'avais deux huit. T'avais pas d'affaire pantoute à me "raiser."

Normand: Quelle différence que ça peut faire, Joe? Quoi c'est que ça t'a couté? Une couple de cennes?

Joseph: C'est pas ça qui compte. Chu tanné de donner mon argent à du monde qui savent pas jouer. Ça fait que joue pu, c'est tout! *(Il se lève et va s'asseoir sur une chaise au fond.)*

Eva: Roger, veux-tu prendre sa place, chéri?

Roger: Non, merci. Si j'veux m'faire chanter des bêtises, j'va r'tourner dans l'armée.

Eva: *(A* Alma*, qui vient de revenir de l'assistance)* Toué, Alma, veux-tu jouer?

Alma: Non. Y commence à être tard, là. Pi chu pas encore sur l'piton, t'sais. J'pense qu'on est aussi ben de s'en aller, Joe.

Jeannette: *(Rapidement)* Si vite? Y est encore de bonne heure, t'sais.

Joseph: Penses-tu encore qu'a va venir, Jeannette?

Jeannette: Oui!

Joseph: Y est déjà neuf heures et demie. Ça fait trois heures qu'on attend. Pour moué, ça f'rait longtemps qui seraient icit, si a était pour venir.

NORMAND: *(To* EVA*)* What did she say when you saw her, Eva?

EVA: Well, she said she was going to invite Jerry, but she wasn't sure how he was going to take it.

YVONNE: Why? I don't see why he'd take it badly.

EVA: I guess Jerry's been planning this for quite a while. He made reservations at Fantini's with a birthday cake and everything. And then, they were going to that rock concert at the Opera House. I guess it took him months just to get tickets.

JOSEPH: That's not what I call a concert. It takes more than noise and screaming and jumping around to make a concert. I can't believe they actually pay money to see that crap.

ANDRÉ: Maybe they'll come afterwards.

EVA: I don't think so, André. The concert goes until one thirty or two in the morning.

Pause

JEANNETTE: Well, I still say she'll be here. She hasn't missed one of her parties yet, and she's not going to start now.

JOSEPH: Great. Then, go ahead and hang around here for nothing, if you want. I'm going home. Come on, Alma. *(*JOSEPH *and* ALMA *cross to door up left. Going out)* That's what happens when you let kids today make decisions. There's not one of them who gives a damn about the parents and relatives who gave them everything they've got. *(Good-bys to everyone.* JOSEPH *and* ALMA *exit.)*

ANDRÉ: I'd better go, too. I've got to get up early tomorrow. We're going on a pilgrimage to LaSalette with Father Paquette after church, and I've got a bunch of things to get ready.

NORMAND: *(À* EVA*)* Quoi c'est qu'a dit quand tu l'as vue, Eva?

EVA: Ben, a dit qu'a allait inviter Jerry à v'nir, mais a savait pas trop comment y allait prendre ça.

YVONNE: Pourquoi? J'voué pas pourquoi y prendrait ça mal.

EVA: Ben, ça d'l'air que ça faisait longtemps que Jerry plannait ça. Y avait fait des réservations chez Fantini's avec un birthday cake pi tout. Pi après ça, y étaient pour aller à un concert à l'Opera House. Y paraît que ça pris des mois pour avoir ces billets-là, t'sais.

JOSEPH: Maudite musique d'énervés. Ça fait ainque mener du train, pi y paient d'l'argent pour aller écouter ça!

ANDRÉ: Tedben qui vont v'nir après.

EVA: Ah, j'pense pas, André. Ça finira pas avant une heure et demie ou deux heures du matin, ça, c't'affaire-là.

Pause

JEANNETTE: Ben moué, j'dis qu'a va v'nir. A pas manqué une de ses parties jusqu'asteur, pi a manquera pas celui-là.

JOSEPH: Ben, vous pouvez rester icit à niaiser toute la soirée, vous autres, mais moué, j'm'en va. Viens-t'en, Alma. *(*JOSEPH *et* ALMA *se dirigent vers la porte à gauche. En sortant)* C'est ça qui arrive quand on laisse les jeunes décider des affaires eux autres-mêmes. Y en a pas un qui pense à ses parents. *(Au revoir à tous.* JOSEPH *et* ALMA *sortent.)*

ANDRÉ: J'pense que j'va partir, moué étou. Faut que j'me lève de bonne heure demain. On fait un pélérinage à Lasalette avec le Père Paquette après les messes, pi j'ai en masse à préparer.

EMILIEN: *(Still in the audience. To* CHARLOTTE *who is also still in the audience)* What do you say, dear? I think we'd better take off, too.

YVONNE: What's the hurry? There's still lots of food.

CHARLOTTE: *(Coming up from the audience)* Ooof! I couldn't eat another bite. Everything was delicious!

EMILIEN: *(Coming up from the audience)* Hey, Normand, do you want to watch the game at our house tomorrow?

NORMAND: Sure. It's always fun to watch the Red Sox lose another one.

EMILIEN: O.k., we'll see you then. Good night, everybody. *(*EMILIEN *and* CHARLOTTE *cross to door up left and exit.)*

NORMAND: Looks like only the true believers are left.

ALICE: *(Puts away her cards. To* JEANNETTE*)* How can you still think she'll be here?

JEANNETTE: She'll be here! I know Connie. I know her better than any of you. She'll be here for sure.

EVA: Well, I think we'll go across the street and wait at home. What do you think, Roger?

ROGER: Yeah. Might as well.

EVA: She'll probably stop there anyway before coming over here. That way, we can all come back together. *(She gets up and crosses to the door up left.)*

YVONNE: Hey, Eva, don't forget your serving tray.

EMILIEN: *(Qui est encore parmi l'assistance. A* CHARLOTTE *qui est également parmi l'assistance)* Nous autres, aussi, j'pense qu'on va s'en aller, hein, bonnefemme?

YVONNE: Pressez-vous pas. Y a encore en masse à manger.

CHARLOTTE: *(En revenant de l'assistance)* Ah, moué, j'pourrais pas. J'ai trop mangé comme c'est là. Tout était assez bon!

EMILIEN: *(En revenant de l'assistance)* Viens-tu chez nous voir la game, demain après-midi, Normand?

NORMAND: Sure. J'aime toujours ça voir les Red Sox perdre.

EMILIEN: O.k., comme ça. Good night, tout le monde! *(Adieux de tous.* EMILIEN *et* CHARLOTTE *sortent par la porte à gauche.)*

NORMAND: Ça ben l'air que c'est rienque les fidèles qui restent.

ALICE: *(Se lève et met ses cartes de côté. A* JEANNETTE*)* Penses-tu encore qu'à va venir, là, toué?

JEANNETTE: Oui, a va venir! J'la connais, moué, Connie. A va venir, ça c'est certain.

EVA: Ben, nous autres, j'pense qu'on va l'attendre chez nous. Quoi c'est que tu penses, toué, Roger?

ROGER: Ouais. Allons-y.

EVA: Anyway, a va probablement arrêter à maison chez nous avant de venir icit. On reviendra tout ensemble comme ça. *(Elle se lève et se dirige vers la porte à gauche.)*

YVONNE: Oublie pas ton plat, Eva.

JEANNETTE: Right. It's in the kitchen. I'll go get it. *(She goes to get up.)*

EVA: No, no. Don't bother. I'll get it when we come back. *(To* NORMAND*)* How about a nightcap, Normand?

NORMAND: Weeeellll . . . maybe just a little one. Tomorrow's a busy day for me, too.

EVA: Come on, then. Good night, you three.

EVA, ROGER, *and* NORMAND *exit up left. Pause.* JEANNETTE *and* ALICE *start picking up bowls, glasses, ashtrays, etc. and bringing them into the kitchen. They should exit and enter two or three times each.* YVONNE *is still sitting at the table down left. She takes a deck of cards and starts playing solitaire.*

JEANNETTE: *(While working)* It must be nice to be able to sit while everybody else is working.

ALICE: *(Also working)* I hope you don't have to be a good worker to get into heaven because I know someone who's goin' to hell for sure.

YVONNE: I'm really getting fed up with you two. If you're so determined to have me work, why do you always tell me to get out of the way when I try to do something?

JEANNETTE: Because you can't do anything right. Worse still, you won't even learn how to do anything right.

YVONNE: Well, it keeps me from doing a lot of things for nothing . . . like throwing parties for people who don't bother to show up.

JEANNETTE: She'll be here!

YVONNE: Talk about making a fool of yourself. All those people, your

JEANNETTE: Ah, oui. Y est dans cuisine. J'va aller le chercher. *(Elle va pour se lever.)*

EVA: Non, non. Dérange-toué pas. J'va l'amener mèque qu'on revienne. *(A* NORMAND*)* Veux-tu passer chez nous prendre un p'tit "night cap," Normand?

NORMAND: Tedben rienque un p'tit. Moué aussi, j'ai en masse à faire demain.

EVA: Viens-t'en, comme ça. Good night, hein, vous-autres.

Adieux de tous. EVA, ROGER, *et* NORMAND *sortent par la porte à gauche. Pause.* JEANNETTE *et* ALICE *se mettent à ramasser plats, cendriers, verres, etc., et les porter à la cuisine. Elles doivent sortir et rentrer deux ou trois fois.* YVONNE, *toujours à la table à gauche, prend le jeu de cartes et commence un jeu de patience.*

JEANNETTE: *(En travaillant)* Ça doit être beau d'avoir l'temps de s'assir pendant que les autres travaillent.

ALICE: *(Même jeu)* J'espère que Saint Pierre demande pas d'ambition pour pouvoir entrer au ciel, parce que j'sais quèqu'un qui est damné certain.

YVONNE: Ah, que vous êtes plattes, vous-autres. Si vous voulez tellement que j'vous aide, pourquoi que vous m'disez toujours de m'ôter dans les jambes quand j'essaie de faire quèque chose?

JEANNETTE: Parce que tu sais rien faire. Pire que ça, tu veux même pas apprendre à rien faire!

YVONNE: Ça m'empêche de faire des affaires pour rien . . . comme donner des parties pour du monde qui viennent pas.

JEANNETTE: A va v'nir!

YVONNE: Parle de niaiser. Tout ce monde-là, ton gâteau . . . Ouais, c'tait

cake ... Yep. It was a beautiful party, all right. There was only one thing missing: the guest of honor.

JEANNETTE: I tell you she'll be here!

ALICE: She'd better hurry up. Pretty soon, it won't even be her birthday any more.

JEANNETTE: You heard what Eva said? Jerry's been planning this for quite a while, so I'm sure that Connie doesn't want to disappoint him. But she doesn't want to disappoint us either. So I think they're going to go out to eat. That'll make Jerry happy. Then, they'll come here.

ALICE: You think they're not going to go to the concert at all?

JEANNETTE: *(Crosses to the table down left with a deck of cards, sits on a chair stage right of the table, and starts to play a game of solitaire)* That's right. And I don't understand why everybody else left. Connie likes to spend her birthdays with her family, not with a bunch of strangers at the Opera House. You'll see. She won't let us down. The concert starts at ten. She'll be here before then.

ALICE: *(Sitting on one of the straight chairs stage right)* Well, I hope she decides not to come.

JEANNETTE: *(Sarcastic)* Well, now we all see just how much you love your niece. You don't even want her to come to her own birthday party.

ALICE: *(Also sarcastic, looking around the room)* And a great party it is, too.

YVONNE: You can't be serious, Alice. Why wouldn't you want her to come?

ALICE: Because she's not a little girl any more. Because she's not eleven any more. Because she's old enough to spend her birthday anyway she pleases ... with or without us.

un ben beau party. C't'un peu de valeur que l'invitée d'honneur y était pas, par exemple.

JEANNETTE: A va v'nir, j'te l'dis!

ALICE: A est aussi ben de s'dépêcher. Ben vite, ça sera même pu sa fête.

JEANNETTE: T'as entendu quoi c'est qu'Eva a dit? Jerry, ça fait longtemps qui a "planné" ça. Chu certain que Connie veut pas le désappointer. Mais a veut pas nous désappointer, nous-autres non plus. Ça fait qui vont aller manger. Ça, ça va faire plaisir à Jerry. Pi après, y vont v'nir icit.

ALICE: Tu penses qui vont manquer le concert?

JEANNETTE: *(Se dirige vers la table à gauche avec un deuxième jeu de cartes et s'assoit sur la chaise à la droite de la table. Elle commence un jeu de patience.)* Oui, pi j'comprends pas pourquoi tous les autres sont partis. Constance, a aime passer sa fête avec sa famille, pas avec une bande d'é-trangers à l'Opera House. Tu vas voir. A nous désappointera pas. Le concert commence à dix heures. A va être icit avant ça.

ALICE: *(S'assoit sur une chaise à droite de la salle)* Ben moué, j'espère qu'a vienne pas.

JEANNETTE: *(Ironique)* Bon, ben on voué que tu l'aimes gros, ta nièce. Tu veux même pas qu'a vienne à son party.

ALICE: *(Ironique de son tour. Regarde autour d'elle)* Beau party, j'te l'dis.

YVONNE: Mais t'es pas sérieuse, Alice. Pourquoi c'est que tu voudrais pas qu'a vienne?

ALICE: Parce que c'est pu une p'tite fille. Parce qu'a pu onze ans. Parce qu'a est assez vieille pour passer sa fête comme a veut . . . avec ou sans nous-autres.

Jeannette: And you think that THIS is what she wants . . . going out to dinner alone, going to a concert alone?

Alice: What do you mean, alone? Did Jerry suddenly fall off the face of the earth?

Jeannette: You know what I mean. She's not with her family.

Yvonne: Right. If she wanted to go out to eat for her birthday, she should have told us. It would've been fun for all of us to go out together.

Jeannette: And Jerry could have come, too, . . . our treat. He wouldn't have had to worry about where the money was going to come from. But if you ask me, she's only doing this to make Jerry happy. If she could do what she really wanted, she'd be here with us.

Yvonne: *(Dreamily)* And after dinner, we could have come back here and had the cake and played cards . . .

Alice: Just like we did last year, and the year before and the year before that.

Jeannette: What's wrong with that? Everybody has fun at Connie's parties . . . Connie most of all. She was never one to go to all the teenage hang outs. She always liked to spend time with adults . . . people who were older than her. It didn't bother her at all. Not like other kids. She was always more mature.

Yvonne: Yep. She always seemed older than her age. Never thought of herself. She always tried to please everybody else.

Alice: But people change.

Jeannette: No, they don't! Not Connie, anyway. Not that much. *(She looks at the clock.)* By ten o'clock, she'll be here.

JEANNETTE: Tu peux pas m'dire que c'est ça qu'a veut . . . aller dîner toute seule pi aller à un concert toute seule.

ALICE: Quoi c'est que tu veux dire, toute seule? Jerry est-ti mort subitement, lui?

JEANNETTE: Tu sais c'que j'veux dire. C'est pas avec la famille.

YVONNE: Oui. Si a voulait sortir manger pour sa fête, a aurait dû nous le dire. Ça aurait été le fun de sortir tout ensemble.

JEANNETTE: Pi Jerry aurait pu v'nir, lui étou, pi on aurait payé pour lui. Ça aurait été ben meilleur pour lui, vu qui a pas de job. Mais pour moué, a sort ainque pour faire plaisir à Jerry. Si a pouvait faire quoi c'est qu'a voulait, a s'rait icit, avec nous-autres.

YVONNE: *(Rêveuse)* Pi après ça, on aurait pu revenir icit pour le gâteau, pi pour jouer aux cartes . . .

ALICE: Pareil comme on a fait l'année dernière, pi l'année d'avant, pi l'année d'avant ça.

JEANNETTE: Y a rien de mal là-dedans. Tout le monde avait du fun aux parties à Connie . . . surtout Connie. C'était pas une pour sortir ainque avec des jeunes, ça. Elle a toujours aime ça être avec le grand monde . . . du monde qui était plus vieux qu'elle. Ça bâdrait pas pantoute. Pas comme les autres jeunes. A était toujours plus raisonnable.

YVONNE: Ouais. On dirait qu'a était plus vieille, plus grandie que les autres. A pensait jamais à elle-même. A voulait toujours faire plaisir aux autres.

ALICE: Mais ça change, ça, du monde!

JEANNETTE: Non, ça change pas! Pas Connie, au moins. Pas autant que ça. *(Elle regarde la pendule.)* A dix heures, a va être icit.

ALICE: Ah, well if you think people don't change, I've got a story to tell you. I once knew a girl. She wasn't a ravishing beauty, but she had boyfriends enough. She was sweet and polite and thoughtful. She could sing and dance. She was in plays and musicals. People even used to ask her and her sisters to sing at meetings of the Ladies of Saint Anne, and other parish get togethers. She was always out having a good time. (JEANNETTE *starts to realize that* ALICE *is talking about her.*) Do you know what happened to that girl? Today she's an old maid who sits around the house smoking one cigarette after another . . . and who has all sorts of sicknesses that no one can cure . . . and who coughs and whines and cries and sneaks around drinking vodka from a hidden bottle all day long. Now, people have to beg her to go out. And you're telling me that that people don't change?

JEANNETTE: *(Coughing)* It's not my fault I'm sick. You're never the same, after you've been sick. But at least, I do my work around the house. *(She indicates* YVONNE.*)* Not like some people I know.

YVONNE: But what does all of this have to do with Connie? Maybe she's changed but she's not sick.

ALICE: Not yet.

YVONNE: What do you mean?!?

JEANNETTE: She doesn't have any idea what she means.

ALICE: Oh no? You've never wondered why you only started getting sick after mama told you not to go out with Bernie any more?

JEANNETTE: That had nothing to do with anything!

ALICE: On no?

JEANNETTE: No! Because if you remember, it was only after mama died that I started getting really sick.

ALICE: Ah, ben si tu penses que l'monde change pas, j'va t'donner un p'tit exemple. Une fois, moué, j'connaissais une fille. C'tait pas une beauté, mais a avait des boyfriends. A était fine, polie, raisonnable. A chantait ben, pi a dansait ben. On y demandait même d'être dans des pièces pi des "musicals." On y demandait de chanter avec ses soeurs à des meetings des dames de Sainte Anne, pi à des soirées. J'te dis qu'a sortait pi a n'avait, du fun! *(JEANNETTE commence à comprendre qu'ALICE parle d'elle. Elle se baisse la tête.)* Sais-tu quoi c'est qui est arrivé à c't'a fille-là? J'va te l'dire. Aujourd'hui, c't'une vieille fille qui fume une cigarette après l'autre . . . pi qui a toutes sortes de maladies que personne peut guérir . . . pi qui tousse pi qui se plaint pi qui pleure pi qui prend du vodka à cachette. Asteur, faut qu'a se fasse prier pour sortir. Pi tu veux me faire accraire que le monde change pas?

JEANNETTE: *(Toussant)* C'est pas ma faute si chu malade. Ça change une personne en masse, ça, des maladies. Au moins, j'fais mon ouvrage icit. *(Elle indique YVONNE.)* Pas comme des autres que j'connais.

YVONNE: Mais quoi c'est que ça l'a à faire avec Connie, tout ça? Tedben qu'a changé, mais a est pas malade.

ALICE: Pas encore.

YVONNE: Quoi c'est que tu veux dire?!?

JEANNETTE: A l'sais pas, quoi c'est qu'a veut dire.

ALICE: Ah non? Tu t'es jamais demandé pourquoi que c'est rienque après que maman t'as défendu de sortir avec Bernard que t'a commencé à être malade?

JEANNETTE: C'avait rien à faire avec ça!

ALICE: Ah non?

JEANNETTE: Non! Parce que si tu t'en souviens, c'tait ainque après la mort à maman que j'ai commencé à être vraiment malade.

ALICE: Right. But the little aches and pains? The little "I just don't feel very goods". All those little visits to the doctor. They all started when Bernie got married. You even had to stop working at the mill. When you were taking care of mama, it wasn't too bad. You had something to keep you busy. But all of a sudden, you found yourself all alone all day. You had time to think about what you were doing and what you had done.

JEANNETTE: Great! And now a word from our amateur psychiatrist.

ALICE: Fine. Don't believe me, but . . .

JEANNETTE: That's right. I don't believe you. I loved mama. It was no sacrifice to take care of her. And even if she hadn't told me not to, I don't think I would have married Bernie anyway.

ALICE: Why not?

JEANNETTE: Why not?!? Because he was a worthless son of a bitch, that's why not! Even when we were engaged, he'd go out on me with other girls.

ALICE: Maybe it's because he was sick of waiting. He kept asking you to set a date for your wedding. You never did. One day, you'd say yes, the next day you'd say no, and most of the time, you'd just say you didn't know. There wasn't much else poor Bernie could do. I think he knew that mama would win out in the end anyway.

JEANNETTE: You're damned right she won and I'm glad. *(Sarcastic)* We would have made a wonderful couple, that's for sure. That's not the kind of life I wanted.

ALICE: *(Also sarcastic)* And this is?

JEANNETTE: *(Angry)* Boy, you're starting to get on my nerves! Yes, this is

Alice: Ouais. Mais les p'tites maladies, là? Les p'tites plaintes? Les p'tites visites au docteur? Ça tout commencé quand Bernard s'est marié. Y a même fallu que tu arrêtes de travailler au moulin. Quand tu prenais soin de maman, c'tait o.k. T'avais toujours quèque chose pour te tenir occupée. Mais tout à coup, tu t'es trouvée toute seule. T'avais le temps de penser à quoi c'est que tu faisais, pi quoi c'est que t'avais fait.

Jeannette: Bon, v'là la "psychiatrist" qui est arrivée!

Alice: T'as beau pas me craire, si tu veux pas mais . . .

Jeannette: Non, j'te cré pas. Moué, je l'aimais, maman. C'tait pas un sacrifice pour moué de prendre soin d'elle. Pi même si a me l'avait pas défendu, j'pense pas que j'aurais marié Bernard anyway.

Alice: Pourquoi pas?

Jeannette: Pourquoi pas?!? C'tait un maudit vaurien. C'est ça pourquoi pas! Même quand on était engagé, y sortait avec d'autres filles.

Alice: C'est parce qui était tanné d'attendre. Quand y te demandait si t'allais choisir une date pour votre mariage, un jour tu disais "oui," l'autre jour c'tait "non," pi la plupart du temps, c'tait "Je l'sais pas." Quoi c'est que tu voulais qui fasse? J'pense qui a ben vu que maman allait gagner à fin anyway.

Jeannette: Oui, c'est elle qui a gagné, pi chu ben contente. (Ironique) J'aurais eu une belle vie avec lui, j'te l'dis.

Alice: (Ironique de son tour) Pi la vie que t'as asteur est ben meilleure, hein?

Jeannette: (En colère) Eh, que t'es tannante! Oui, a est meilleure . . .

the kind of life I wanted . . . because whatever I've done in life, I've done it for other people. It would have been real easy to be selfish . . . not to listen to mama and take her advice. But that's not how I was raised. That's not the example that mama set for us. *(She starts to cry.)* It wasn't easy, you know. My suffering means that there's a lot of days in Purgatory I won't have to spend. But I'm glad that at least one of us can say that we tried to follow mama's example. *(She stops crying. Takes a handkerchief from her sleeve and blows her nose)* There! Satisfied? You made me cry. Now, leave me alone! Yvonne was right. None of this has anything to do with Connie.

JEANNETTE *takes her glass, gets up, and exits down right. Pause. She returns with a full glass, crosses to the table, sits, and resumes her game of solitaire.*

Pause

ALICE: Jeannette.

JEANNETTE: *(Exasperated)* What now?!?

ALICE: Did you love Bernie?

JEANNETTE: What kind of stupid question is that? *(Pause. More softly)* You know I loved him.

ALICE: And do you think that Connie loves Jerry?

YVONNE: Great. We're into guessing games now. We don't know if she loves him. Nobody's asked her.

ALICE: Let's say they're in love. Don't you think it's better for them to spend time together talking, getting to know each other better, and having fun with people their own age rather than hanging around with a bunch of senile old maids.

parce que quoi c'est que j'ai fait, moué, dans la vie, j'l'ai fait pour les autres. C'aurait été ben façile de penser rienque à moué-même, de désobéir à maman. Mais c'est pas comme ça que j'ai été élevée, moué. C'est pas l'exemple que maman m'a donné. A jamais pensé à elle-même, maman, pi moué non plus. *(Elle se met à pleurnicher.)* Ça pas été facile, t'sais. J'te dis que je n'ai éffacé, des journées au purgatoire. Mais chu ben contente qui a au moins une de ses filles qui a essayé être comme maman. *(Un temps. Elle arrête de pleurnicher. Elle sort un mouchoir de sa manche et se mouche.)* Bon. Es-tu satisfaite, là? Tu m'as fait pleurer. Asteur, laisse-moué tranquille! Yvonne, a était correcte. Tout ça, ça rien à faire avec Connie anyway.

JEANNETTE *prend son verre, se lève, et sort à droite. Un temps. Silence. Elle revient avec un verre plein, se dirige vers la table, s'assoit, et recommence son jeu de patience.*

Pause

ALICE: Jeannette.

JEANNETTE: *(Irritée)* Quoi c'est que tu veux asteur?

ALICE: L'aimais-tu, Bernard?

JEANNETTE: Quelle sorte de mautadite question que c'est ça? *(Un temps. Plus douce)* Tu sais ben que je l'aimais.

ALICE: Pi penses-tu que Connie aime Jerry?

YVONNE: Bon, c'est l'heure des devinettes. On sait pas si a l'aime. On y a pas demandé.

ALICE: Disons qui s'aiment. Tu penses pas que c'est mieux qui passent leur temps ensemble à parler, pi à se connaître pi à avoir du fun avec du monde de leur âge ... plutôt que de venir icit pâtir avec des vieux?

JEANNETTE: They can have just as much fun here. We're not that old and we're certainly not senile.

YVONNE: If you ask me, the only reason they go out alone is because they'd be ashamed to do what they do together in front of us.

ALICE: Listen, Yvonne. The only thing they can't do here is spend time with each other. The only thing that matters, anyway.

YVONNE: They can't spend time together here?!?

ALICE: Not easily. The minute they walk in the door, the aunts take one off this way and the uncles take the other one off the other way and they don't see each other again all night.

JEANNETTE: That never kept Connie from bringing her other boyfriends here. They did everything with the family.

ALICE: And then, after three visits, they'd mysteriously disappear. Connie would never hear from them again.

YVONNE: There she goes again.

ALICE: *(Ignores* YVONNE*)* That's why I said what I did. That's why I hope Connie doesn't show up tonight. At her age, she should spend time planning her future . . . not sitting around playing cards.

YVONNE: And you don't care that she may be planning it with a Protestant who doesn't even have a job?

ALICE: I wouldn't care of she was planning it with someone who had one eye, three legs, and a half dozen noses. Connie's the one who should decide if she's going to date him. It's her choice, and nobody else's.

JEANNETTE:Y auraient pu avoir du fun aussi ben icit. On est pas si vieux que ça.

YVONNE: Ben moué, j'pense que la seule raison qui sortent tout seul c'est parce qui auraient honte de faire quoi c'est qui font ensemble en avant de nous-autres.

ALICE: Ecoute,Yvonne. La seule chose qui font tout seul qui pourraient pas faire icit, c'est de se parler. La seule chose importante, anyway.

YVONNE: Y peuvent pas se parler icit?!?

ALICE: C'est tough en mautadit. En arrivant, les tantes en prennent un, pi les oncles, l'autre, pi c'est good bye pour les reste de la soirée.

JEANNETTE: Ça jamais empêché Connie des amener icit avant, ses boyfriends.Y faisaient tout avec la famille.

ALICE: Pi ça les prenait pas longtemps de sacrer leur camp après ça, non plus.Trois visites icit, pi Connie les voyait pu.

YVONNE: A recommence là-dessus, asteur.

ALICE: *(Elle ignore* YVONNE.*)* C'est pour ça que j'ai dit quoi c'est que j'ai dit. C'est pour ça que j'espère que Connie vienne pas à soir. A son âge, a devrait passer son temps à jouer à l'amour ou à l'avenir, pas aux cartes.

YVONNE: Pi ça te fait rien si a joue avec un protestant qui a même pas de job?

ALICE: Ça m'ferait rien si y avait ainque un oeil, pi trois pattes, pi une dizaine de nez. C'est Connie qui devrait décider si a va le voir ou non. C'est son choix à elle, pas à personne d'autre.

JEANNETTE: That's all well and good, but Connie can't just think of herself. Eva would die for sure if Connie married a Protestant.

ALICE: Ah, we're back to killing off mothers again.

JEANNETTE: And you saw how upset Joe was when he heard about all this.

YVONNE: And what about us? Maybe you don't care, but I'm upset about this whole thing . . . and so's Jeannette.

ALICE: If that's true, it calls for a celebration. It's the first time you two have agreed on anything in thirty years. But, come on, now. Think about it. Connie's not going to spend the rest of her life with Eva or Joe or us, I hope. What difference does it make what we think and how we feel? The important thing for her is to be happy.

YVONNE: You can't make yourself happy by hurting other people.

JEANNETTE: That's true. It's better to suffer than to hurt those who love us.

YVONNE: And you can't tell me that Connie can't do better than that. If she really tried. If she really looked around . . .

ALICE: If, if, if! We could "if" all day long and it wouldn't help. It's what's going on right now that's important. And right now, Connie's going out with Jerry.

YVONNE: And it's a shame.

JEANNETTE: I agree. This might surprise you a bit, Alice, but we can't shut off our feelings like you do. We still love our Connie. And it hurts us when we see that she's getting ready to throw her whole life away.

ALICE: How touching! Well I have one thing that you don't. Maybe you

JEANNETTE: C'est ben beau de dire ça, mais a peut pas penser rienque à elle-même, c't'a fille-là. Eva, ça la tuerait si Connie mariait un protestant.

ALICE: Bon. On est encore rendu au tuage de mères.

JEANNETTE: Pi Joe, t'as vu comment ça y fait d'la peine quand y entendu qu'a sortait avec.

YVONNE: Pi nous autres, là. Tedben que toué, ça t'fait rien, mais ça me fait d'la peine, moué . . . pi a Jeannette étou.

ALICE: Si c'est vrai, ça, on devrait célébrer. C'est la première fois dans trente ans que vous vous accordez ensemble. Mais, voyons. Connie, a passera pas le reste de sa vie avec Eva, ou avec Joe, ou avec nous-autres, j'espère. Quoi c'est que ça peut ben faire quoi c'est qu'on pense. L'important pour elle, c'est d'être heureuse.

YVONNE: On peut pas être heureuse si on fait d'la peine aux autres.

JEANNETTE: C'est vrai, ça. Ça vaux mieux de souffrir que de faire d'la peine à ceux qui nous aiment.

YVONNE: Pi tu peux pas m'dire que Connie peux pas trouver mieux que ça. Si a essayait, là. Si . . .

ALICE: Si, si, si ! C'est pas les "si" qui comptent. C'est quoi c'est qui se passe asteur. Pi asteur, Connie sort avec Jerry.

YVONNE: Pi c'est ben de valeur.

JEANNETTE: Ouais. Ça t'surprendrait tedben, Alice, mais nous autres, on est pas des sans-coeur comme toué. On l'aime encore, notre Connie. Pi ça nous fait quèque chose quand on voué qu'a est prête à gaspiller sa vie.

ALICE: C'est-ti donc beau ! Ben moué, j'ai une affaire que vous avez pas,

don't think it's very important, but I've got it. It's called trust. Out of this whole family, I'm the only one who trusts that little girl enough to leave her alone. Oh, it's great to say that she's soooo sweet, and soooo polite, and soooooo mature. But none of you believe a damn word of it. Because the minute she does something you don't like, Pow! . . . suddenly, she turns into an heartless, selfish ogre.

YVONNE: No one's saying that.

ALICE: Don't have to say it. It's been clear all day. If Connie is as mature as you all say, then she'll make the right choice. But she won't be able to unless you leave her alone and let her make the choice. Not one of you here asked Connie what she wanted today. It IS her birthday, after all. No. Everybody was much too busy telling her what she had to do, and how much she would hurt all of us if she didn't do it. *(Pause)* That's why I hope she doesn't show up tonight. *(Pause)* Because if she does show up, it'll mean that you've won . . . just like mama used to win . . . time after time after time. *(Pause. She looks over at JEANNETTE.)* I'm afraid it's going to be a very expensive victory.

Pause

JEANNETTE: *(Nervous)* What time us it?

YVONNE: *(Looking at the clock)* Ten past ten.

Pause

ALICE: *(Softly)* Put the cake away, Jeannette. *(Pause)* We can take it over to Eva's tomorrow.

Pause

JEANNETTE: *(She coughs.)* Anyone want to play cards?

vous autres. Tedben qu'vous pensez que c'est pas diable important, mais je l'ai. Ça s'appelle la confiance. De tout le monde qui a passé icit, aujourd'hui, chu la seule qui aie confiance assez dans c't'a p'tite fille-là pour la laisser tranquille. Ah, c'est ben beau de dire qu'a est fine, pi polie, pi raisonnable ... mais pour moué, vous créez pas ça. Parce que la minute qu'a fait quèque chose que vous aimez pas, bang! ... tout à coup, c't'une p'tite sans-coeur.

Yvonne: On a jamais dit ça.

Alice: Pas besoin de l'dire. Ça s'est vu toute la journée. Si Connie est si raisonable que vous dites, a va ben choisir. Mais a pourra rien faire si on la laisse pas tranquille ... si on y donne pas la chance de faire son choix. Y a pas un chat qui a demandé à Connie quoi c'est qu'a voulait, elle, aujourd'hui. C'tait sa fête, pourtant. Non. Tout le monde était trop occupé à y dire quoi faire, pi comment de peine qu'a ferait à tout le monde si a le faisait pas. *(Un temps)* C'est pour ça que j'espère qu'a vienne pas, à soir. *(Un temps)* Parce que si a vient, ça veut dire que vous avez gagné, vous autres ... comme maman gagnait toujours avant. *(Un temps. Elle regarde Jeannette.)* J'ai ben peur que c'est une victoire qui va coûter cher.

Pause

Jeannette: *(Nerveuse)* Quelle heure qui est, donc?

Yvonne: *(Regarde la pendule)* Dix heures et dix.

Pause

Alice: *(Plus douce)* Serre ton gâteau, Jeannette. *(Un temps)* Tu pourras l'emporter chez Eva demain.

Pause

Jeannette: *(Elle tousse. Bas)* Qui c'est qui veux jouer aux cartes?

YVONNE *puts away her deck of cards and gets ready to play.* JEANNETTE *starts to shuffle the cards.* CONSTANCE *enters up left. At first, no one notices her. She hesitates for a moment. Finally, she crosses to the table and sits next to* JEANNETTE. JEANNETTE *notices* CONSTANCE. *She hesitates for a moment, pats her hand a couple of times, and keeps shuffling the cards. Pause.*

JEANNETTE: *(To* ALICE*)* Do you want to play or not?

ALICE *hesitates. She crosses to the table and sits.* JEANNETTE *starts to deal the cards.*

Curtain

YVONNE *met son jeu de cartes de côté et se prépare à jouer.* JEANNETTE *commence à battre les cartes.* CONSTANCE *entre à gauche, inaperçue. Elle hésite pour un moment. Enfin, elle va s'asseoir à la table à côté de* JEANNETTE. JEANNETTE *aperçoit* CONSTANCE. *Elle hésite un instant, lui caresse les mains deux ou trois fois, et continue à battre les cartes. Un temps.*

JEANNETTE: *(A* ALICE*)* Joues-tu, toué?

ALICE *hésite. Elle se dirige vers la table et s'assoit.* JEANNETTE *commence à donner les cartes.*

Rideau

SANS ATOUT

No Trump

Pièce en trois actes / A drama in three acts

CAST OF CHARACTERS

GÉRARD, *Middle-class Franco-American, 64 years old*

JULIETTE, *Gérard's wife, also 64*

LOUIS, *Gérard and Juliette's brother-in-law, 69 years old*

HILDA, *Juliette's sister, 70 years old*

THE TELEVISION, *Hypnotic anglophone presence*

PERSONNAGES

GÉRARD, *Bourgeois franco-américain,* 64 ans

JULIETTE, *Bourgeoise franco-américaine, épouse de Gérard, 64 ans*

LOUIS, *Beau-frère de Gérard et de Juliette, 69 ans*

HILDA, *Soeur de Juliette, 70 ans*

LE TÉLÉVISEUR, *Présence anglophone hypnotique*

SETTING

The action of the play takes place in GÉRARD *and* JULIETTE'S *house during the two days preceding Thanksgiving Day, and on the holiday itself. The scene depicts the kitchen and the living room of the house. The kitchen is up left and takes up about a third of the stage. It has a table and four chairs, counter space, a sink, a refrigerator, a stove, and cupboards. The living room takes up the rest of the stage. There is a table against the wall up right with a telephone. Above the table are pictures of* GÉRARD *and* JULIETTE'S *children and grandchildren. A couch is located down left with two small tables on each side and a coffee table in front. A television set, seen from the rear, is down right center. Two easy chairs face the television set on each side. Between the two chairs is a small table with newspapers, magazines, and the all-important remote control. The decor is typical of a middle class Franco-American home of the 80s or 90s. A door up center leads outside. Another door down right leads to the bedrooms.*

Important note: The television is a key character in the play. The audience should always be aware of its presence and its influence. When I first wrote the play, I thought it would be enough to show flickering lighting, reflected on the walls, to depict changes in the picture. I was wrong. It's not enough. Instead, I suggest showing slides of the "shows" that GÉRARD *and* JULIETTE *are watching on the backstage wall. As needed, the slides could change quickly or not at all. In the sections of the play where the TV plays a key role (soap operas, hockey game, parade), the images must reflect the content. The most important thing to keep in mind is that the dominant role of the TV in* GÉRARD *and* JULIETTE'S *lives must be apparent to the audience. Otherwise, the play doesn't work.*

MISE EN SCÈNE

L'action de la pièce se passe dans la maison de GÉRARD *et* JULIETTE *pendant les deux jours avant la Fête de l'Action de Grâce (Thanksgiving), et la journée même de la fête. La scène représente la cuisine et le salon de la maison. La cuisine se trouve à gauche, vers l'arrière-scène, et doit prendre à peu près un tiers de la scène entière. Il a y une table et quatre chaises, un comptoir, un évier, un frigo, et un poêle. Le salon occupe le restant de la scène. Il y a une table près du mur à l'arrière-scène à gauche avec téléphone, verreries, plats, etc. La table est surmontée de photos de la famille. Il y a un divan à droite avec deux petites tables de chaque côté. Il y a aussi une table basse en avant du divan. A l'avant-scène, légèrement à droite, se trouve Le Téléviseur qu'on voit de dos. Deux fauteuils sont placés "en avant" et de chaque côté du téléviseur. Il y a aussi une table entre les fauteuils avec une télécommande. Le tout est décoré avec un goût petit bourgeois franco-américain. Une porte à l'arrière-scène au centre mène à l'extérieur. Une porte/sortie à l'avant-scène à droite mène aux chambres à coucher.*

Note de l'auteur à propos de la mise en scène: Le Téléviseur est un personnage essentiel de la pièce. L'assistance doit toujours se rendre compte de sa présence et de son influence. En écrivant la pièce, je pensais qu'il suffisait de montrer les changements d'intensité, reflétés dans la salle, pour indiquer des changements d'images. J'avais tort, et c'est devenu évident au cours de la première représentation de la pièce. Ce que je suggère maintenant c'est de projeter des diapositives sur un écran/mur à l'arrière scène. Ces diapositives pourraient changer très lentement . . . ou pas du tout . . . pendant les dialogues où la télé n'entre pas en jeu. Pour les sections de la pièce où la télé joue un rôle principal (Téléromans, partie de hockey, parade, etc.), on devrait changer les images assez rapidement pour suivre le texte. D'une façon ou d'une autre, le rôle du téléviseur doit être évident à l'assistance. Autrement, cette pièce ne peut pas réussir.

ACT I

Late afternoon in November. Fairly dim lighting. GÉRARD *is sitting in front of the TV in the easy chair on the right. He is almost hypnotized by the TV show.* JULIETTE *is sitting in the easy chair on the left. She is reading* The National Enquirer. *Every once in a while, she interrupts her reading to glance at the TV.*

WOMAN 1: *(On TV. Weepy)* Oh, Sibyl . . . I think Lance is . . . is . . . gay! *(She bursts into tears.)*

JULIETTE *lowers* The Enquirer *and watches.*

WOMAN 2: *(On TV)* So that's why Bruce is blackmailing him.

WOMAN 1: *(Weepy)* Yes! Lance knows that if people find out he's gay, his career as the football coach of Central High is over . . . finished! *(She bursts into tears once again.)*

JULIETTE *goes back to reading* The Enquirer.

WOMAN 2: But why did Lance steal that money from the team's uniform fund?

WOMAN 1: I don't know. But I do know that he's gone to see Bruce . . . and he took THE GUN! *(She bursts into tears.)*

JULIETTE *lowers* The Enquirer *and glances at the TV. We hear a flourish of organ music. She goes back to her reading.*

ANNOUNCER: Join us again tomorrow for the continuing story of "When We Were Young and Beautiful."

ACTE I

L'après-midi. Éclairage assez sombre. GÉRARD *est dans le salon, assis sur le fauteuil à droite. Il est presque hypnotisé par ce qui se passe à la télévision.* JULIETTE *est également dans le salon, assise sur le divan à gauche. Elle est en train de lire "Le National Enquirer." De temps à autre, elle jette un coup d'oeil à la télé.*

FEMME 1: *(A la télé. Pleurnichant)* Oh, Sybil . . . I think Lance is . . . is . . . gay! *(Elle éclate en sanglots.)*

JULIETTE *baisse son journal et regarde la télé.*

FEMME 2: *(A la télé)* So that's why Bruce is blackmailing him.

FEMME 1: *(Même jeu)* Yes! Lance knows that if people find out he's gay, his career as the football coach of Central High is over . . . finished! *(Elle éclate de nouveau en sanglots.)*

JULIETTE *se remet à lire son journal.*

FEMME 2: But why did Lance steal that money from the team's uniform fund?

FEMME 1: I don't know. But I do know that he's gone to see Bruce . . . and he took THE GUN! *(Elle éclate en sanglots.)*

JULIETTE *baisse son journal et regarde la télé. On entend la musique d'orgue.* JULIETTE *se remet à lire son journal.*

ANNONCEUR: Join us again tomorrow for the continuing story of "When We Were Young and Beautiful."

Organ music. Gérard *reaches for the remote control and changes the channel.*

Announcer: *(In the middle of the ad)* So, if dingy floors are killing your family's social life . . . making you and your loved ones incapable of establishing meaningful, interpersonal relationships with the world around you . . . use Lino-Shine, the easy-to-use wax that makes your floors—and the world—take a shine to YOU! Now, stay tuned for the continuing saga of an American family as we present the exciting, day-time drama: "Alone Together."

The volume goes down.

Gérard: You'll see. I bet you she won't be able to keep her baby.

Juliette: *(Lowering the newspaper)* What?

Gérard: Samantha. I bet you she won't be able to keep her baby.

Juliette: Oh, come on. People don't go around just giving their babies away. If you ask me, she'll find a way to get the money to pay those people off.

Gérard: Well fifty thousand bucks isn't chicken feed. Besides, Jerry borrowed it from some Mafia guy . . . and you know how the Mafia can be when they don't get their money.

Juliette: But that baby is so cute.

Gérard: That's not going to make a bit of difference. She won't be able to keep him. You'll see!

The volume goes up.

Man 1: Hiya, baby.

Samantha: *(Icily)* What do you want?

Musique d'orgue. GÉRARD *prend la télécommande et change le canal.*

ANNONCEUR: *(Au milieu de son annonce)* So, if dingy floors are killing your family's social life . . . making you and your loved ones incapable of establishing meaningful, interpersonal relationships with the world around you . . . use Lino-Shine, the easy-to-use wax that makes your floors—and the world—take a shine to YOU! Now, stay tuned for the continuing saga of an American family as we present the exciting, day-time drama: "Alone Together."

Le son du téléviseur s'adoucit.

GÉRARD: Tu vas voir. A pourra pas garder son bébé.

JULIETTE: *(Qui baisse son journal)* Hein?

GÉRARD: Samantha. Tu vas voir qu'a pourra pas garder son bébé.

JULIETTE: Mais, voyons. Ça se donne pas comme ça, des bébés. Pour moué, a va trouver d'l'argent pour payer ça, c'monde-là.

GÉRARD: Ben, cinquante mille piastres, c'est pas des épelures d'oignons, ça. A part de ça, Jeremy a emprunté ça d'un gars qui est avec le Mafia. C'est pas patient, ça, des gars comme ça.

JULIETTE: Oui, mais son bébé est si cute.

GÉRARD: Cute ou pas cute, a pourra pas le garder, tu vas voir.

Le son du téléviseur devient plus fort.

HOMME 1: Hiya, baby.

SAMANTHA: *(Froide)* What do you want?

MAN 2:Your autograph. *(The two men laugh.)* What d'ya think we want?

MAN 1:Your husband borrowed some money from a friend of ours. Lots of money.

SAMANTHA:You know my husband's dead.

MAN 2:Yeah, we heard. It's not every day that a guy dies from breast cancer.

MAN 1:That's why we're here . . . to protect our friend's investment.

SAMANTHA:You'll get your money!

MAN 2: No problem there. We always do.

MAN 1:The question is "when." Ya see, your husband had promised to pay us last week.

MAN 2:And our friend gets very impatient when people don't pay on time.

MAN 1:And when he gets impatient, he can do some real nasty things. So, if he doesn't get that money by tomorrow . . .

SAMANTHA: *(Shocked)* Tomorrow?!?! How can I get fifty thousand dollars by tomorrow?!?

MAN 2:That ain't our problem.

MAN 1: Look, baby, we ain't unreasonable. Maybe we can work somethin' out. Ya see, our friend has this little problem. He wants to have a kid. He wants one real bad . . . but . . . well . . . he can't.

MAN 2:And he can't adopt a kid either, 'cause them social worker types don't like the kind of work he does.

HOMME 2: Your autograph. *(Les deux hommes rient.)* What d'ya think we want?

HOMME 1: Your husband borrowed some money from a friend of ours. Lots of money.

SAMANTHA: You know my husband's dead.

HOMME 2: Yeah, we heard. It's not every day that a guy dies from breast cancer.

HOMME 1: That's why we're here . . . to protect our friend's investment.

SAMANTHA: You'll get your money!

HOMME 2: No problem there. We always do.

HOMME 1: The question is "when." Ya see, your husband had promised to pay us last week.

HOMME 2: And our friend gets very impatient when people don't pay on time.

HOMME 1: And when he gets impatient, he can do some real nasty things. So, if he doesn't get that money by tomorrow . . .

SAMANTHA: *(Ahurie)* Tomorrow?!?! How can I get fifty thousand dollars by tomorrow?!?

HOMME 2: That ain't our problem.

HOMME 1: Look, baby, we ain't unreasonable. Maybe we can work somethin' out. Ya see, our friend has this little problem. He want to have a kid. He wants one real bad . . . but . . . well . . . he can't.

HOMME 2: And he can't adopt a kid either, 'cause them social worker types don't like the kind of work he does.

Man 1: Now, here you are, a woman alone with a kid you really can't take care of . . .

Samantha: *(Furious)* You can't mean . . . *(She bursts into tears.)* No! Not my baby! Not my baby!

Man 2: Seems to me you ain't got much of a choice. Think about it. We'll be back.

A baby cries. Samantha *bursts into tears once more. Organ music.*

Juliette: It's a shame, isn't it?

Gérard: *(Exaggerated. As if he had won a bet)* See?!? See?!? What did I tell you? She's going to have to sell her baby to that Mafia guy.

Juliette: It's a crying shame.

Gérard: It's the only way she can pay him off.

Lights dim everywhere except on Juliette. *The TV becomes practically inaudible. Pause. When* Juliette *speaks, she directs her remarks primarily to the audience.*

Juliette: It's a shame, alright. But that's life. You work, and you work, and you work and what do you end up with? After years of breaking your back, you end up right back where you started . . . and that's only if you're lucky. It's when I see things like that on TV that it really sinks in. You should see Samantha's baby. He's so cute with his big blue eyes, and his curly blond hair, and his pink cheeks. A real living doll. And already, he's finding out how tough life can be. That little baby never hurt a soul. Seems to me that it's always the ones who deserve it least who suffer the most. Poor innocent babies. Sometimes, I'll read an article in here *(she indicates* The National Enquirer*)* and it'll make me sick because it's so unfair and so mean. *(She searches for an article in the paper.)* Here,

HOMME 1: Now, here you are, a woman alone with a kid you really can't take care of . . .

SAMANTHA: *(En colère)* You can't mean . . . *(Elle éclate en sanglots.)* No! Not my baby! Not my baby!

HOMME 2: Seems to me you ain't got much of a choice. Think about it. We'll be back.

On entend un bébé qui pleure. SAMANTHA *éclate en sanglots de nouveau. Musique d'orgue.*

JULIETTE: C'pas drôle, hein?

GÉRARD: *(Exagéré. Comme s'il avait gagné un pari)* Tu voué?!? J'te l'ai dit, hein? Là, y va falloir qu'a vende son bébé à c'gars-la.

JULIETTE: C'pas drôle, hein?

GÉRARD: C'est la seule manière qu'a va pouvoir le payer.

L'éclairage devient plus sombre partout, sauf sur JULIETTE. *Le son du téléviseur disparaît presque. Un temps. Quand* JULIETTE *parle, elle s'adresse surtout à l'assistance.*

JULIETTE: Non, c'pas drôle certain, ça, la vie. Tu travailles, pi tu travailles, pi tu travailles . . . pi quoi c'est que ça t'donne? Après des années, t'es rendu à même place que t'étais quand t'as commencé. Pi ça, c'est rienque si t'es chanceux. C'est quand on voué des affaires comme ça sur l'TV qu'on réalise ça. Le p'tit bébé à Samantha, y est assez cute. Des beaux yeux bleus, des cheveux blonds tous frisés, des joues rouges . . . une vrai p'tite catin. Pi ça souffre déjà. C't'enfant-là a jamais fait de mal à personne, ça. On dirait même que c'est eux-autres qui souffrent le plus. Pauvres p'tits innocents. Des fois, j'lis des affaires icit *(elle indique son journal)* pi ça m'enrage assez . . . j'peux pu y penser. J'viens mal. *(Elle cherche dans le journal.)* Tiens, par exemple,

listen to this if you think I'm crazy. *(She keeps on searching.)* It's right here on page . . . mmmmm *(still searching)* . . . page twelve. It says, "Mother kills two children. Incin . . . incener . . . *(she has trouble pronouncing the word)* . . . Incencerates them in gas oven." *(She lowers the paper.)* What kind of mother would do something like that? Kill her own little children! *(She reads from the article again.)* It says here, "Poverty cited as cause in woman's deranged act." Can you imagine? Killing your own babies just because you're poor? It's a good thing mothers were different when we were young, because there probably wouldn't be a single one of us alive out of the twenty kids my mother had. *(Indicating the article in the newspaper)* This woman was a regular Rockefeller compared to us. No car, no electricity, no money. No gas oven either, that's for sure. Maybe that's the only reason we're still here. And we were as dumb as we were poor. Especially me. *(Pause)* I was the youngest of them all. So all my older sisters used to love to torture me. They'd always invent some kind of errand for me to do. Most of the time, it meant going to old lady Josée's house. And, besides being our neighbor, old lady Josée was the meanest witch in town. My friends and I were so scared of her that we'd run across the street if we saw her coming towards us on the sidewalk. And of course, the only way for us to get to school was to go right by her house. Well, I tell you, we'd start running about a hundred feet before her house . . . and we wouldn't slow down until a hundred feet past it. Anyway, my older sisters would always send me to old lady Josée's house to borrow something or other, like flour, or butter, or sugar. Most of the time, it was just to see what I'd do, because they didn't really need anything. Well, let me tell you, I would try to put off going for as long as I could. I'd wait and wait and wait until one of them finally told me how mad papa would be if I didn't go. Well, for all of us, there was nothing worse than making papa mad. So off I'd go . . . but I sure wouldn't go very fast. Once I got there, I'd knock at the door and go in and stand there without saying a word because I was just too scared. I'd just stand there near the door and stare at the floor . . . until old lady Josée would get around to asking me what I wanted. Sometimes, I'd stay there for ten . . . fifteen . . . even twenty minutes before the old hag talked to me. And most of the time, when she looked at me with those cold little black eyes of hers, I'd be so scared that I'd forget why I was there in the first place. So I'd start

icit . . . *(elle continue à chercher)* . . . c't'à la page, euh . . . *(même jeu)* . . .
tiens, à page douze. Ça dit "Mother kills two children. Incin . . .
incener . . . *(elle a des difficultés à prononcer le mot)* . . . Incencerates them
in gas oven." *(Elle baisse le journal.)* Quelle sorte de mère que ça
prend pour faire des affaires comme ça. Tuer des p'tits enfants*! (Elle
regarde le journal de nouveau.)* Ça dit icit: "Poverty cited as cause in
woman's deranged act." Ça-ti du bons sens, ça, tuer des enfants parce
qu'on est pauvre?!? Une chance que les mères étaient différentes
quand on était jeunes, nous-autres, parce qui n'aurait pas un de la
vingtaine que ma mère a eu qui s'rait en vie aujourd'hui. Parle d'être
pauvre! Pas de char, pas d'électricité, pas d'argent. Pi pas de poêle à
gaz, non plus. C'est tedben pour ça qu'on est encore icit. Pi on était
aussi bête qu'on était pauvre. Moué, surtout. *(Pause)* Moué, j'tais la
plus jeune. Pi les plus vieilles inventaient des commissions pour
moué, surtout chez grand'mère Josée. Pi grand'mère Josée, elle, a
était déplaisante. On en avait assez peur qu'on changeait de bord
quand on la voyait venir vers nous autres sur le trottoir. Pi quand y
fallait passer devant sa maison pour aller à école, j'te dis qu'on courait
aussi vite qu'on pouvait. Ben, les plus vieilles, eux-autres, y m'en-
voyaient toujours emprunter quèque chose chez grand'mère Josée.
La plupart du temps, c'tait rienque pour rire de moué, parce qu'y
avaient pas besoin de rien. Ben, là, j'te l'dis que ça m'pesait sur le dos.
J'attendais pi j'attendais jusqu'à temps qui me disent que papa allait
être ben fâché si j'y allais pas. Pi pour nous-autres, faire fâcher papa,
y avait rien de pire. Ça fait que j'partais, pi j'te dis que j'prenais mon
temps. Une fois arrivée, j'frappais à porte, pi j'entrais, pi j'avais
encore assez peur que j'disais pas un mot. J'restais plantée là, près d'la
porte, à regarder le plancher . . . jusqu'à temps que grand'mère Josée
me demande quoi c'est que j'voulais. Des fois j'restais là pour dix,
quinze, vingt minutes avant qu'a me dise quèque chose. Pi la plupart
du temps, quand a me regardait avec ses p'tits yeux noirs pi durs,
j'avais assez peur que j'oubliais pourquoi y m'avaient envoyée là. Dans
c'temps-là, j'me mettais à brailler, pi j'courais chez nous. Pi quand y
me voyaient arriver, là, les plus vieilles riaient assez qui pissaient dans
leurs culottes. C'est pas drôle, hein, faire peur à du monde comme
ça? *(Pause)* Mais le plus drôle, c'est que j'y allais toujours. Même si

crying and then I'd run back home. Then, those sisters of mine would see me and they'd laugh so hard, they'd pee their pants. Imagine. Scaring people like that and enjoying it. Funny, isn't it? *(Pause)* But what's even funnier is that I always went. Even if I knew we didn't really need anything . . . even if I knew they only wanted to torture me . . . even if it scared me to death . . . I always went to old lady Josée's. *(Pause. She smiles.)* If you asked me why I did it without ever complaining, without ever saying no, without giving someone a good swift kick in the rear, I don't think I could tell you. *(Pause)* Even worse, if one of my older sisters walked into this room right now and told me to go borrow a cup of flour from old lady Josée, I think I'd probably do it. How dumb can you get? And I wasn't the only one. The whole family was like that. Come to think of it, the boys were even worse. Well, they had to help papa out on the farm, so none of them ever went to school. But a couple of us younger girls did. We even graduated from high school. So one day, Françoise decides she's going to teach Xavier how to read and write in English. She should have known that Xavier was about as dense as this table. *(Knocks the top of the table next to her)* Anyway, they'd been going at it for months when one day, she asks him to spell the word "run." Three little letters. One little word. Well Xavier sat there and concentrated real hard for at least five minutes before he said anything. Then, he started: "t . . . h . . . e: run!" *(She laughs.)* Can you imagine being that thick? "T . . . h . . .e: run!" But what could we do? We were all stuck in our fields on our farms in the boonies. Think about it. No central heat, no radio, no TV, no food lots of time. We were lucky to see a Model T twice a year. We never went out. We never saw anybody. We never even knew what was going on the other side of our tiny town. We never saw a newspaper. But even if we had seen one, it wouldn't have helped a heck of a lot, 'cause most of the family couldn't read or write. No wonder I'm afraid of everything. Even today, it takes me hours to cross the street. And forget about driving a car. I never could learn how . . . and I never will. Sometimes, I think we just weren't meant to live in a world like this. We should have all been born a century earlier. Take poor Uncle Exior when he went to Louise's house for supper. Louise got married to an Irishman and moved to Connecticut. She thought she was a big deal and she wanted to show her relatives that she really knew how to live. So when

j'savais qu'on avait besoin de rien . . . même si j'savais qui voulaient
ainque rire de moué . . . même si j'avais si peur que j'voulais mourir
. . . j'y allais toujours, chez grand'mère Josée. *(Pause. Elle rit à elle-
même.)* Si on m'demandait asteur pourquoi j'faisais ça, sans me plaindre, sans jamais dire non, sans donner un beau coup de pied à
quèqu'un, j'aurais pas de réponses. *(Pause)* Pire que ça, si une des plus
vieilles rentrait icit aujourd'hui, pi me disait d'aller emprunter d'la
farine chez grand'mère Josée, j'pense que j'l'f'rais encore. Faut pas
être ben smarte, pour faire des affaires comme ça, hein? Pi, j'tais pas
la seule. Toute la famille était comme ça. J'pense que les gars, y
étaient encore pires. Ça avait pas été à école, ça, parce que fallait qui
aident à papa sur la ferme. Mais une couple de nous-autres, les filles,
on est allée, pi on a même graduée d'la high school. Ça fait que
Françoise décide qu'a va enseigner l'anglais à Xavier . . . lui qui avait
la tête dure comme du ciment. Ça faisait des mois qui étudiait, pi un
jour, Françoise y demande d'épeler le mot "run." C'est pas tough,
épeler ça, "run." Mais a fallu que Xavier pense à son affaire pour cinq
minutes au moins. Après ça, y commence: "t . . . h . . . e: run!" *(Elle
rit.)* Ça-ti du bons sens, être bête comme ça. "T . . . h . . .e: run!" Mais
quoi c'est que vous voulez. On était pris dans nos champs dans les
concessions. Hey, pensez-y. Pas de chauffage, pas de radio, pas de TV,
pas de manger ben des fois. On était chanceux si on voyait un Model
T deux fois par année. On sortait pas. On voyait pas de monde. On
savait même pas quoi c'est qui se passait de l'autre côté du town. On
avait pas de papiers. Pi même si on en avait eu, la plupart de la famille
savait pas lire, ça fait que ça aurait pas aidé diable. C'est pas sur-
prenant qu'on sait rien faire pi qu'on a peur de tout. Même aujour-
d'hui, ça me prend deux heures pour traverser une rue. Pi conduire
une auto . . . ça, j'ai jamais pu apprendre ça, pi je l'apprendrai jamais.
On dirait qu'on était pas fait pour vivre dans c'monde-cit. On aurait
du v'nir au monde pendant le siècle passé. Prends pauvre mon oncle
Exior quand y est allé chez Louise. Louise, elle, a marié un anglais pi
a déménagé à Connecticut. A se pensait ben smarte, j'te l'dis. Pi a
voulait montrer à ses parents qu'a savait comment vivre. Ça fait que,
quand toute une gang de nous-autres l'ont visitée, a nous a fait à
souper. Pi pour commencer, a nous a servi du bouillon chaud dans

a bunch of us showed up at her house, she made us an elegant dinner. And to start off, she served us consommé in demitasses. Uncle Exior took one look at the cup, figured it was coffee, put cream and sugar in it, and drank it all in one gulp. And after dinner, Louise brought out some finger bowls and Uncle Exior drank those, too. *(Pause. Dreamily)* Poor Uncle Exior.

The lights come up somewhat. We hear the sound of the TV.

ANNOUNCER: I'm sorry, Mrs. Johnson. You selected "butt" number one. That's Jennifer's . . . and on Jennifer's butt, over that lovely designer swimsuit are painted our nasty, little words: "The End." That means you don't get the trip, you don't get the car, you don't get the money . . . AND you lose all of your social security checks. Heh, heh, just a little joke on that last item, there, Mrs. Johnson. What a good sport she is, folks. But we do have great parting gifts for you.

JOHNSON: *(In a trembling, little old lady voice)* What is it? What is it?

ANNOUNCER: Isn't that cute, folks. Johnny, tell Mrs. Johnson what she's won.

JOHNNY: It's a complete collection of designer jeans . . . one for every day of the week . . . and . . . a lifetime supply of Minnow Paws cat food, the scrumptious diet that will keep your cat feeling and looking younger.

ANNOUNCER: Well, Mrs. Johnson, I don't know what an 84 year-old like yourself will do with those designer jeans, but from what I hear about poverty among senior citizens, that cat food will sure come in handy, won't it?

JOHNSON: Oh, thank you. Thank you very much.

ANNOUNCER: Isn't that sweet. Folks, let's have a big hand for Mrs. Elvira Johnson. Well, that's all the time we have for today. But join us again tomorrow when we play "No Ifs, Ands . . . or Butts"!!!

des demi-tasses. Pi mon oncle Exior, lui, y regarde ça, pi y met du sucre pi d'la crème là-dedans, pi y boué ça d'une gorgée. Pi après le repas, Louise nous emporte des "finger bowls" ... pi mon oncle Exior boué ça étou. *(Pause. Rêveuse)* Pauvre mon oncle Exior.

L'éclairage devient moins sombre. Le son du téléviseur devient plus fort.

ANNONCEUR: I'm sorry, Mrs. Johnson. You selected "butt" number one. That's Jennifer's ... and on Jennifer's butt, over that lovely designer swimsuit are painted our nasty, little words: "The End." That means you don't get the trip, you don't get the car, you don't get the money ... AND you lose all of your social security checks. Heh, heh, just a little joke on that last item, there, Mrs. Johnson. What a good sport she is, folks. But we do have great parting gifts for you.

JOHNSON: *(Voix tremblante de petite vieille)* What is it? What is It?

ANNONCEUR: Isn't that cute, folks. Johnny, tell Mrs. Johnson what she's won.

JOHNNY: It's a complete collection of designer jeans ... one for every day of the week ... and ... a lifetime supply of Minnow Paws cat food, the scrumptious diet that will keep your cat feeling and looking younger.

ANNONCEUR: Well, Mrs. Johnson, I don't know what an 84 year-old like yourself will do with those designer jeans, but from what I hear about poverty among senior citizens, that cat food will sure come in handy, won't it?

JOHNSON: Oh, thank you. Thank you very much.

ANNONCEUR: Isn't that sweet. Folks, let's have a big hand for Mrs. Elvira Johnson. Well, that's all the time we have for today. But join us again tomorrow when we play "No Ifs, Ands ... or Butts"!!!

The volume goes down.

GÉRARD: *(Yawning and stretching)* What's for supper tonight?

JULIETTE: I made some soup.

GÉRARD: Mmmmm. Good ol' home made soup.

JULIETTE: There's some TV dinners, too if you want something more.

GÉRARD: Nope. Home made soup will be just fine. *(He starts to get up.)*

JULIETTE: No, no. Stay. I'll get you some. I've got to turn the thermo-stat up anyway. It's getting chilly in here. *(She gets up and goes into the kitchen. She gets ready to serve the soup.)*

The TV volume goes up.

ANNOUNCER: Yes, folks, this Reverend John T. Pointer spiritual self help kit . . . COMPLETE with the simplified Bible, the popular and uplift-ing simplified life of Christ, and your inspirational guide to happiness entitled "Tis Much, Much, Much Better to Give Than To Receive" can be yours for this amazing low price today. And for our Spanish-speak-ing friends, 'Ola! hermanos y hermanas! . . . this same beautiful kit is available in Spanish. But hurry! Supplies are limited!! Call NOW to order!!! *(The telephone rings. GÉRARD can't figure out if the sound is coming from the TV or from his own phone.)* And if you give us your credit card number before midnight tonight, *(The telephone rings again. Same dilem-ma for GÉRARD)* this beautiful painting of our Lord and Savior, Jesus Christ, done on the finest velvet, will be yours ABSOLUTELY FREE. *(GÉRARD reaches for the remote control and turns the TV down.)* Remember, just send three hundred and seventy . . . *(The telephone rings again. GÉRARD finally realizes that it's his phone. He gets up, crosses up center to the phone and answers it.)*

GÉRARD: Hello? *(Pause)* Hi, George, my boy. How are you? *(Pause)* How

Le son du téléviseur s'adoucit.

GÉRARD: *(Baillant)* Quoi c'est qui a pour souper, à soir?

JULIETTE: J'ai fait d'la soupe.

GÉRARD: Mmmmm. D'la bonne soupe.

JULIETTE: Y a des TV dinners, si tu veux quèque chose d'autre.

GÉRARD: Non, non. Pas besoin. D'la bonne soupe, ça va être assez. *(Il va pour se lever.)*

JULIETTE: Non, non. Reste assis. J'va t'en emporter. Faut que j'alle remonter la fournaise, anyway. J'frissonne. *(Elle se lève et va dans la cuisine. Elle se prépare à servir de la soupe.)*

Le son du téléviseur devient plus fort.

ANNONCEUR: Yes, folks, this Reverend John T. Pointer spiritual self help kit . . . COMPLETE with the simplified bible, the popular and uplifting simplified life of Christ, and your inspirational guide to happiness entitled "Tis Much, Much, Much Better to Give Than To Receive" can be yours for this amazing low price today. And for our Spanish-speaking friends, 'Ola! hermanos y hermanas! . . . this same beautiful kit is available in Spanish. But hurry! Supplies are limited!! Call NOW to order!!! *(Le téléphone sonne. GÉRARD ne sait pas si c'est à la télé ou chez lui.)* And if you give us your credit card number before midnight tonight, *(Le téléphone sonne. Même jeu.)* this beautiful painting of our Lord and Savior, Jesus Christ, done on the finest velvet, will be yours ABSOLUTELY FREE. *(GÉRARD prend la télécommande et baisse le son.)* Remember, just send three hundred and seventy . . . *(Le téléphone sonne de nouveau et GÉRARD se rend compte que c'est chez lui. Il se lève et va au téléphone à l'arrière-scène.)*

GÉRARD: *(Au téléphone)* Allô? *(Pause)* Allô, mon Georges. Comment ça

about Mary and the kids? *(Pause)* Good, good. *(Pause)* Oh, not bad for a couple of old relics. *(Small laugh)* What do you think of this weather? I've never seen anything like it. We haven't had a November this bad in a long time. So what's new? *(Longer pause)* Well, we were hoping you would come, but . . . *(Pause)* Sure, we understand. Hold on a minute. Mom will talk to you. *(Loud)* Juliette! It's George! *(To the phone)* She'll be right here. We were just getting ready to have supper. *(Silence. The audience must realize that* Gérard *doesn't know what to say.)* Er . . . and the kids, they're all o.k.? *(*Juliette *enters and goes to the phone.)* Ah, here she is. *(He hands the phone to* Juliette.*)* They're not coming. *(He crosses to "his" easy chair and sits.).*

Juliette: *(On the phone)* Hello? George? How are you, my sweetheart? *(Pause)* And Mary and the kids? *(Pause)* Your kids are all so cute . . . every one of them. Did Sherry like the dress we sent for her birthday? *(Pause)* Unhuh. *(Pause)* Oh, she's such a little lady. You'd swear that she was five years older than she is. *(Pause)* Unhuh. *(Pause)* Unhuh. *(Pause)* Well, not too bad for a couple of old relics. So you won't be coming for Thanksgiving? *(Pause)* Of course, we understand. *(Pause)* Oh, I'm sure Normand and Paul will make it. They always do. *(Pause)* O.k., then. *(Pause. She lowers her voice slightly.)* Listen, George, try to write us a letter every once in awhile. It doesn't take long and it makes your dad so happy. It's not funny, you know. All we do is sit around all day and watch each other get older. When we get a letter from you, it makes our whole day. *(Pause)* O.k. *(Pause)* O.k., and Happy Thanksgiving to all of you, too. *(Pause)* Bye.

Juliette *hangs up the phone and returns to the kitchen. She puts two bowls of soup on a tray and comes back to the living room. She puts one bowl on the table next to* Gérard. *She crosses to the couch down left and puts her bowl on the coffee table. She sits and starts eating her soup. Pause.*

Gérard: It's too bad they can't come.

Juliette: Well, I can understand why. Their first Thanksgiving in their new house. It's only natural they'd want to spend it there.

va? *(Pause)* Mary pi les enfants, eux-autres? *(Pause)* Good, good. *(Pause)* Ah, pas pire pour des vieux. *(Petit rire)* Fait pas beau, hein? Nous-autres, icit, ça pas de bons sens. Ça fait longtemps qu'on a pas eu un novembre comme ça. Pi à part de ça? *(Pause plus longue que les autres)* Ah? Ben, on vous attendait mais . . . *(Pause)* Ben oui, on comprend. Attends une minute, là. Ta mère va te parler. *(Fort)* Juliette! C'est Georges! *(Au téléphone)* A vient, là. On vient juste de préparer à souper. *(Silence. On doit voir que* GÉRARD *ne sait plus quoi dire.)* Euh . . . pi les enfants, eux-autres? *(*JULIETTE *entre et va au téléphone.)* Tiens. V'là ta mère. *(Il donne le combiné à* JULIETTE. *A voix basse à* JULIETTE*)* Y viennent pas. *(Il va au fauteuil à droite et s'assoit.)*

JULIETTE: *(Au téléphone)* Allô? Georges? Comment ça va, mon p'tit? *(Pause)* Pi Mary, pi les enfants? *(Pause)* C'est assez cute, ces enfants-là. Sherry a-ti aimé la robe qu'on a envoyé pour sa fête? *(Pause)* Oui? *(Pause)* Ah, a se présente assez ben. On dirait que c'est une grande fille déjà. *(Pause)* Oui. *(Pause)* Oui. *(Pause)* Ah, pas pire pour des vieux. Comme ça, vous venez pas pour Thanksgiving? *(Pause)* Ben oui, on comprend. *(Pause)* Oui, ça devrait que Normand pi Paul viennent. Y viennent toujours. *(Pause)* O.k., comme ça. *(Pause. Elle baisse sa voix légèrement.)* Écoute, Georges, écris donc des fois, hein? Ça prend pas de temps, pi ça fait assez plaisir à ton père. C'est pas drôle, t'sais. On est pris icit à se regarder faire. Quand y a une lettre de vous-autres, ça fait toute sa journée. *(Pause)* O.k. *(Pause)* O.k., pi Happy Thanksgiving à vous-autres étou. *(Pause)* Bye.

JULIETTE *accroche le combiné et se rend à la cuisine. Elle met deux bols de soupe sur un tabouret et retourne au salon. Elle met un bol sur la table à côté de* GÉRARD. *Elle se rend au divan à droite, met son bol sur la table basse. Elle s'assoit et commence à manger sa soupe. Un temps.*

GÉRARD: C'est de valeur qui viennent pas, hein?

JULIETTE: Ah, ça se comprend. Leur premier Thanksgiving dans leur maison neuve. C'est naturel qui veulent rester là.

GÉRARD: It just won't be the same without George and the kids.

JULIETTE: Well, Normand and Paul and their families should manage to keep us busy for awhile.

GÉRARD: Are you sure they're coming?

JULIETTE: Come on. Of course they're coming. They always do.

GÉRARD: *(Dreamily and a little sad)* It'll be the first time we won't be all together for Thanksgiving.

JULIETTE: Cheer up, Gérard. We can still have fun. Besides, it will mean less for me to fix. I'm not as young as I used to be, you know.

GÉRARD: *(Suddenly harsh)* Juliette, I don't want you saying things like that. Our children are our children. It sounds like you don't want any of them to come.

JULIETTE: *(Hurt)* That's not what I meant. You know there's nothing I wouldn't do for those kids. But there's no use crying over spilt milk. *(Pause. Indicating GÉRARD's bowl)* Ready for some more?

GÉRARD: *(Watching TV. Distracted)* What?

JULIETTE: Ready for some more soup?

GÉRARD: *(Still distracted)* No. No, Thanks.

JULIETTE: Was it good?

GÉRARD: What?

JULIETTE: The soup. Was it good?

GÉRARD: Me semble que ça sera pas pareil sans Georges pi les enfants.

JULIETTE: Ben, entre Normand, pi Paul, pi leurs familles, ça devrait nous tenir ben occupé.

GÉRARD: Es-tu certaine qui vont venir, eux-autres?

JULIETTE: Mais voyons. Ben sûr qui vont venir. Y viennent toujours.

GÉRARD: *(Rêveur et un peu triste)* Ça va être la première fois qu'on est pas tout ensemble pour Thanksgiving.

JULIETTE: Voyons, Gérard. On va avoir du fun quand même, tu vas voir. A part de ça, ça va me donner moins à préparer. Chu pas si jeune que j'tais, t'sais.

GÉRARD: *(Soudain dur)* Juliette, j'veux pas que tu parles comme ça. Nos enfants, c'est nos enfants. A t'entendre parler, on dirait que tu veux pas qui viennent.

JULIETTE: *(Blessée)* Non, c'est pas ça que j'voulais dire, Gérard. Ces enfants-là, y a rien que j'ferais pas pour eux-autres. Ça, tu l'sais ben. Mais ça sert à rien de se faire pâtir à propos de quèque chose qu'on peut pas changer. *(Un temps. Elle indique le bol de GÉRARD.)* En veux-tu d'autre?

GÉRARD: *(Il regarde la télé. Distrait)* Hein?

JULIETTE: Veux-tu d'autre soupe?

GÉRARD: *(Même jeu)* Non. Non, merci.

JULIETTE: A était-ti bonne?

GÉRARD: Hein?

JULIETTE: La soupe. A était-ti bonne?

GÉRARD: Very good.

JULIETTE: It wasn't too salty?

GÉRARD: What?

JULIETTE *gets up, takes her bowl and* GÉRARD's, *and takes them to the kitchen.*

JULIETTE: *(From the kitchen)* Want some dessert?

GÉRARD: *(Still distracted)* What?

JULIETTE: *(Louder)* Do you want some dessert?!? *(Pause.* GÉRARD *doesn't answer.* JULIETTE *returns to the living room, takes* The National Enquirer *from her easy chair, crosses to the couch, sits, and begins to read. Pause)*

GÉRARD: What's for dessert?

JULIETTE: *(Reading the paper)* What?

GÉRARD: What's for dessert?

JULIETTE: *(She sighs.)* There's donuts and Tootsie Rolls.

Pause

GÉRARD: Do you know where the Tootsie Rolls are?

JULIETTE: In the kitchen. *(Pause.* GÉRARD *doesn't move. She sighs. She gets up, goes into the kitchen and takes out a bag of Tootsie Rolls from a drawer. She comes back into the living room and places the bag of Tootsie Rolls on the table next to* GÉRARD.) There.

GÉRARD: What?

JULIETTE: There . . . the Tootsie Rolls you wanted. *(She takes a handful and returns to sit on the couch down left.)*

Gérard: Ah, oui.

Juliette: A était pas trop salée?

Gérard: Hein?

Juliette *se lève, prend son bol et le bol de* Gérard, *et se rend à la cuisine.*

Juliette: *(De la cuisine)* Veux-tu du dessert?

Gérard: *(Distrait)* Hein?

Juliette: *(Plus fort)* Veux-tu du dessert?!? *(Un temps.* Gérard *ne répond pas.* Juliette *revient au salon et s'assoit sur le divan. Elle reprend son journal et se met à lire. Un temps)*

Gérard: Quoi c'est qui a pour dessert?

Juliette: *(Qui lit le journal)* Hein?

Gérard: Quoi c'est qui a pour dessert?

Juliette: *(Elle pousse un soupir.)* Y a des donuts, pi des Tootsie Rolls.

Un temps

Gérard: Les Tootsie Rolls, où c'est qui sont?

Juliette: Dans la cuisine. *(Un temps.* Gérard *ne bouge pas. Elle pousse un soupir. Elle se lève, se rend à la cuisine, et sort un sac de Tootsie Rolls d'un tiroir. Elle revient au salon et dépose le sac de Tootsie Rolls sur la table, à côté de* Gérard.*)* Tiens.

Gérard: Hein?

Juliette: Tiens, les Tootsie Rolls. *(Elle en prend une poignée et va s'asseoir sur le divan.)*

GÉRARD: Ah.

The television gets louder. JULIETTE *takes a deck of cards and starts a game of solitaire on the coffee table.*

ANNOUNCER: And now, it's time for "To Honor And Obey!" . . . the exciting game show where two total strangers from our studio audience meet, get to know each other, and get married right here on our stage . . . making them eligible to win cash and prizes worth over twenty-five thousand dollars!!!

JULIETTE: *(To the audience)* What will they think of next? Imagine. Giving money to people just for getting married. Now, that's crazy. *(Pause. After thinking about it)* Wait! It may not be as crazy as it looks. At least, these people might have a better chance of making it in life. You can buy a lot of Tootsie Rolls with twenty-five thousand dollars. It might even be worth marrying somebody you don't give a damn about, then getting a divorce right away and splitting the money. And with all the dumb things they have on TV now, they'll probably come up with another show that'll pay you another twenty-five thousand for getting a divorce. Yep. That's not crazy at all. I wonder what Gerry would think. Hey, Gérard. *(Pause. No answer. Louder)* Gérard!!

GÉRARD: What?

JULIETTE: What do you say you and me go on that show?

GÉRARD: Right. We'd be quite a sight.

JULIETTE: Wouldn't be any worse that that old man and old lady that were on a couple of weeks ago. How old were they?

GÉRARD: She was eighty-five and he was ninety-two.

JULIETTE: Is that all? I thought they were older than that. Anyway, you know what Dear Abby says: "You're never too old to try."

GÉRARD: Ah.

Le son du téléviseur devient plus fort. JULIETTE *prend un jeu de cartes et se met à jouer à un jeu de patience sur la table basse.*

ANNONCEUR: And now, it's time for "To Honor And Obey!" . . . the exciting game show where two total strangers from our studio audience meet, get to know each other, and get married right here on our stage . . . making them eligible to win cash and prizes worth over twenty-five thousand dollars!!!

JULIETTE: *(A l'assistance)* Tiens. Les v'là pris à donner de l'argent pour se marier, asteur. Ça-ti du bon sens? *(Pause. Elle repense son affaire.)* Oui! Ça n'a en masse, du bon sens. Au moins, c'monde-là vont avoir la chance de faire quèque chose dans vie. Pensez-y. Vingt-cinq mille piastres. Ça n'achète des Tootsie Rolls, ça. Ça vaudrait même la peine de se marier à quèqu'un qu'on aime pas, prendre le vingt-cinq mille, se divorcer tout de suite, pi séparer l'argent en deux. Avec tout ce qui se passe à TV asteur, y aurait tedben un autre show qui donnerait un autre vingt-cinq mille pour se divorcer. Ouais, c't'une ben bonne idée. J'pense que j'va proposer ça à bonhomme, là. Hey, Gérard. *(Un temps. Pas de réponse. Plus fort)* Gérard!!

GÉRARD: Hein?

JULIETTE: Veux-tu aller sur ce show-là, toué pi moué?

GÉRARD: Ouais. On s'rait ben cute.

JULIETTE: Pas plus cute que le p'tit vieux pi la p'tite vieille qui ont eu là-dessus, v'là deux semaines. Quel âge qui avaient, eux-autres?

GÉRARD: Elle, a avait quatre-vingt-cinq, pi lui, y avait quatre-vingt-douze.

JULIETTE: C'est-ti toute? J'pensais qui étaient plus vieux que ça. Anyway, tu sais quoi c'est que Dear Abby dit: "You're never too old to try."

GÉRARD: Yeah. But she also says . . . and that was just yesterday, too: "There's no fool like an old fool." That's what we'd be, you and me. A pair of real old fools.

JULIETTE: Well, maybe it's time we acted foolish. God knows we've earned the right to act out and have a little fun after everything we've been through. Lord almighty! *(Pause)* We just don't have a clue, I guess. *(Pause)* We certainly don't have a clue when it comes to making money. But it's worse than that. It's almost like we don't have a clue about what to do or what to say or how to live or anything. Now that's sad. Not like the Livingstons. They had a house in town, a big camp on the lake, another house on the ocean . . . and they were always riding around in these big Cadillacs. It was seven years after we got married before we got our first car. And it wasn't even a car. It was a truck that came with the store when we bought it. People would order their food on the phone and Gerry would deliver it in the truck. I remember it only had a driver's seat, so I'd sit on cushions and pillows on the floor. And the Livingstons had maids and cooks. Mrs. Livingston didn't have to lift a finger for anything. That's what I call knowing how to live. They had hired me to take care of the children and there wasn't a weekend where we didn't do something exciting or fun. We'd go skiing in the winter . . . and sailing in the summer. Sometimes, we'd go horseback riding. And then there were always plays and concerts and dances. Those kids used to do more in a month than I've done my whole life. It's not funny, you know. I hate to think about it because it makes me want to take to drink. *(Pause)* We just don't have a clue. Mister Livingston didn't work a day in his life. Sure, he'd go to an office and write a few letters and talk to people on the phone. But that's not what I call that work. Not the kind of work we've had to do all of our lives, at least. Anyway, neither one of them did any work and they had money coming out of their ears. They didn't even know what to do with it all. Now here's Gerry and me, working night and day for years and years just to get by. And most of the time we got by with not a lot to spare. *(Pause)* We must have been dreaming when we bought that store. We thought it was the end of our problems. No more bosses yelling at us, no more layoffs, no need to work in those damned shoe

GÉRARD: Ouais, mais a dit aussi . . . pi ça, c'tait hier, dans le papier: "There's no fool like an old fool." C'est ça qu'on s'rait, nous-autres, moué pi toué. Des "old fools" ben mal!

JULIETTE: Ben, tedben que c'est le temps qu'on en fasse, nous-autres, des folies. On mérite certainement une p'tite folie ou deux après tout ce qu'on a enduré, Seigneur! *(Pause)* Ça doué qu'on ait pas le tour. *(Pause)* On a certainement pas le tour de faire d'l'argent, ça c'est certain. Pi ça va plus loin que ça. On dirait qu'on sait pas comment se faire une vie, même. C'est grave, ça. Pas comme les Livingstons. Eux-autres, y avaient une maison en ville, un gros camp sur le lac, une autre maison à mer . . . pi ça conduisait toujours des grosses Cadillacs. Nous-autres, ça nous a pris sept ans après qu'on se marie avant d'avoir une char. Pi c'tait pas même une char. C'tait un truck pour délivrer les ordres qu'on avait acheté avec le magasin. Y avait rienque un siège. Moué, j'm'assisais sur des coussins pi des oreillers qu'on mettait sur le plancher. Pi les Livingstons, ça avaient des maids pi des cooks. Madame Livingston faisait rien presque. Mais ça savait comment se faire une vie. Moué, là, y m'avaient engagée pour prendre soin des enfants, pi y avait pas un week-end qu'on faisait pas quèque chose. L'hiver, on allait skier. L'été, on sortait en sailboat pi on passait toute la journée dehors. Des fois, y allaient à cheval, pi d'autres fois, y allaient à des pièces ou des danses ou des concerts. Ces enfants-là, ça faisait plus pendant un mois que j'ai fait, moué, pendant toute ma vie. C'est pas drôle, ça. Faut pas que j'y pense, parce que j'me mettrais à boire. *(Pause)* On a pas le tour, c'est tout. Monsieur Livingston, lui, y travaillait même pas. Ben, y allait dans un bureau, pi y écrivait des lettres, pi y parlait à du monde sur le téléphone. Mais, j'appelle pas ça travailler, moué. Pas travailler comme nous-autres, au moins. Anyway, ça travaillait pas, pi ça avait d'l'argent par dessus la tête. Y savaient même pas quoi c'est faire avec. Pi nous-autres, là, on a travaillé nuit et jour pendant des années pi des années juste pour arriver. Pi la plupart du temps, on arrivait juste, j'te l'dis. *(Pause)* On devait rêver, quand on a acheté ça, c'magasin-là. On pensait que c'tait la fin de toutes nos troubles. Pu de boss pour nous chanter des bêtises, pu de lay offs, pu besoin de travailler au shoe shop ou au moulin de coton. Pi pendant la guerre, le monde qui avait des

shops or cotton mills. And during the war, people who owned little neighborhood grocery stores like ours had made a killing. Yep, it was a like a dream come true. Too bad we woke up . . . and fast. First of all, we were so busy the first couple of years that Gerry couldn't do everything himself. He was trying to be the meat cutter, the delivery man, the stock boy and it just wasn't working. So it wasn't long before I started going in to help him out. That meant that the kids were home alone after school. And lots of times, I'd end up working nights and Saturdays and even Sunday mornings. That's no way to raise kids. Some nights, when we were real busy at the store, we wouldn't eat until nine o'clock at night. The only day we saw them really was on Sunday . . . and even then, we were too tired to do anything with them. You know how boys are. They want to play and run around and get out and do things. Sunday was the only day I had to clean and do the laundry and cook for the week. But what could we do. We never had a choice. We both had to work hard or starve. Oh, sometimes Gerry tried to play with them but he had statements to send out and the books to keep. *(Pause)* Sometimes, I wonder what it did to those boys, to be alone like that day after day. *(Pause)* But we were lucky. They all turned out fine. Each one of them has a good job. They all married nice girls and they all have the cutest kids. Oh, sure, they have a few problems like everybody else, but not like Gerry and me had. *(Pause. She sighs.)* Like I said, we don't have a clue. It just seems that everything happens for the best for everybody else. For us, it always happens for the worst. When we bought the store, the only big chain store in town was the A&P. But that didn't last long. After awhile, there were five of them. And those chain stores could sell everything for less than we could. Problem was, you couldn't charge anything. You had to pay cash. So you know what people used to do? When they had money, they'd go to the A&P or the Stop & Shop. And when they were broke, they'd come to us and charge it. And then they'd never pay. We'd have to chase them for months just to get our money. That's why so many of the neighborhood grocery stores closed down. Nobody ever paid them. The only reason we held out was because both Gerry and me worked. When things got tough, we'd lay off people, and work harder ourselves. I even learned how to cut meat. *(Pause)* Then, after awhile, everything

magasins de groceries comme ça ont fait assez d'argent que c'est pas
drôle. Ouais, c'tait un vrai rêve. J'te dis qu'on s'est réveillé vite. Pour
commencer, avec toute la besogne qu'on avait pendant les premières
années, Gérard pouvait pas toute faire tout seul. Fallait qui coupe la
viande, pi qui ordre les affaires, pi qui délivre les ordres aux maisons. Ça
fait que ça pas pris de temps avant que j'commence à travailler pour y
aider. Ça, ça voulait dire que les enfants étaient tous seuls après l'école.
Pi souvent, fallait qu'on travaille le soir, pi le samedi, pi le dimanche
matin. C'est pas vraiment une façon d'élever des enfants, ça. Y a ben
des soirs, quand on était ben pressé au magasin, on soupait pas avant
neuf heures du soir. La seule journée qu'on les voyait, ces enfants-là,
c'tait le dimanche ... pi ordinairement, on était trop fatigué pour rien
faire avec eux-autres. Hey, trois gars, ça veut jouer, ça. Ça veut sortir.
Ça veut faire quèque chose. Pi moué, j'avais ainque c't'a journée-là
pour cleaner, pi faire des lavages, pi faire à manger pour la semaine.
Mais quoi c'est que tu veux. On avait pas de choix. Fallait travailler
fort, tous les deux, ou ben crever. Ah, Gérard essayait de jouer avec eux-
autres des fois, mais lui, étou, y avait des "bills" à envoyé, pi ses comptes
à faire. *(Pause)* J'me demande des fois si ça y eux a pas fait quèque chose,
aux gars, d'être tout seuls comme ça. *(Pause)* Mais on a été chanceux.
C'est tous des bons gars. Ça tous des bonnes jobs. Ça marié des femmes
ben smartes, pi leurs enfants sont tous assez cute. Ah, y ont leurs pro-
blèmes comme tout le monde, mais pas comme on avait, nous-autres.
(Pause. Elle pousse un soupir.) Comme j'vous dit, on a pas le tour. Me
semble que, pour les autres, tout arrivait pour le mieux ... pi pour nous-
autres, tout arrivait pour le pire. Quand on a commencé, nous-autres,
y avait rienque le A&P en ville comme gros magasin. Mais ça changé,
ça pas pris de temps. Après une secousse, y en avait cinq. Pi tu sais que
ces gros magasins-là, ça pouvait vendre tout à ben meilleur marché que
nous-autres. Mais ça donnait pas de crédit. Fallait payer "cash." Ça fait
que savez-vous quoi c'est que l'monde faisait? Quand y avaient de l'argent, y allaient au A&P ou au Stop & Shop. Pi quand y en avaient pas,
y venaient chez nous pi y chargeaient ça. Pi après ça, y payaient pas.
Fallait courir après notre argent pour des mois de temps. C'est pour ça
que tant de p'tites groceries ont fermé. Y pouvaient pu continuer. Là
seule raison qu'on a enduré, nous-autres, c'est parce qu'on travaillait

changed again. And again, it meant a change for the worse for us. Some younger people with money started buying up the neighborhood stores and they started staying open until midnight almost seven days a week. Thanksgiving, Christmas, the Fourth of July . . . seemed like they were always open. And they'd make pizzas and grinders and all kinds of other things. But by that time, we felt we had worked hard enough. We were already worn out. We weren't going to start spending every waking hour at the store. And making pizzas is fine, but do you have any idea how much one of those pizza ovens costs? Besides, we would have had to move everything around, build a new wall, and reinforce the foundation. It just wasn't worth it. Anyway, we didn't have the money because we had just replaced two of the old coolers that had broken down. *(Pause)* Oh, it's not like we didn't try anything new. But when things start to go wrong . . . I remember when those two showed up. We were just starting to get back on track after Gerry's first heart attack and the time when the furnace broke during the night and everything in the store froze solid. So these two guys come along and show us this new gadget. It was a little microwave oven that you used to heat up sandwiches that they provided. It was much better than pizzas, they said. That's right. "The wave of the future," they called it. "Put those pizza places right out of business." So Gerry and I go to the bank and borrow five thousand dollars. One thousand for the oven, and the rest for "extensive" . . . no, that wasn't it. "Expanded" . . . Oh, what the hell did they call it? *(Pause)* Ah, got it! It was "exclusive" something or other, and it meant that we had to buy everything from them and that nobody else in town would have a set up like ours. Exclusive, my eye! Two months after they took our money, we stopped by Pomerleau's market and there was the same damned oven with the same damned sandwiches. And those sandwiches of theirs were made days ahead of time. They all tasted like cardboard. But what could we do? We had already paid them. But I'll tell you one thing. I hope those two guys get sent right to hell . . . and end up having to eat their damned sandwiches for all eternity. That's what I call a punishment. You see what I mean? We don't have a clue, do we? It's just not right. *(Pause)* We even got taken when we finally sold the store off. First of all, it wasn't in the right section of town. And then, depending on who

toutes les deux. On laissait aller du monde, pi on travaillait plus fort, nous-autres-mêmes. J'ai même appris à couper la viande. *(Pause)* Ben après une secousse, ça changé encore . . . pi pour nous-autres, encore pour le pire. Y a des jeunes avec d'l'argent qui ont acheté des p'tites groceries, pi y ont commencé à être ouverts jusqu'à minuit le soir pi sept jours par semaine, presque. Thanksgiving, Noël, le quatre de juillet . . . c'tait toujours ouvert, ça. Pi ça vendait des pizzas, pi des grinders, pi toutes sortes d'autres affaires. Nous-autres, on avait déjà travaillé assez fort. On était déjà rendu à bout. On était pas pour commencer à passer toute notre vie au magasin. Pi les pizzas, c'est ben beau, mais savez-vous comment ça coûte, ça, un fourneau pour les pizzas? Pi à part de ça, aurait fallu tout changer dans le magasin . . . bâtir un nouveau mur, mettre du ciment nouveau en cave. Ça valait pas la peine. Pi dans c'temps-là, on avait pas d'argent anyway, parce qu'on venait juste de remplacer deux vieux coolers. *(Pause)* Ah, c'est pas qu'on a pas essayé des affaires différentes. Mais quand ça se met à aller mal . . . J'm'en souviens quand c'est gars-là sont arrivés. On commençait juste à prendre le dessus après la première attaque de coeur de Gérard, pi après la journée où la fournaise s'était brisée pi tout avait gelé. Ces deux gars-là nous arrivent, pi y nous montrent c't'a nouvelle affaire-là. C'tait un p'tit fourneau, pi on faisait réchauffer des sandwichs, là-dedans. Ça allait être ben mieux que rienque des pizzas, y nous ont dit. Ah, oui. "The wave of the future," y ont appelé ça. "Put those pizza places right out of business." Ça fait que nous-autres, on va à banque, pi on emprunte cinq mille piastres. Mille piastres pour le fourneau, pi le restant pour "extensive" . . ., non, c'tait pas ça. "Expanded" . . . Comment c'est qui ont appelé ça? *(Pause)* Ah, oui, c'tait "exclusive" quèque chose, pi ça voulait dire qu'on achetait tout d'eux-autres, pi c'tait rienque nous-autres en ville qui aurait c't'a machine-là. Ben, t'sais, deux mois après qu'on leur a donné notre argent, on est entré chez le magasin à Pomerleau, pi on a vu la même maudite machine. "Exclusive," my eye! Pi leurs sandwichs, c'tait tout applati, pi cassé . . . pi ça goûtait comme du carton. J'te l'dis qu'on s'est ben fait fourrer avec ça. Mais quoi c'est que tu veux? On les avait déjà payés. Mais j'te dis que j'voudrais ben les voir pâtir en enfer, ces deux gars-là. Pi comme punition, y devraient être forcés de manger leur maudits sandwichs à longeur de journée. Voyez-vous quoi c'est

you talked to, it was either too big or too small or too old. We finally ended up getting rid of it for less than we paid thirty-five years ago. But we were so fed up that we didn't give a damn. At least, we'd be able to retire. *(Pause. She gives a short, bitter laugh.)* I remember some nights, when we were working late, I'd think about how well off we'd be when we retired. We'd travel, we'd go out, we'd finally get a chance to do things we'd never done before. And I could stay in bed until noon if I wanted to. That would be the life! *(Pause)* Well, here we are . . . and the only thing I've been able to do out of everything I dreamed about is stay in bed. All we do is stay here all day long and watch each other and get in each other's way. I think we were better off when we were working. *(Pause)* The kids tell us to spend the winters in Florida, and go out to eat, and have fun. But we can't. They don't understand that having fun is expensive. It takes everything we have just to get by . . . especially the way taxes and electricity and oil have gone up. It's a good thing the house is all paid for, because otherwise, I really don't know what we'd do. *(Pause. She looks at a picture of her grandchildren on the coffee table.)* It's a good thing we have these kids. It's probably the only thing that keeps us going. That little one of Paul's with her big eyes, she's so cute and so sweet. She'll stay on my lap for hours at a time without moving. And they're all so smart. It's a good thing we've got them, because without them, life would be pretty sad and pretty dull. *(Pause)* We don't have a clue, that's for sure. Ah, to live like the Livingstons. Seems like they were always so happy and so well off. *(Pause. She looks at the cards from her game of solitaire.)* But for me, life is a little like poker. I've never been able to understand poker. I can spend all night watching people play, but it doesn't help. I don't understand any better. Sometimes, when they need someone else for their games, they ask me to play. I hate to . . . but I play anyway. Sometimes I win. Sometimes I lose. But it's not the losing that bothers me. What bothers me is that I don't understand why. I don't know why I win. I don't know why I lose. Life's just like that too. But what can I do? I'm too old now to start changing. *(Pause)* There are lots of nights when I dream about the years I spent with the Livingstons. I was making good money . . . and got food and clothes and housing too. I think that was the happiest time of my life. Maybe that's why I think about it so often. *(Pause)* But, what can you do?

que j'veux dire? On a pas le tour, hein? Ça pas de bon sens. *(Pause)* On s'est même fait fourrer quand on l'a vendu, ce maudit magasin-là. Pour commencer, c'tait pas dans la bonne partie d'la ville. Après ça, le monde disait que c'tait trop p'tit . . . ou trop grand . . . ou trop vieux. On s'en est débarrassé enfin . . . pour moins qu'on avait payé pour. Mais on était si tanné qu'on s'en foutait ben. Au moins, on pourrait se retirer. *(Pause. Rire amer)* J'm'en souviens que des soirs, quand j'travaillais encore, j'pensais qu'on serait ben mèque on se retire. On prendrait des voyages, on sortirait, on f'rait des affaires qu'on avait jamais eu le temps de faire avant. Pi moué, j'pourrais rester au lit jusqu'à midi. Là, on serait ben! *(Pause)* Ben, nous v'là retirés . . . pi la seule chose que j'peux faire de toute ce que j'ai rêvé c'est de rester couchée tard. A part de ça, on reste icit à longueur du jour à se regarder faire, pi se mettre dans les jambes. J'pense qu'on était mieux quand on travaillait. *(Pause)* Les enfants nous disent d'aller en Floride, pi de sortir manger, pi d'avoir du fun. Mais on peut pas. Y réalisent tedben pas, mais ça coûte cher, ça, du fun. Nous-autres, ça prend tout rienque pour arriver avec quoi c'est que ça coûte asteur pour l'électricité, pi le chauffage. Une chance que la maison est payée, parce que j'sais pas quoi c'est qu'on ferait. *(Pause. Elle regarde une photo des ses petits enfants sur la table.)* Mais une chance qu'on a ces enfants-là. C'est la seule chose qui nous tient aller. La plus p'tite à Paul avec ses grands yeux . . . a est assez cute pi assez fine. A reste assis sur moué pour des heures de temps, pi a grouille même pas. Pi y sont tous assez smartes. Une chance qu'on les a, parce que j'te dis que la vie s'rait ben triste sans eux-autres. *(Pause)* On a pas le tour . . . ça, c'est certain. Vivre comme les Livingstons, là . . . Me semble qui d'vaient être assez ben, eux-autres. *(Pause. Elle regarde les cartes du jeu de patience qu'elle joue.)* Mais la vie, c'est un peu comme le poker pour moué. Le poker, j'ai jamais compris ça. J'peux passer toute la soirée à regarder le monde jouer au poker, mais ça aide pas. J'comprends pas mieux. Des fois, quand y a du monde qui manque, y me font jouer. J'viens assez mal . . . mais j'joue pareil. Des fois j'gagne. Des fois j'perds. Mais ce qui m'tracasse, c'est pas de perdre. Ça me tracasse de jamais comprendre. Je comprends pas pourquoi j'gagne. J'comprends pas pourquoi que j'perds. C'est la même chose dans la vie. Mais quoi c'est que vous voulez? Chu trop vieille pour changer asteur. *(Pause)* Des fois, là, quand

The TV gets louder.

ANNOUNCER: . . . and remember, you're only as strong as the deodorant you use. So if your demanding lifestyle needs that male power and strength, use . . . (GÉRARD *reaches for the remote control and changes the channel.)*

ANNOUNCER: . . . Yes, folks! Bouncy whole wheat bread contains absolutely NO preservatives, NO artificial ingredients. Bouncy has none of those unnatural by-products which many of you find so objectionable in ordinary processed bread. So insist on Bouncy . . . the all natural, whole wheat bread. And for those of you who prefer an enriched, batter-whipped, white bread, remember that regular Bouncy is still available wherever better breads are sold. Now, stay tuned for "Salt Lake City," as crime, lust, jealousy, sex, greed, and unnatural acts explode within the calm exterior of a devout, Mormon community.

GÉRARD *watches television.* JULIETTE *keeps playing her game of solitaire. Tableau.*

Curtain

j'rêve, j'pense au temps que j'ai passé avec les Livingstons. J'tais ben payée . . . pi à part de ça j'tais nourrie, pi chauffée, pi habillée. J'pense que c'tait là que j'tais le plus content. C'est tedben pour ça que j'y pense si souvent. *(Pause)* C'pas drôle, hein?

Le son du téléviseur devient plus fort.

ANNONCEUR: . . . and remember, you're only as strong as the deoderant you use. So if your demanding lifestyle needs that male power and strength, use . . . *(Gérard prend la télécommande et change de canal.)*

ANNONCEUR: . . . Yes, folks! Bouncy whole wheat bread contains absolutely NO preservatives, NO artificial ingredients. Bouncy has none of those unnatural by-products which many of you find so objectionable in ordinary processed bread. So insist on Bouncy . . . the all-natural, whole wheat bread. And for those of you who prefer an enriched, batter-whipped, white bread, remember that regular Bouncy is still available wherever better breads are sold. Now, stay tuned for "Salt Lake City," as crime, lust, jealousy, sex, greed, and unnatural acts explode within the calm exterior of a devout, Mormon community.

GÉRARD *regarde la télévision.* JULIETTE *joue à son jeu de patience. Tableau.*

Rideau

ACT II

The next evening. Same setting as in the first act. When the curtain goes up,
GÉRARD, JULIETTE, LOUIS, *and* HILDA *are seated around the kitchen table
playing cards. Their conversation should be fairly loud and lively. The TV is on
in the living room. We should see reflections of the picture changes or slides rep-
resenting moments from some TV show on the back wall.*

HILDA: Here you go! *(She slams the table each time she plays a card.)*
Trump! Trump! And trump again!!!

HILDA *and* JULIETTE *laugh heartily.*

HILDA: Those men don't stand a chance tonight, do they?

JULIETTE: That's for sure. That's the fifth game in a row we've won. *(To*
LOUIS *and* GÉRARD*)* What's wrong with you two tonight?

LOUIS: There's nothing wrong with us. But there's not much we can do
when you two start cheating, right, Gérard?

HILDA: Wow. Talk about reaching for an excuse. Juliette, we'd better let
them win a couple of games or else they'll sit there and pout the rest
of the night and most of next week.

LOUIS: You don't have to let us win. We're more than able to do it on
our own.

JULIETTE: You could have fooled me.

LOUIS: If only Gérard would start getting some decent cards . . .

HILDA: Watch out, Gérard. He's looking for somebody to blame . . . and
it isn't himself.

ACTE II

Le soir du jour suivant. Même décor que dans le premier acte. Éclairage sombre. Au lever du rideau, GÉRARD, JULIETTE, LOUIS, et HILDA sont assis autour de la table de la cuisine, et sont en train de jouer aux cartes. Leur conversation doit être assez forte et mouvementée. Dans le salon, Le Téléviseur fonctionne toujours. On devrait voir les reflets imprécis des changements d'images sur le mur du fond.

HILDA: Tiens! *(Elle frappe la table d'une façon décisive chaque fois qu'elle joue une carte.)* Atout! Atout! Pi atout!!!

HILDA *et* JULIETTE *rient.*

HILDA: J'te l'dis qu'on les arrange, ces hommes-là, à soir, hein?

JULIETTE: Ouais. Ça fait cinq games de file qu'on gagne. *(Aux hommes)* Quoi c'est que vous avez, à soir, vous-autres?

LOUIS: On a rien. C'est vous-autres qui trichez. C'est tout, hein, Gérard?

HILDA: Bon, y va commencer là-dessus asteur. Juliette, on est aussi ben de les laissez gagner un couple de games si on veut pas qui nous boudent pour le reste d'la semaine.

LOUIS: Pas besoin de nous laisser gagner. On est ben capable de l'faire nous-autres-mêmes.

JULIETTE: Ben, ça pas d'l'air à ça.

LOUIS: Si Gérard commençait à avoir des bonnes cartes, là . . .

HILDA: Bon, attention à toué, Gérard. Y va tout mettre ça sur ton dos.

Juliette: Gérard, can you turn the TV down please? I can't even hear myself think. More peanuts, Hilda?

Gérard: How about another drink, Louis?

Louis: *(He puts his arm behind his back and acts as if* Hilda *were twisting it.)* Ouch, woman!!! Enough . . . enough! O.k.! I'll have another one. *(He gives his glass to* Gérard.*)* But everyone can see it's only because she's forcing me to.

Hilda: Ah, the nerve of the man!

Juliette: *(Impatient)* Gérard, will you please turn that TV down!

Gérard: In a minute. *(He crosses to the counter and starts making the drinks.)* Let me just make these drinks. After all, first things first. Now stop jabbering away and deal. *(He give a glass to* Louis *and goes into the living room with his own. He crosses to the TV and stops for a minute to see what's on. The TV gets louder.)*

Announcer: We've got Mrs. Benitez safely tucked away in our sound proof booth and our cameras are recording her every move. What she doesn't know is that she'll soon be getting a phone call saying that her 15 children have been kidnapped. The kidnapers, who are really members of our "People Are Stupid" staff, will tell her that the only way to get her kids back is to pay a ransom of one million dollars . . . by nine o'clock tonight! *(He snickers.)* Then, we'll send her out in the street to beg for the money. Naturally, one of our "People are Stupid" staff will agree to give her the money . . . *(he snickers)* but not until one minute PAST nine. When she rushes in here, we'll show her pictures of mutilated bodies and tell her that she was just a little too late. We hope to prove . . . as we have so often in the past . . . that People Are Stupid! Now, Mrs. Benitez is . . .

Mrs. Benitez: AY, madre de dios!!!!

JULIETTE: Gérard, va donc baisser le TV., hein? On peut presque pas s'entendre parler. Hilda, veux-tu encore des peanuts?

GÉRARD: Pi toué, Louis, veux-tu une autre drink?

LOUIS: *(Il met son bras derrière lui. Fait comme si* HILDA *lui tordait le bras)* Ouch, bonnefemme!!! Arrête ... arrête! O.k.! J'va en prendre une. *(Il donne son verre à* GÉRARD.*)* Mais tu voué que c'est ainque parce qu'a me force.

HILDA: Ah, y est pas endurable, c't'homme-là.

JULIETTE: *(Impatiente)* Gérard, veux-tu baisser c'TV-là!

GÉRARD: Oui, oui. *(Il se dirige vers le comptoir de la cuisine et commence à préparer les coups.)* Laisse-moué faire les drinks, là. Après tout, faut s'occuper des affaires importantes pour commencer. Arrête de parler, pi brasse. *(Il donne un verre à Louis et va au salon avec son verre. Une fois arrivé, il s'arrête pour un moment pour regarder le programme à la télé. Le son du téléviseur devient plus fort.)*

ANNONCEUR: We've got Mrs. Benitez safely tucked away in our sound proof booth and our cameras are recording her every move. What she doesn't know is that she'll soon be getting a phone call saying that her 15 children have been kidnapped. The kidnappers, who are really members of our "People Are Stupid" staff, will tell her that the only way to get her kids back is to pay a ransom of one million dollars ... by nine o'clock tonight! *(Il rit un peu sans le vouloir.)* Then, we'll send her out in the street to beg for the money. Naturally, one of our "People are Stupid" staff will agree to give her the money ... *(il rit un peu sans le vouloir)* but not until one minute PAST nine. When she rushes in here, we'll show her pictures of mutilated bodies and tell her that she was just a little too late. We hope to prove ... as we have so often in the past ... that People Are Stupid! Now, Mrs. Benitez is ...

MRS. BENITEZ: AY, madre de dios!!!!

ANNOUNCER: Well, it looks like the fun has already begun. Let's look in as . . .

JULIETTE: *(From the kitchen. Loud)* Gérard, what on earth are you doing?

GÉRARD: I'm coming.

HILDA: Hurry up! We're itching to beat you two again!

GÉRARD *reaches for the remote control to turn the TV off, but he manages to change the channel instead. We hear the end of the American national anthem.*

GÉRARD: *(Loud. To* LOUIS*)* Hey, Louis, there's a game on tonight.

JULIETTE: Forget about the damned game and get over here. We haven't finished playing cards.

GÉRARD: O.k., o.k. *(He goes to turn off the TV, but the sound of the telephone ringing interrupts him. He hesitates. He looks at the TV. The phone rings again.* GÉRARD *hesitates again. The phone rings for a third time.)*

JULIETTE: Gérard, are you going to answer that or not?

GÉRARD: O.k., o.k. *(He crosses to the phone without turning off the TV. Answering the phone)* Hello? *(Pause)* Well hello, Normand. How are you, son? *(Pause)* And Elaine and the kids? *(Pause)* Oh, not too bad for a couple of old relics. What do you think of this weather? I've never seen anything like it. We haven't had a November this bad in a long time. We've already got six inches of snow on the ground. So what's new? *(Longer pause)* Well, we were hoping you would come, but . . . I guess things like that happen. *(Pause)* Sure, we understand. Hold on a minute. I'll get your mother. *(Loud. To the kitchen)* Juliette! It's Normand! *(On the phone)* Here she comes. *(Pause)* Oh, not much. Hilda and Louis came over tonight. *(Pause)* Playing cards, just like we always do. *(Pause)* Oh, they're both fine. Want to talk to them? *(Pause.* JULIETTE *arrives next to* GÉRARD.*)* Well, here's your mother. *(He hands the phone to* JULIETTE *and slowly heads for the kitchen.)*

ANNONCEUR: Well, it looks like the fun has already begun. Let's look in as . . .

JULIETTE: *(De la cuisine. Fort)* Gérard, quoi c'est que tu fais?

GÉRARD: J'viens, là.

HILDA: Dépêche-toué! On veut vous "beater" encore!"

GÉRARD *prend la télécommande pour fermer le Téléviseur, mais il change de canal plutôt. On entend la dernière partie de l'hymne national américain.*

GÉRARD: *(Fort. A* LOUIS*)* Tiens, Louis, y a une game, à soir.

JULIETTE: Laisse la mautadite game pi viens jouer aux cartes.

GÉRARD: O.k., o.k. *(Il va pour fermer le téléviseur, mais le son du téléphone l'interrompt.* GÉRARD *hésite. Il regarde le téléviseur. Le téléphone sonne de nouveau.* GÉRARD *hésite de nouveau. Le téléphone sonne une troisième fois.)*

JULIETTE: Gérard, veux-tu répondre au téléphone!

GÉRARD: O.k., o.k. *(Il va au téléphone sans avoir fermé le téléviseur. Au téléphone)* Allô? *(Pause)* Ah, tiens, allô, Normand. Comment ça va, mon gars? *(Pause)* Pi Elaine pi les enfants? *(Pause)* Ah, pas pire . . . pour des vieux. Y fait pas beau, hein? Nous-autres icit, ça pas de bon sens. Ça fait longtemps qu'on a pas eu un novembre comme ça. On a déjà six pouces de neige icit. Pi à part de ça? *(Pause plus longue que les autres. Après un temps,* GÉRARD *regarde d'une façon assez triste vers la cuisine.)* Ah, ben, on vous attendait mais. . . quoi c'est que tu veux? Des affaires comme ça, ça arrive. *(Pause)* Ben oui, on comprend. Attends une minute, là. Ta mère va t'parler. *(Il baisse le récepteur. Fort)* Juliette! C'est Normand! *(Au téléphone)* A vient, là. *(Pause)* Ah, pas grand chose. Hilda pi Louis sont icit à soir. *(Pause)* Ben, on joue aux cartes, comme de coutume. *(Pause)* Ah, y sont pas pires. Veux-tu leur parler? *(Pause.* JULIETTE *arrive près de* GÉRARD*.)* O.k., ben v'là ta mère. *(Il passe le combiné à* JULIETTE *et se rend lentement à la cuisine.)*

JULIETTE: *(To* Gérard*)* What's wrong?

Gérard: They're not coming.

JULIETTE: *(On the phone)* Hello, Normand, my sweetheart. How is everything? *(Pause)* And Elaine and the kids? *(Pause)* Has Bobby started hockey practice yet? *(Pause)* And how about the baby . . . oh, I really should stop calling her that. She's four years old after all. Is she still taking dancing lessons? *(Pause)* You don't know how lucky you are to have kids like those. *(Pause)* Oh, we're o.k. Hilda and Louis came over tonight. *(Pause)* Yep, they're fine, too. So you won't be able to make it tomorrow? *(Longer pause)* Of course, we understand. Work is work and you can't always do what you want when you've got a job. Especially with both of you working. *(Pause)* Oh, I know it's hard. Your dad and I did it for thirty-five years. I don't blame you at all. *(Pause)* Well, it's not going to be the same this year, that's for sure. George isn't coming either. *(Pause)* Well, you know they just bought a house, so they want to spend Thanksgiving there. *(Pause)* Oh, I'm sure Paul will be here. They always make it. *(Pause)* Well, we'll all eat more turkey, I guess. *(Pause)* No, I'm sure that Paul and Cécile will be here. Anyway, it's too long a trip for us to go down there. Your dad just hasn't been the same since those two heart attacks. Every little thing tires him out. *(Pause)* O.k., then. *(Pause)* Unhuh. *(She lowers her voice a little.)* Listen, Norm, how about writing us a letter every once in a while. It doesn't take long and it gives your dad such a thrill. It's not funny, you know, when you get old like us. We never go out any more. When we get a letter from you, it makes our whole day. *(Pause)* Well, I hope you're planning on coming for Christmas! I've already started buying gifts for all the kids. *(Pause)* Unhuh. *(Pause)* O.k., and Happy Thanksgiving to all of you, too. *(Pause)* Bye-bye. *(She hangs up the phone and stays motionless for a few moments. All we hear is the TV.)*

Louis: Well if nobody's going to play cards, I'm going to watch the game! *(He gets up, goes into the living room with his glass, and sits in the easy chair stage right. Loud)* Gérard! Come here! They're playing the Flyers.

JULIETTE: *(A GÉRARD)* Quoi c'est qui a, donc?

GÉRARD: Y viennent pas.

JULIETTE: *(Au téléphone)* Allô, Normand, mon p'tit chou. Comment ça va? *(Pause)* Pi Elaine pi les enfants? *(Pause)* Bobby a-ti commencé à pratiquer son hockey? *(Pause)* Pi la p'tite, a doué pu être p'tite, asteur . . . a danse-ti encore? *(Pause)* J'te dis que vous êtes chanceux d'avoir des enfants comme ça, vous-autres. *(Pause)* Ah, pas pire. Hilda pi Louis sont icit, à soir. *(Pause)* Oui, y s'arrangent pas pire. Comme ça, vous venez pas demain? *(Pause plus longue que les autres)* Ben oui, on comprend. Des jobs, là, on peut pas toujours faire ce qu'on veut avec ça, surtout quand vous travaillez tous les deux. *(Pause)* Oui, j'sais que c'est tough. On l'a fait pour quarante ans, nous-autres. J'vous blâme pas pantoute. *(Pause)* Ben, ça d'l'air que ça va être un peu triste, c't'année. Georges vient pas. *(Pause)* Ben, y viennent juste d'acheter leur maison, t'sais, pi y veulent passer Thanksgiving là. *(Pause)* Oui, Paul va venir, chu certaine. Y viennent toujours, eux-autres. *(Pause)* Ben, on va manger plus de dinde, c'est tout. *(Pause)* Non, chu certaine que Paul pi Cécile vont venir. Anyway, descendre là, ça s'rait trop loin pour nous-autres à voyager. Tu sais, ton père, là, depuis ses attaques de coeur, y fatigue vite. *(Pause)* O.k., comme ça. *(Pause)* Oui. *(Elle baisse la voix légèrement.)* Ecoute, Normand, écris donc des fois, hein? Ça prend pas de temps, pi ça fait assez plaisir à ton père. T'sais, c'est pas drôle, être rendu comme nous-autres. On sort presque pas. Ça nous fait assez plaisir quand on a une p'tite note de vous-autres. *(Pause)* Ben, j'espère que vous allez v'nir pour Noël! J'ai déjà commencé à acheter les cadeaux aux enfants. *(Pause)* Oui. *(Pause)* O.k., comme ça. Pi Happy Thanksgiving, vous-autres, étou. *(Pause)* Bye-bye. *(Elle raccroche le combiné et reste immobile pour quelques instants. Silence, sauf le son du téléviseur)*

LOUIS: Ben si y a personne qui va jouer aux cartes, icit, moué, j'va aller watcher la game! *(Il se rend au salon avec son verre et s'assoit sur le fauteuil à droite. En regardant la télévision. Fort)* Gérard! Viens voir ça! Y jouent contre les Flyers.

Pause. GÉRARD *gets up from the kitchen table, goes to the living room with his glass in his hand, and sits in the easy chair stage left. Pause.* JULIETTE *returns to the kitchen and sits at the table. Pause.* GÉRARD *goes to take a drink and realizes that his glass is empty.*

GÉRARD: Damn, I don't know why but hockey games always make me thirsty. How about you, Louis?

LOUIS: I think it has something to do with ice.

LOUIS *gives his glass to* GÉRARD *who gets up and goes into the kitchen. He starts making the drinks.* JULIETTE *interrupts her conversation with* HILDA *and watches him.* GÉRARD *goes back to the living room with two full glasses, gives one to* LOUIS, *and sits.*

GÉRARD: There you go. *(Lifting his glass)* Cheers!

LOUIS *lifts his glass half-heartedly and drinks.* GÉRARD *drinks his practically in one gulp.* HILDA *and* JULIETTE *come into the living room just in time for* JULIETTE *to notice the fast drink. She hesitates for a moment. Then she and* HILDA *sit on the couch down left and continue a conversation.*

LOUIS: It's about time you got back. You missed two goals.

GÉRARD: For who?

LOUIS: For the Flyers. Looks like the Bruins are going to take it on the chin tonight.

HILDA: *(Who heard)* Just like you two playing cards.

LOUIS: Leave me alone, woman. We'll even everything up next week, right Gérard?

GÉRARD: You bet!

Un temps. On voit GÉRARD *se lever de la table dans la cuisine. Il entre au salon, verre à la main, et s'assoit sur le fauteuil à gauche. Un temps.* JULIETTE *va à la cuisine et s'assoit à la table. Un temps.* GÉRARD *va pour boire et se rend compte que le verre est vide.*

GÉRARD: Maudit, t'sais des hockey games, ça me donne toujours envie de boire, ça. Toué, Louis?

LOUIS: J'pense que c'est la glace qui nous donne des idées.

LOUIS *donne son verre à* GÉRARD *qui se lève et va à la cuisine. On le voit en train de préparer les coups.* JULIETTE *interrompt sa conversation avec* HILDA *et le regarde faire.* GÉRARD *rentre au salon avec deux verres pleins, donne un verre à* LOUIS, *et s'assoit.*

GÉRARD: Tiens. *(Il lève son verre.)* A ta santé, mon vieux!

LOUIS *lève son verre d'une façon distraite et boit.* GÉRARD *vide son verre presque d'un trait.* HILDA *et* JULIETTE *entrent au salon juste à temps pour que* JULIETTE *puisse apercevoir les actions de* GÉRARD. *Elle hésite un moment.* HILDA *et* JULIETTE *s'assoient sur le divan à gauche. Elles parlent toujours.*

LOUIS: C't'à peu près le temps que tu arrives. T'as déjà manqué deux goals.

GÉRARD: Pour qui?

LOUIS: Pour les Flyers. Ça d'l'air que les Bruins vont en manger une bonne, à soir.

HILDA: *(Qui a entendu)* Ça va être un peu comme vous-autres aux cartes.

LOUIS: Bâdre-moué pas, bonnefemme. On va se reprendre la semaine prochaine, hein Gérard?

GÉRARD: Oui, ça, c'est certain.

GÉRARD *goes to take a drink and realizes that his glass is empty. He gets up and heads toward the kitchen.* JULIETTE *sees him and interrupts her conversation with* HILDA.

JULIETTE: *(Sternly)* Gérard! *(He stops at the sound of her voice.)* Be careful. You know what the doctor said.

GÉRARD: Come on, dear. It's a holiday tonight. And Thanksgiving eve only happens once a year. *(He goes into the kitchen.* JULIETTE'*s stare follows him.)*

HILDA: *(Trying to distract her)* You know, you're welcome to spend the day at our house tomorrow. We've got more food than we'll ever be able to eat. I made three pies today, and a huge ham, and . . .

JULIETTE: Oh, no, Hilda. Paul and his family are coming and we should be here.

HILDA: Well, they can come along, too. It certainly won't be any bother . . . and we'll have a great time, all of us together.

JULIETTE: Thanks, Hilda, but Thanksgiving is meant for families. I'm sure you'd rather spend the day with your kids than with us.

HILDA: Juliette, you're my little sister. You're as much family as anybody else. And Paul's been coming over to our house ever since he was a little boy. He's not exactly a stranger either.

There is a long and painful silence. GÉRARD *enters with a full glass and crosses to sit in the easy chair, while* JULIETTE'*s stare follows his every step. She then goes back to her conversation with* HILDA.

LOUIS: Yep. I tell you they're gonna take it on the chin tonight. They're playing like a bunch of girls. *(Pause.* LOUIS *sits up and points to the TV.)* See! See! What did I tell you? He might as well have handed him the puck on a silver platter! Can you believe it?!? *(Pause. Loud, to the TV)* Stop him, you stupid sonofabitch!

GÉRARD *va pour boire et se rend compte que son verre est vide. Il se lève et se dirige vers la cuisine.* JULIETTE *l'aperçoit et interrompt sa conversation avec* HILDA.

JULIETTE: *(Assez sévèrement)* Gérard! *(Celui-ci s'arrête au son de sa voix.)* Fais attention à toué, là. Tu sais quoi c'est que l'docteur a dit.

GÉRARD: Ben voyons, Juliette, c'est fête, à soir. Après tout, ça arrive ainque une fois par année, ça, la soirée de Thanksgiving. *(Il sort.* JULIETTE *le suit de son regard.)*

HILDA: *(Qui essaie de la distraire)* Tu sais, vous pouvez venir chez nous demain. Du manger, on va n'avoir en masse. J'ai fait trois tartes aujour- d'hui, pi un gros jambon, pi . . .

JULIETTE: Non, non, Hilda. Paul pi sa famille vont venir, pi on devrait être icit.

HILDA: Ben qu'ils viennent, eux-autres, étou. J'te dis que ça dérangera pas. Pi on aurait du fun, tout ensemble.

JULIETTE: Merci, Hilda, mais Thanksgiving, c'est pour la famille. Chu certain que vous-autres, vous aimeriez mieux ça passer la journée avec votre famille, qu'avec nous-autres.

HILDA: Voyons, Juliette, t'es ma p'tite soeur. T'es autant ma famille que les autres. Pi Paul, lui, ça fait depuis qui est p'tit qui vient chez nous. Y est pas exactement un étranger, lui non plus.

Silence assez long et pénible. GÉRARD *entre avec un verre plein et va s'asseoir sur le fauteuil à gauche, pendant que* JULIETTE *suit chaque pas. Elle retourne ensuite à sa conversation silencieuse avec* HILDA.

LOUIS: Ouais. J'te l'dis qui vont en manger une bonne, à soir. Ça joue comme des filles. *(Pause.* LOUIS *indique le téléviseur.)* Tiens! Tiens! Regarde, là! Y a presque donné la maudite puck! Ça-ti du bon sens?!? *(Pause. Fort, au téléviseur)* Arrêtez-les, baptême!

HILDA: *(Interrupting her conversation. To* LOUIS*)* No swearing tonight, Louis. Please! *(She goes back to her conversation.)*

GÉRARD: *(Who keeps drinking)* Nobody plays like Montreal. If you ask me, the Canadiens are the only real team in the whole league.

LOUIS: Hey, the Bruins aren't too bad when they use their sticks for something else besides picking their nose. *(He goes to take a drink and notices that his glass is empty.* GÉRARD *notices, too.)*

GÉRARD: Ready?

LOUIS: Yeah, but make it quick before my old lady gets a chance to bitch and moan.

GÉRARD *takes his glass and* LOUIS' *and gets up. He just manages to turn around to head for the kitchen when* JULIETTE'*s voice stops him.*

JULIETTE: Gérard!

GÉRARD: *(Trying to defend himself)* It's for Louis, dear. And it just wouldn't be polite of me to let him drink alone.

JULIETTE: Alright, but make it a weak one, o.k.? *(*GÉRARD *continues toward the kitchen without answering.)* Gérard!?!

GÉRARD: *(A little like a beaten dog)* O.k., o.k., I'll make it weak. *(He goes to the kitchen and starts making the drinks.)*

JULIETTE: *(To* HILDA*, explaining)* You know the doctor said he could drop dead any time if he wasn't careful. His heart is still pretty weak, so it wouldn't take much. *(She glances quickly toward the kitchen.)* He just can't do whatever he wants to . . . like he did in the old days, you know. *(Pause. She glances quickly toward the kitchen again. Worried)* Gérard?!?

GÉRARD: What is it?

HILDA: *(Elle interrompt sa conversation. A* LOUIS*)* Commence pas à sacrer, là, toué! *(Elle retourne à sa conversation.)*

GÉRARD: *(Qui boit toujours)* Ben, j'te l'dis que ça joue pas comme Montréal, ça. Les Canadiens, ça, ça sait comment jouer comme du monde.

LOUIS: Ben, les Bruins sont pas pires non plus quand y servent pas de leurs batons rienque pour se décrotter le nez. *(Il va pour boire et s'aperçoit que son verre est vide.* GÉRARD *le remarque aussi.)*

GÉRARD: En veux-tu une autre?

LOUIS: Oui, mais vas-y vite avant que ma bonnefemme dise quèque chose.

GÉRARD *prend son verre et celui de* LOUIS *et se lève. Il arrivera juste à se tourner pour aller à la cuisine quand la voix de* JULIETTE *l'arrêtera.*

JULIETTE: Gérard!

GÉRARD: *(Il essaie de se défendre.)* C'est pour Louis, Juliette. Pi moué, là . . . ben ça serait pas poli de le laisser boire tout seul.

JULIETTE: Ben, fais-là pas forte, hein? *(*GÉRARD *continue vers la cuisine sans répondre.)* Gérard!?!

GÉRARD: *(Un peu comme un chien battu)* Non, non. J'la ferai pas forte. *(Il entre à la cuisine et prépare ses coups.)*

JULIETTE: *(A* HILDA, *comme explication)* Tu sais que le docteur y a dit qui pourrait mourir si y faisait pas attention. Son coeur est encore faible, t'sais, pi ça prendrait pas gros, j'te l'dis. *(Elle jette un regard vers la cuisine.)* Y peut pas faire tout ce qui veut, c'thomme-là. *(Un temps. Elle jette un regard vers la cuisine encore une fois. Un peu inquiète)* Gérard?!?

GÉRARD: Quoi c'est?

JULIETTE: Are you o.k.?

GÉRARD: *(Comes back into the living room with the full glasses)* Of course, I'm o.k. I don't know why you keep worrying about nothing. *(He goes to the easy chair, gives a drink to* LOUIS, *and sits.* JULIETTE *continues her conversation with* HILDA.*)*

GÉRARD: *(To* LOUIS*)* Anything exciting happen?

LOUIS: Nothing. Goddamn Bruins can't do a Goddamn thing!

HILDA: *(Interrupting her conversation)* Louis! I told you. Don't swear! *(She goes back to her conversation.)*

GÉRARD: I tell you these kids today aren't worth shit.

LOUIS: *(Lost in the game)* What?

GÉRARD: *(Louder)* I said that these young players today aren't worth shit. *(Louder still. To* LOUIS*)* What do you think?

JULIETTE: *(Interrupting him)* Don't talk so loud, Gérard. You'll wake the dead.

LOUIS: *(Distracted)* Ah, kids are kids. Always have been. Always will be.

The lights dim, except on GÉRARD. *It looks as though* GÉRARD *is talking to* LOUIS, *but he's really addressing most of his lines to the audience. He must appear to be feeling the effects of the drinks he's been gulping down.*

GÉRARD: Oh, you know what I mean. Take those players, for example. They don't want to do a thing, but they still want to get paid hundreds of thousands of dollars a years. Think about it, Louis. I know I sure would have like to get paid hundreds of thousands of dollars a year to work one hour a night, three nights week, six months a year like these

JULIETTE: Es-ti o.k.?

GÉRARD: *(Il se rend au salon avec les verres pleins.)* Ben, oui, chu o.k. Quoi c'est que tu penses, donc? *(Il va s'asseoir et donne un verre à* LOUIS. JULIETTE *continue sa conversation silencieuse avec* HILDA.*)*

GÉRARD: *(A* LOUIS*)* Y ont-ti fait quèque chose?

LOUIS: Non. J'te dis qui sont plattes en Christ!

HILDA: *(Elle interrompt sa conversation. A* LOUIS*)* J't'ai demandé de pas sacrer, Louis! *(Elle retourne à sa conversation.)*

GÉRARD: J'te dis que les jeunes aujourd'hui, là, ça vaut pas d'la colle.

LOUIS: *(Qui regarde la partie)* Hein?

GÉRARD: *(Plus fort)* J'te dis que les jeunes aujourd'hui, là, ça vaut pas d'la colle. *(Encore plus fort. A* LOUIS*)* Tu penses pas?

JULIETTE: *(L'interrompant)* Parle pas donc si fort, Gérard. Tu vas réveiller les morts.

LOUIS: *(Distrait)* Ah, les jeunes, c'est les jeunes. Y sont comme y ont toujours été.

L'éclairage devient plus sombre, sauf sur GÉRARD. GÉRARD *doit faire comme s'il parlait à* LOUIS, *mais il s'adresse surtout à l'assistance. Il doit donner l'impression qu'il est un peu ivre.*

GÉRARD: Non, mais tu sais quoi c'est que j'veux dire. Regarde ces joueurs-là. Ça veut rien faire, pi ça veut se faire payer des cinq cent mille piastres par année. Non, mais c'est vrai. Pense à ça, Louis. Moué, j'aurais ben aimé ça, me faire payer cinq cent mille piastres pour travailler une heure par soir, trois soirs par semaine, six mois par année,

guys. *(Pause)* It sure wasn't like that for us when we were young. When I started at the mill, they gave me fifty cents a week. Of course, I was only twelve, and I worked only on Saturday, but I still had to wash every damn window in that damn mill. And all they paid us was fifty cents. At least it was better than working on those machines. *(Pause)* Hey, Louis, that's how you got your start, right? Working on those damned weaving machines? . . . *(Pause)* How old were you when you started at the mill, anyway?

Louis: *(Distracted)* What?

Gérard: *(Louder)* How old were you when you started working at the mill full time?!?

Juliette: Gérard, I thought I asked you not to talk so loud.

Louis: *(Distracted)* Fifteen.

Gérard: Yep. You graduated from Amoskaeg University . . . and probably with honors. Well, do you know what I'd do with my fifty cents? I'd ask the guy who paid us to give me the whole fifty cents in pennies. Then, I'd divide the pennies in half. Twenty-five cents in this pocket here. Twenty-five cents in the other one. When I walked down the street and heard all those pennies jingling, I felt like the richest man on earth. That's something these kids will never know. After all, what can they do? Ask to get their hundreds of thousands of dollars in one dollar bills? *(He suddenly finds the idea very funny and starts laughing.)* Now, that's a good one. Ask for hundreds of thousands of singles. *(He keeps laughing.)* And I know something else that those poor young hockey players will miss out on. They'll never get to know hunger. *(He's still laughing.)* Not like I knew hunger anyway. When I was young, she was probably the only true friend I had. *(Still laughing)* I think I almost married her. *(He has a fit of hysterical laughter. He takes a quick look at* Juliette.*)* Come to think of it, I probably would have been better off with her. *(Suddenly stops laughing)* No, that's not true. Juliette has been a good wife. I don't know what I would have done without her. *(Pause)* Ah, that's not true either. I know

comme ces gars-là. *(Pause)* J'te l'dis que nous-autres, c'tait pas comme ça, hein? Moué, quand j'ai commencé au moulin, j'gagnais cinquante cennes. Ben j'avais ainque douze ans, pi j'travaillais ainque le samedi . . . mais y nous faisaient laver toutes les châssis dans c't'a maudite place-là. Pi y nous payaient cinquante cennes. Mais c'tait mieux que de travailler sur les machines. *(Pause)* Hey, Louis, c'est ça que tu faisais, ça, hein? Tu travaillais sur leurs maudites machines . . . *(Pause)* Quel âge que t'avais quand t'as commencé au moulin, toué?

LOUIS: *(Distrait)* Hein?

GÉRARD: *(Plus fort)* Quel âge que t'avais quand t'as commencé au moulin full time?!?

JULIETTE: Gérard, me semble que j't'ai demandé de pas parler si fort.

LOUIS: *(Distrait)* Quinze ans.

GÉRARD: Oui. T'as gradué d'Amoskaeg University, toué. Ben, sais-ti quoi c'est que j'faisais avec mon cinquante cennes, moué? J'allais à banque pi j'faisais changer ça en cennes noires. Pi là, j'divisais ça en deux. Vingt-cinq cennes dans c't'a poche-cit, pi vingt-cinq cennes dans l'autre. Quand j'marchais pi j'entendais le train que toutes ces cennes-là menaient, j'me pensais l'homme le plus important du monde. Ça, c'est quèque chose qui connaîtront jamais, ces gars-là. Après tout, quoi c'est qui vont faire? Faire changer leurs cinq cent mille piastres en billets d'une piastre? *(Soudain, il trouve l'idée comique et se met à rire.)* Ça, c'est bon. Changer leur cinq cent mille piastres en billets d'une piastres. *(Il rit d'avantage.)* Pi, j'sais une autre chose qui connaîtront jamais. Ouais, ces pauvres joueurs de hockey-là connaîtront jamais la faim. *(Il rit toujours.)* Pas comme moué, j'l'ai connue. Quand j'tais jeune, c'tait la seule chum que j'avais. *(Il rit.)* J'pense que chu venu proche à la marier. *(Il lui prend un fou de rire. Il jette un regard vers* JULIETTE.*)* Asteur que j'y pense, tedben que j'aurais été mieux amanché avec elle. *(Il rit toujours. Soudain sérieux)* Non, non. C'est pas vrai, ça. Juliette, c'est un bonne femme. Je l'sais pas quoi c'est que j'aurais fait

damn well what I would have done. I'd never have bought that damned store. *(Pause)* Maybe we'd be happy now. Maybe we'd actually have something. Maybe we wouldn't have to scrimp, and worry, and go without, and struggle just to get by. *(Pause)* I could have made it in the world. I'm not dumb. When I was in the army, a captain even went out of his way to tell me how smart I was. "You've got brains, soldier. You'll go a long way." That's what he said. And captains are nobody's fools, you know. They're good judges of character. *(Pause)* And this guy was an American, so you know he wasn't just blowing smoke. "You'll go a long way." *(Pause)* And I could have, too. When I was discharged, the army was ready to pay for my college education and everything. *(Sarcastic)* But no. *(He indicates* JULIETTE. *His voice keeps getting louder and louder.)* She didn't want me to. She didn't know how we'd get by and whether it was worth it or not and *(tries to imitate* JULIETTE's *voice)* look at the wonderful business the Boisverts' built up for their little store. Just look how well off they are with their biiig car and their biiig house.

JULIETTE: Gérard, I don't know what's wrong with you tonight. Louis is only three feet away from you and he's not deaf, you know. You don't have to scream.

GÉRARD: *(Continues more quietly)* It's true we already had two kids . . . and college takes time to finish. And she wasn't the only one who didn't like the idea. No. My whole wonderful family ganged up against me. I wasn't as smart as the others and it was going to be too hard for me and I was just going to waste a lot of time and money. After all, a father's duty doesn't include going to college. *(Sermonizing)* No. A father's duty is to put food on the table . . . even if he has to work sixty hours a week . . . even if he doesn't have time to play with his kids . . . even if it kills him. That's what happened to my dad. Do you know how old he was when he died? Forty-nine. No disease, no accident, nothing. He was just worn out. Poor dad. He used to love to sing and dance and have his little drink. At the end, he couldn't do a thing. He was too worn out. *(Pause)* What kind of a life is that?!? Poor dad. *(Pause. Getting back to his original idea. Imitating a wise older brother)* "You know, Gérard, my boy, there are lots of people who didn't go to college

sans elle. *(Pause)* Non, ça, c'pas vrai non plus. Je l'sais ben quoi c'est que j'aurais fait. J'aurais jamais acheté c'maudit magasin-là. *(Pause)* Tedben qu'on s'rait heureux, asteur. Tedben qu'on aurait quèque chose. Tedben qu'on aurait pas besoin de ménager, pi s'en passer, pi faire attention ainque pour arriver. *(Pause)* J'aurais pu faire quèque chose, moué. Après tout, chu pas si épais que ça. Dans l'armée, là, c'est même un capitaine qui m'la dit. Y a dit: "You've got brains, soldier. You'll go a long way." Oui, c'est ça qui a dit. Pi des capitaines, c'est pas des niaiseux, ça. Y connaissent ça, les hommes. *(Pause)* Pi c'tait un Américain, c'gars-là, ça fait que tu sais qui disait pas ça ainque pour s'entendre parler. "You'll go a long way." *(Pause)* Pi j'aurais pu le faire, étou. En sortant, là, l'armée aurait payé mon collège, pi tout. *(Ironique)* Ah, mais non. *(Indique* JULIETTE *de la tête. Il parle de plus en plus fort.)* Elle, a voulait pas. A savait pas comment on était pour s'arranger, pi a pensait pas que ça valait la peine, pi *(il essaie d'imiter la voix de* JULIETTE*)* regarde le beau magasin à Boisvert. Regarde comment y sont ben avec leur grosse machine, pi leur grosse maison!

JULIETTE: Gérard, j'sais pas quoi c'est que t'as, à soir. Louis, y est juste à côté de toué, pi y est pas sourd, t'sais. T'as pas besoin de crier.

GÉRARD: *(Continue plus bas)* C'est vrai qu'on avait deux enfants déjà . . . pi le collège, ça prend du temps. Pi c'tait pas rienque elle qui me chiaulait. Non. Y avait toute ma belle famille. J'tais pas aussi smarte que les autres, pi on allait avoir d'la misère, pi j'allais perdre mon temps. Après tout, le devoir d'un père de famille, c'est pas d'aller au collège. *(Il sermonise.)* Non. Le devoir d'un père de famille c'est de mettre du manger sur la table . . . même si y travaille des soixante heures par semaine . . . même si y a pas l'temps de jouer avec ses enfants . . . même si ça le tue . . . C'est ça qui est arrivé à mon père, t'sais. Sais-ti quel âge qui avait, quand y est mort, mon père? Quarante-neuf ans. Pas de maladie, pas d'accident, pas rien. Y était rendu à bout, c'est tout. Pauvre papa. Y aimait-ti donc ça danser, pi chanter, pi prendre un coup. A fin, là, c'tait rendu qui pouvait pu rien faire. Y était trop fatigué. *(Pause)* C'est-ti une vie, ça?!? Pauvre papa. *(Pause. Il revient à son idée originale. Imite la voix d'un frère sage)* "Tu sais, mon p'tit Gérard, y a en masse du

and who made lots of money." That's what my brother Léo would tell me. "And look at all those who went to college and are struggling just to get by." So I didn't go to college and I struggled for years just to get by. Léo and all those others who kept giving me advice never thought of that one, I guess. If they did, they never told me. At least if they had given me a choice. If they had sat me down and said, "You're not going to college and you'll struggle for the rest of your life," maybe it would-n't have been so bad. But no. A neighborhood store was perfect for someone like me. That's where I could make some real money. That's where I could really be happy. *(He laughs bitterly.)* Look at me. I've had two heart attacks. I have trouble even moving my fingers because of the arthritis I caught while cutting meat in the cooler all day long. I'm so worn out that I catch every little sickness that's going around and dozens of others. Yep. The true picture of happiness. *(Pause)* Well I made sure my kids went to college. You'd think they'd be grateful, wouldn't you? Right! They never write. They never call. We see them only on the holidays and even then it's almost like it's only out of duty or guilt. *(Pause)* We're not smart enough for them, I guess. That's the way it goes in life. *(Pause)* It's a good thing we had the grandchildren. There were always a couple running around here during the summer or during vacations. *(Pause)* But they get older, too. Now, most of them want to spend their time with friends. We're not smart enough for them, either. Now, only Paul's kids spend a week with us during the summer. And it won't be long before they get tired of us, too.

Pause. Lights go up. GÉRARD *goes to take a drink and realizes that his glass is empty. He looks over at* LOUIS' *glass and sees that it's empty as well. He takes both glasses and gets up shakily. He staggers a little as he turns to go to the kitchen.* JULIETTE *notices.*

JULIETTE: Gérard!

GÉRARD: We've got to have a night cap, Juliette.

JULIETTE: Gérard, I don't think you . .

monde qui sont pas allés aux collège pi qui font en masse d'argent."
C'est ça que mon frère Léo me disait. "Pi regarde tous ceux qui sont
allés au collège, pi qui crèvent." Ça fait que moué, chu pas aller au collège, pi j'crève. Pour moué, y avaient pas pensé à c't'a possibilité-là,
mon grand frère pi tous les autres qui me chiaulaient. Si y ont pensé,
y m'l'ont jamais dit. Au moins, si y m'avaient donné un choix. Au
moins, si y m'avaient dit: "Tu vas pas aller au collège, pi tu vas crever,"
me semble que ça aurait pas été si pire. Mais non. Une grocerie, c'tait
fait pour moué, ça. Là, j'allais en faire, d'l'argent. Là, j'allais être content. *(Rire amer)* Regarde-moué. J'ai eu deux attaques de coeur. J'peux
presque pu m'grouiller les mains parce que j'ai poigné l'arthrite en
coupant la viande dans le cooler. J't'assez rendu au bout que j'prends
toutes les maladies qui se passent, pi une dizaine d'autres. Ouais. J't'un
vrai portrait du bonheur. *(Pause)* Ben, mes enfants, y sont allés au collège, eux-autres. Ça, j'ai fait certain de ça. Tu penserais qu'ils
apprécieraient ça, hein? Pantoute. Y écrivent pas. Y téléphonent pas.
On les voué presque pas. Ah, y viennent aux fêtes . . . mais même là,
on dirait que ça les force. *(Pause)* On est pas assez smartes pour eux-
autres, ça d'l'air. C'est comme ça que c'est, dans la vie. *(Pause)* Une
chance qu'on avait les p'tits, par exemple. Pendant les vacances, là, y en
avait toujours une couple icit. *(Pause)* Mais ça vieillit aussi, les enfants.
Asteur, la plupart d'eux-autres veulent passer leur temps avec leurs
chums. *(Rire amer)* On est rendu trop plattes pour eux-autres, étou. Y
a rienque les enfants à Paul qui viennent passer une semaine avec
nous-autres. Pi ça prendra pas longtemps avant qui se tannent de nous-
autres, eux-autres étou.

Pause. L'éclairage devient moins sombre. GÉRARD *va pour boire et se rend
compte que son verre est vide. Il regarde le verre de* LOUIS, *qui est également
vide. Il prend les deux verres et se lève avec un peu de difficulté. Il chancelle
un peu. Il va pour se tourner.* JULIETTE *l'aperçoit.*

JULIETTE: Gérard!

GÉRARD: Faut ben prendre une "night cap," Juliette.

JULIETTE: Gérard, j'pense pas . . .

GÉRARD: Blame it on the Bruins. They're driving us to drink. That's how bad they're playing. *(He staggers toward the kitchen.* JULIETTE's *stare follows him every step of the way. He goes into the kitchen and starts making the drinks. He could start singing "Prendre un p'tit coup" or "Hail, hail the gang's all here" or some other drinking type song. Suddenly, he drops a glass that shatters on the kitchen floor.)*

JULIETTE: Gérard?!?!

GÉRARD: *(He starts picking up pieces of the glass.)* It's o.k. Everything's o.k.

GÉRARD *starts singing again.* JULIETTE *gets up and goes into the kitchen. We should see her giving* GÉRARD *hell without really being able to hear what she is saying.* GÉRARD *could try to defend himself occasionally without much luck with a "Come on, Juliette" or a "I only had a couple." He looks like a dog being reprimanded by his master.*

HILDA: *(In a stage whisper)* Louis. *(Pause)* Louis. *(He doesn't hear her. Louder)* Louis! Louis!

LOUIS: What? What is it?

HILDA: I think we'd better go.

LOUIS: *(Distracted. Still watching the game)* What?

HILDA: I think we'd better go.

LOUIS: But the game isn't over yet.

HILDA: *(Indicating what's going on in the kitchen)* Forget the stupid game. Let's go!

LOUIS: Alright, alright. It looks like the sons of bitches won't be able to get out of their own shit tonight anyway.

Gérard: Blâme ça sur les Bruins. Y jouent assez mal qui nous forcent à boire. *(Il se dirige lentement et en chancelant un peu vers l'entrée de la cuisine.* Juliette *suit chaque pas. Il entre dans la cuisine et commence à préparer les coups. Il se met à chanter "Prendre un p'tit coup." Soudain, il échappe un verre, qui se casse sur le plancher.)*

Juliette: Gérard?!?!

Gérard: *(Il se met à ramasser le verre.)* C't'o.k. C't'o.k.

Gérard *se met à chanter de nouveau.* Juliette *se lève et entre dans la cuisine. On devrait la voir en train d'engueuler* Gérard *sans pouvoir entendre exactement ce qu'elle dit.* Gérard *peut essayer de se défendre de temps à autre sans succès avec des "Voyons, Juliette." Il doit donner l'impression d'un chien battu.*

Hilda: *(A voix basse)* Louis. *(Pause)* Louis. *(Il ne l'entend pas. Plus fort)* Louis! Louis!

Louis: Hein? Quoi c'est que tu veux?

Hilda: J'pense qu'on devrait partir.

Louis: *(Distrait)* Hein?

Hilda: J'pense qu'on devrait partir.

Louis: Mais la game est pas finie.

Hilda: *(Indiquant la cuisine)* Oublie ta mautadite game. Viens-t-en, là.

Louis: O.k., o.k. Ça d'l'air qui vont rester pris dans marde anyway, enfants de chiennes de Bruins!

HILDA: Louis! You know I don't like it when you swear like that.

HILDA *and* LOUIS *get up.* HILDA *starts picking up trays, glasses, etc.* JULIETTE *and* GÉRARD *come back into the living room.* GÉRARD *carries a full glass in each hand.*

JULIETTE: What are you two doing?

HILDA: We'd better be going, Juliette.

JULIETTE: Nonsense. Stay a little longer. Louis, the game isn't even over yet. Go on. Have a seat.

HILDA: No, we really have to go, Juliette. I've still got a whole bunch of things to get ready tomorrow. And if I don't get to bed soon, I know I'll never be able to get up in time.

GÉRARD: *(Heads for the easy chairs)* Too bad, Louis. I was on my way with a couple of night caps for us.

LOUIS: The way the damned Bruins played tonight, they would have helped ease the pain. But when the old lady here wants to go, there's no stopping her. Right, woman?

HILDA: *(She heads for the kitchen with trays, ashtrays, etc.)* Not if you keep blabbing all night. Move it!

JULIETTE: *(She follows* HILDA.*)* Don't do that, Hilda. We have to clean up tomorrow morning anyway.

LOUIS: *(He heads for the door up center.)* Well, Gérard, we'll get our revenge next week, right? And remember, no more mister nice guy. Those women have just won their last game of cards.

JULIETTE: Gérard, go get their coats. They're in the bedroom.

Hilda: Louis! Tu sais que j'aime pas ça quand tu sacres comme ça.

Hilda *et* Louis *se lèvent.* Hilda *commence à ramasser plats, cendriers, etc.* Juliette *et* Gérard *entrent au salon.* Gérard *tient un verre plein dans chaque main.*

Juliette: Mais, quoi c'est que vous faites, vous-autres?

Hilda: J'pense que c'est le temps de partir, Juliette.

Juliette: Mais non, restez, voyons. Louis, la game est même pas finie. Assis-toué, là.

Hilda: Non, faut vraiment partir, là, Juliette. Moué, j'ai assez d'affaires à préparer demain que c'est pas drôle. Si j'me couche pas, là, j'me lèverai jamais en temps.

Gérard: *(Il se dirige vers les fauteuils.)* C'est de valeur, Louis. J'nous apportais justement notre night cap.

Louis: D'la façon que les Bruins ont joué à soir, c'aurait aidé. Mais quand la bonnefemme veut décoller, on décolle. C'est vrai, ça, hein, bonnefemme?

Hilda: *(Elle se dirige vers la cuisine avec des plats, cendriers, etc.)* Pas si tu restes planté là. Grouille!

Juliette: *(Elle suit* Hilda.*)* Laisse donc ça, Hilda. On va ramasser ça demain matin.

Louis: *(Il se dirige vers la porte à l'arrière-scène.)* Ben, Gérard, on se reprendra la semaine prochaine, hein? Pi souviens-toué que la charité, c'est fini. On laisse pu ces femmes-là gagner une game de cartes.

Juliette: Gérard, veux-tu aller chercher le coat à Hilda?

JULIETTE, HILDA, *and* LOUIS *are together at the door up center. They don't notice when* GÉRARD *takes* LOUIS' *drink and gulps it down. He wipes his lips and exits right. He comes back quickly with two coats. He crosses to the door, gives* LOUIS *his coat, and helps* HILDA *with hers. He should always walk rather unsteadily.*

HILDA: *(During* GÉRARD's *business)* You know the invitation to come to our house for dinner tomorrow is still open. And there's no problem with Paul and his family. We have lots of room and lots of food. *(Putting on her coat)* Thank you, Gérard.

JULIETTE: Thanks, Hilda. *(To* GÉRARD, *indicating the* TV*)* Gérard, will you turn that damned thing down? I can't even hear myself think. *(*GÉRARD *crosses to the* TV, *takes the remote control from the small table, and turns down the sound. He starts watching the hockey game.)* But it just wouldn't be the same if we didn't spend Thanksgiving here. Besides, we'll still have fun with Paul and the kids. You know how cute those kids are. And they're really the only little ones we have left. *(Pause)*

LOUIS: Well . . . are we goin' or stayin'?

HILDA: We're goin', we're goin'! *(*LOUIS *exits up center. Quietly to* JULIETTE*)* Listen, Juliette, give me a call tomorrow.

JULIETTE: Sure.

HILDA: To wish us a happy Thanksgiving.

JULIETTE: Sure.

HILDA *and* JULIETTE *exit up center.* GÉRARD *watches them leave. He crosses to the easy chairs, takes his own drink, and gulps it down.*

JULIETTE: *(From off)* Gérard! Come say good night!

GÉRARD: I'm coming. I just wanted to make sure they hadn't forgotten anything.

Juliette, Hilda, *et* Louis *sont ensembles à la porte à l'arrière-scène. Ils ne voient pas* Gérard *qui prend le verre de* Louis *et le boit d'un trait. Il s'essuie la bouche et sort à droite. Il revient presqu'immédiatement avec le manteau d'*Hilda. *Il va à la porte et aide* Hilda *à mettre son manteau.*

Hilda: *(Pendant le jeu de* Gérard*)* Tu sais que vous pouvez encore venir chez nous demain, si vous voulez. Pi y a pas de problème avec Paul, pi sa famille. On a en masse d'la place chez nous. *(En mettant son manteau.)* Merci, Gérard.

Juliette: Ben, merci, Hilda. *(A* Gérard*)* Gérard, veux-ti baisser ce maudit TV-là? On peut même pas s'entendre. *(*Gérard *se dirige vers le téléviseur, prend la télécommande de la petite table, et baisse le son. Il se met à regarder la partie de hockey.)* Mais me semble que ça serait pas Thanksgiving si on passait pas ça icit. Pi avec Paul pi les enfants, là, on va avoir du fun, quand même. Ça sera pas comme c'était, mais on va avoir du fun, quand même. Tu sais comment cute qui sont, ses enfants. Pi c'est vraiment les seuls p'tits qui nous restent. *(Silence)*

Louis: Ben on y va-ti, ou on y va-ti pas?

Hilda: O.k., o.k., décolle! *(*Louis *sort par la porte à l'arrière-scène. A voix basse à* Juliette*)* Écoute, Juliette, appelle-moué demain, hein?

Juliette: Oui.

Hilda: Rienque pour nous souhaiter une bonne Thanksgiving.

Juliette: O.k., là.

Hilda *et* Juliette *sortent par la porte à l'arrière-scène.* Gérard *les voit partir. Il prend son verre et le boit d'un trait.*

Juliette: *(Des coulisses)* Gérard! Viens dire goodnight!

Gérard: Oui, j'voulais rienque être certain qui oublient rien.

He crosses to the door up center and exits. He wobbles and weaves and stag-gers all the way. Pause. We hear a chorus of "good nights, thank yous," etc. from the wings. Pause. Juliette *enters, heads for the kitchen, and starts cleaning up.* Gérard *enters, crosses to the easy chair stage right, and sits heavily. He leans his head back and closes his eyes. Pause*

Juliette: *(Loud. From the kitchen while she's working)* You really should be more careful, Gérard. You know what the doctor said. *(Silence)* It wouldn't take much for you to have another heart attack, you know. And this time, maybe you wouldn't be as lucky. *(Silence)* I can under-stand that you want to have a drink with Louis when we play cards, but you don't seem to know when to stop. *(Silence)* I don't like having to nag you about it all the time, you know. It would be different if you knew how to take care of yourself . . . but, no! I'm always the one who has to say something. *(Silence)* And I have no idea why you thought you had to talk so loud tonight. I'm sure the neighbors were able to hear every word just as well as we could. *(She finishes her work, comes back into the living room, and sits on the couch. Pause)* Are you o.k., Gérard?

Gérard: *(He opens his eyes and sits up.)* Of course, I'm o.k., Juliette. I didn't have that much to drink, you know. You get yourself all worked up for nothing.

Juliette: I don't know, Gérard. Louis can drink as much as he wants. He hasn't had two big heart attacks. You don't have to have a drink just because he's having one.

Gérard: *(Softly)* Come on, Juliette.

Juliette: It's true! *(Silence)* We'll I've had it. I guess I'll turn in. We've still got a lot to do tomorrow. *(Silence)* Gérard? *(Silence. Louder)* Gérard?

Gérard: *(Distracted)* What?

Juliette: Do you think Paul will come tomorrow?

Il se rend à la porte à l'arrière-scène et sort. Il doit marcher d'un pas très incertain. Un temps. On entend des "Bonsoirs, Mercis," etc. des coulisses. Silence. JULIETTE entre et se rend à la cuisine. Elle commence à nettoyer la salle. GÉRARD rentre, va au fauteuil à droite, et s'assoit d'une façon lourde. Il s'accote la tête sur le dossier de la chaise et ferme les yeux. Un temps

JULIETTE: *(Fort. De la cuisine en travaillant)* Tu devrais vraiment faire plus attention, Gérard. Tu sais quoi c'est que l'docteur t'a dit. *(Silence)* Ça prendrait pas grand chose pour que tu aies une autre attaque de coeur, t'sais. Pi c't'a fois-cit, tedben que tu s'rais pas si chanceux que les autres fois. *(Silence)* J'comprends que tu prennes un coup avec Louis quand on joue aux cartes, mais on dirait que tu sais pas quand arrêter. *(Silence)* J'aime pas ça être toujours sur ton dos, comme ça, t'sais. Si tu savais prendre soin de toué même . . . Mais non. C'est toujours moué qui faut qui te dise quèque chose. *(Silence)* Pi je l'sais pas pourquoi tu pensais qu'il fallait parler si fort, à soir. Chu certain que les voisins pouvaient t'entendre aussi ben que nous-autres. *(Elle finit son travail, entre au salon, et s'assoit sur le divan à gauche. Un temps)* Es-tu o.k., là., Gérard?

GÉRARD: *(Il ouvre les yeux et se redresse.)* Ben oui, ch't'o.k., Juliette. J'ai pas bu tant que ça, t'sais. Tu t'occupes pour rien.

JULIETTE: Je l'sais pas, Gérard. Louis, lui, y peut boire autant qui veut. Y a pas eu deux attaques de coeur. T'es pas obligé à prendre un coup rienque parce qui en prend un, lui, t'sais.

GÉRARD: *(A voix basse)* Voyons, Juliette, voyons.

JULIETTE: C'est vrai! *(Silence)* Ben, moué, chu rendue à bout. J'pense que j'va aller me coucher. On a gros à faire demain. *(Silence)* Gérard? *(Silence. Plus fort)* Gérard?

GÉRARD: *(Distrait)* Hein?

JULIETTE: Penses-tu que Paul va venir?

GÉRARD: Of course he'll come. They always come. *(Tenderly)* Don't worry your little head about that, Juliette.

JULIETTE: I don't know. It would be pretty depressing around here if they didn't come. Just the two of us . . . alone . . . on Thanksgiving.

GÉRARD: *(Trying to be cheerful)* Of course they'll be here. They'll be here and we'll have a great time. You'll see. I even bought champagne and everything.

Pause

JULIETTE: Well, I can't keep my eyes open another minute. *(She gets up.)* Are you coming?

GÉRARD: *(Distracted)* What?

JULIETTE: Are you coming to bed?

GÉRARD: In a while. I think I'll watch the game for a little longer.

JULIETTE: *(She crosses to GÉRARD and kisses him on the forehead.)* Well, don't be too late. We have to get up early tomorrow. Good night, my little man. *(She crosses right and exits down right.)*

GÉRARD *notices that the sound is still turned down. He takes the remote control and turns it up. We hear the sounds of a hockey game in progress in the background. Slides of a hockey game should also be shown on the rear wall during* GÉRARD's *monologue. Pause.* GÉRARD *gets up slowly and painfully and goes to the kitchen. He wobbles and weaves and staggers all the way.*

JULIETTE: *(From off)* Gérard!

GÉRARD: Ben, oui, y va venir. Y viennent toujours, voyons. *(Doux)* Occupe-toué pas de ça, Juliette.

JULIETTE: Je l'sais pas. Ça s'rait ben triste icit si y venaient pas. Tous seuls . . . à Thanksgiving.

GÉRARD: *(Il s'efforce d'être gai.)* Voyons. Y vont venir, pi on va avoir du fun, tu vas voir. J'ai même acheté d'la champagne pi toute.

Un temps

JULIETTE: Ben là, j'peux pu me tenir les yeux ouverts. *(Elle se lève.)* Viens-tu, Gérard?

GÉRARD: *(Distrait)* Hein?

JULIETTE: Viens-tu te coucher?

GÉRARD: Non. Pas tout de suite. J'pense que j'va regarder la game pour une secousse.

JULIETTE: *(Elle va à GÉRARD et lui donne un baiser sur le front.)* Ben, couche-toué pas trop tard, là. Faut s'elver de bonne heure, demain. Good night, mon p'tit gars. *(Elle se dirige à droite et sort.)*

GÉRARD se rend compte que le son du téléviseur est encore baissé. Il prend la télécommande et remonte le son. Si possible, on devrait entendre les sons d'une partie de hockey. On devrait aussi entendre un commentaire sans comprendre exactement ce qu'on dit. Je suggère aussi qu'on montre des diapositives d'une partie de hockey sur le mur à l'arrière-scène pendant le monologue de GÉRARD. Un temps. GÉRARD se lève lentement et péniblement, et se rend en chancelant un peu à la cuisine. Un temps.

JULIETTE: *(Des coulisses)* Gérard!

GÉRARD: *(He returns with a glass.)* It's only water, Juliette. I need to take a couple of aspirins. *(He crosses slowly to his easy chair, puts the aspirins that he was holding in his hands in his mouth and takes them with water. He puts the glass down on the table. Pause. He puts his head in hands. Pause. Very loud and in agony)* Dear God!!!

JULIETTE: *(From off)* Gérard?!?

GÉRARD: It's o.k., Juliette. I'm watching the game. The Bruins just scored.

Pause

JULIETTE: *(From off)* Don't stay up too late, o.k., my Gerry?

GÉRARD: O.k. *(Muttering. In a fit of despair)* Dear God, dear God, dear God, dear God! *(Louder)* At least tell me why. I don't mind suffering. I don't mind doing penance. I'm ready to do Your will . . . whatever it may be. But at least tell me why. I know I've sinned, dear God. *(He strikes his chest.)* Through my fault, through my fault, through my most grievous fault. People don't suffer like this if they haven't sinned. But you are a merciful God. You never let Your faithful servants suffer for no reason at all. Help me. I beg You, dear Lord, help me! *(Pause)* I examine my conscience over and over and over again. But I'm weak, dear Lord. I can't think of what I've done for You to punish me like this. I can't find my sin. I've always tried to live like they taught me in school and in church. I never swore, never stole, never cheated, never lied . . . o.k., o.k. a couple of little lies, but I confessed them all, Lord. You know it only too well. I never missed Mass once, not even when I was in the army. *(Pause)* Sometimes, I think it's something I forgot . . . maybe something that happened years and years ago. So I rack my brain to try to remember. But it's no use, Lord. *(Muttering)* It's no use . . . no use at all. *(Loud)* Help me, dear God. Help me find my sin. Is it liquor?!? Tell me and I won't have another drink for as long as I live. It just seems that it can't be anywhere near as bad as what's in the paper

GÉRARD: *(Il revient de la cuisine avec un verre.)* C'est rienque de l'eau, Juliette. J't'après prendre des aspirines. *(Il se dirige lentement vers le fauteuil à droite, met les apirines qu'il tenait dans sa main dans sa bouche, et les prend avec de l'eau. Il pose le verre sur la table. Un temps. Il se met la tête dans les mains. Un temps. Très fort et angoissé)* Seigneur!!!

JULIETTE: *(Des coulisses)* Gérard?!?

GÉRARD: C't'o.k., Juliette. J't'après watcher la game. Les Bruins viennent de faire un point.

Pause

JULIETTE: *(Des coulisses)* Couche-toué pas trop tard, hein, mon p'tit Gérard?

GÉRARD: O.k. *(En murmurant. Au comble du désespoir. Il pourrait aussi pleurer.)* Seigneur, Seigneur, Seigneur, Seigneur . . . *(Plus fort)* Dites-moué pourquoi, au moins. Chu prêt à souffrir. Chu prêt à faire pénitence. Chu prêt à faire n'importe quoi. Mais au moins, dites moué pourquoi. J'l'sais que j'ai péché, Seigneur. *(Il se frappe la poitrine.)* Par ma faute, par ma faute, par ma très grande faute. On souffre pas comme ça sans avoir commis des péchés. Mais Vous êtes miséricordieux, Seigneur. Vous laissez pas souffrir Vos serviteurs fidèles pour rien. Aidez-moué! S'il Vous plaît, aidez-moué! *(Pause)* J'fais mon examen de conscience, mais chu faible, Seigneur. J'peux pas penser à quoi c'est que j'ai fait pour que Vous me punissez tant. J'peux pas trouver mon péché. J'ai toujours essayé de vivre comme on m'a enseigné à l'école pi à l'église. J'ai jamais sacré, j'ai jamais triché, j'ai jamais conté de menteries . . . ah, ben des p'tites, des fois, mais j'les ai toutes confessées, Seigneur. Ça, Vous le savez ben. J'ai jamais manqué la messe pas une fois . . . même quand j'tais dans l'armée. *(Pause)* Des fois, j'pense que c'est quèque chose que j'ai oublié, quèque chose qui est arrivé ça fait ben longtemps. Ça fait que j'pense fort . . . j'essaie de me rappeler. Mais ça vient pas, Seigneur. *(Il murmure.)* Ça vient pas . . . ça vient pas. *(Fort)* Aidez-moué, Seigneur. Aidez-moué à trouver c'péché-là. C'est-ti la

every day. People kill, they steal millions of dollars, they take drugs, they break your Commandments in every imaginable way. Then, we see them on TV with a big smile on their face. They hire some crooked lawyer and they don't even spend any time in jail. *(Louder)* Is that fair?!? Is that suffering?!? Tell me, Lord! Do You make those people suffer as much as I suffer? *(Realizes that he's skirting blasphemy)* Forgive me, Lord. I know that suffering helps expiate our sins. I know that I'm wiping out years of Purgatory. But what kind of sin earned me so much suffering? What sin so angered You that You took my sons away from me? *(Pause)* That's what You did, You know. Sure, they're still physically around, but there's a big, huge wall between them and me . . . because I can't even talk to them. *(Imitating himself in a singsong voice)* "Hello, George, my boy. How's everything? What do you think of this weather?" *(Pause)* Christ! *(Pause)* My sons. My little George . . . Normand . . . Paul, you don't know how much I'd like to be able to really say something to you . . . to take you in my arms and hug you and tell you how much I love you. And after that, we could all sit around the table and talk for as long as we wanted. *(Pause. Bitterly)* Like we never had time to do. *(Pause)* How in the world could we ever have learned to talk to each other? I was always working. And when I got home, either you were all in bed or I was too tired to talk to anybody. I only had time to scold you. Yep. I was there to punish you, that's about all. But that's not how I wanted it to be. That's not what . . . *(Loud)* If you can hear me, please believe me . . . *(softer)* please. That's what I'd like to tell you, my sons. To ask your forgiveness. To tell you that . . . but I won't tell you. *(Pause)* I'll never tell you because You won't let me Lord. *(Pause)* Don't let me suffer any longer, I beg You. Let me do something right for once in my life. Tell me how I've sinned, and let me confess my sin, and let me die in peace, dear God, in peace. Give me a sign . . . something that will show me why I'm being punished. And then, let me speak to my own sons. Give me Your permission, Lord, before it's too late.

Silence. The TV gets louder.

boisson?!? Dites-moué-le pi j'prendrai pu un coup le reste de ma vie. Pourtant, ça peut pas être aussi pire que les affaires qu'on lit dans le papier chaque jour. Ça tue, ça vole des milliers de piastres, ça prend des drugs, ça se débauche. Pi on les voué sur le TV après ça, pi ça d'l'air content comme toute. Y engagent un avocat croche, là, pi y vont même pas en prison. *(Plus fort)* Ça souffre-ti, c'monde-là?!? Dites-moué-le, hein, Seigneur! Ça souffre-ti, ça, comme Vous me voyez souf-frir?!? *(Se rend compte qu'il blasphème presque. Il baisse sa voix.)* Pardon, Seigneur. J'sais que la souffrance va expier nos péchés. J'sais que j'ef-face des années au purgatoire. Mais quel sorte de péché m'a valu tant de souffrances? Quel péché Vous a tellement enragé que Vous m'en-levez mes fils? *(Pause)* C'est ça que Vous avez fait, Vous savez. Ah, y sont encore là, mais y a un mur, un gros maudit mur, entre eux-autres pi moué . . . parce que j'peux même pas leur parler. *(Il s'imite d'une façon niaiseuse.)* "Allô, mon Georges. Comment ça va? Fais pas beau, hein?" *(Pause)* Christ! *(Pause)* Mon p'tit Georges . . . Normand . . . Paul, vous savez pas comment j'aimerais pouvoir vous parler, vous prendre dans mes bras pi vous embrasser pi vous dire comment j'vous aime. Pi après ça, là, on s'assirait toutes autour d'la table pi on parlerait à longeur de la journée. *(Pause. Amer)* . . . Comme on a jamais eu la chance de l'faire. *(Pause)* Comment qu'on aurait pu parler ensemble? J'tais jamais à mai-son. J'travaillais toujours. Pi quand j'arrivais, j'tais toujours trop fatigué. J'avais ainque le temps de vous chicaner. Ouais, j'tais là pour punir, c'est tout. Mais c'pas ça que j'voulais. C'est pas ça qui . . . *(Fort)* Si vous m'entendez, là, croyez-moué . . . *(plus doux)* s'il vous plaît. C'est ça que j'voudrais vous dire, mes p'tits gars. Vous demander pardon. Vous dire que . . . Mais j'l'dirai pas. *(Pause)* J'l'dirai jamais, parce que Vous me laissez pas, Seigneur. *(Pause)* Laissez-moué plus souffir, j'Vous en supplie. Laissez-moué faire quèque chose de ben une fois dans ma vie. Dites-moué quoi c'est que j'ai fait, pi laissez-moué me confesser, pi laissez-moué mourir en paix . . . Seigneur . . . en paix. Mais laissez-moué pas comme ça. Donnez-moué un signe . . . quèque chose qui va me donner une p'tite raison, pi laissez-moué parler à mes enfants. Donnez-moué la permission, Seigneur . . . avant qui soit trop tard.

Silence. Le son du téléviseur devient plus fort.

Announcer: Well, what can you possibly say about a night like this? The Bruins were literally embarrassed out there by a vastly superior Philadelphia Flyers team. But, it goes deeper than that, folks. What can you say about a team that looked so promising at the start of the season . . . that seemed to have everything going for it . . . and that ends up playing the way the Bruins did tonight . . . and the way they've played for the last couple of weeks. Is it luck? Is it skill? Is it aggressiveness? Is it knowing how to capitalize on breaks and the other team's mistakes? Well, whatever it is, the Bruins just don't have it . . . and it shows. This is a team that can't seem to do anything right . . . and the result is the pitiful spectacle we saw tonight. I guess the only consolation is that things have got to get better, 'cause they sure can't get any worse. So, once again, the final score: the Philadelphia Flyers 15, and the Boston Bruins 1.

The TV gets softer. GÉRARD *continues to watch the screen for a moment. Then, he takes the remote control and turns the TV off. Pause. He gets up slowly, crosses to the door down right and exits.*

Curtain

ANNONCEUR: Well, what can you possibly say about a night like this? The Bruins were literally embarassed out there by a vastly superior Philadelphia Flyers team. But, it goes deeper than that, folks. What can you say about a team that looked so promising at the start of the season . . . that seemed to have everything going for it . . . and that ends up playing the way the Bruins did tonight . . . and the way they've played for the last couple of weeks. Is it luck? Is it skill? Is it aggressiveness? Is it knowing how to capitalize on breaks and the other team's mistakes? Well, whatever it is, the Bruins just don't have it . . . and it shows. This is a team that can't seem to do anything right . . . and the result is the pitiful spectacle we saw tonight. I guess the only consolation is that things have got to get better, 'cause they sure can't get any worse. So, once again, the final score: the Philadelphia Flyers 15, and the Boston Bruins 1.

Le son du télévieur s'adoucit. Pause. GÉRARD *regarde le téléviseur. Il prend la télécommande et ferme le téléviseur. Pause. Il se lève lentement, se dirige vers la droite et sort.*

Rideau

ACT III

The following morning. It's Thanksgiving. Same setting as in the two previous acts. When the curtain goes up, JULIETTE is in the kitchen. She is wearing her "Sunday best" dress covered by an apron. She should look like she's very busy getting everything ready for the meal and her guests. The television is on in the living room and we can hear its sounds in the background. After a few moments, GÉRARD enters down right. He is also wearing his "Sunday best"— trousers, shirt and tie. He crosses to the easy chair stage right, sits, and starts watching television. He must seem very nervous.

ANNOUNCER 1: *(Man's voice)* And the next float in our wonderful Thanksgiving Day parade depicts the many contributions that good old-fashioned hard work has made to our American way of life as we see a family gathered around their dying father, while dad's boss is serving the papers to evict them from their shabby, mill-owned house. Yes, folks, this float truly portrays the combination of honest labor and benign capitalism that has made this country the best in the world.

GÉRARD: *(Gets up and crosses to the window up center. To JULIETTE. Loud)* They should have been here by now. It's already quarter of twelve.

ANNOUNCER 1: And this float of the Road Runner pushing Wily Coyote off the cliff is always a favorite with the kids.

GÉRARD: *(Coming back to the easy chair)* They're usually here by ten thirty at the latest. The kids always watch the parades here.

ANNOUNCER 2: *(Woman's voice)* And here's another float that's sure to go over big with the kids. As you can see, this one's animated. Watch how real Fred Flintstone's reaction is when BamBam hits him over the head with the club. And Pebble's laugh is really something else. Let's see if our microphone can pick it up.

ACTE III

Le matin de la journée suivante. C'est Thanksgiving. Même décor que dans les deux actes précédents. Éclairage sombre, mais moins sombre que dans les actes précédents. Au lever du rideau, JULIETTE *se trouve dans la cuisine à l'arrière-scène à gauche. Elle porte une robe "du dimanche" avec un tablier. Elle devrait donner l'impression qu'elle est très occupée à tout préparer pour le repas et sa "visite." On entend le son du téléviseur du salon. Après un temps,* GÉRARD, *habillé en dimanche, entre par la porte à l'arrière-scène, entre au salon, s'assoit, et se met à regarder la télévision. Il doit paraître extrêmement nerveux.*

ANNONCEUR 1: *(Voix d'homme)* And the next float in our wonderful Thanksgiving Day parade depicts the many contributions that good old-fashioned hard work has made to our American way of life as we see a family gathered around their dying father, while dad's boss is serving the papers to evict them from their shabby, mill-owned house. Yes, folks, this float truly portrays the combination of honest labor and benign capitalism that has made this country the best in the world.

GÉRARD: *(Il se lève et va à la fenêtre à l'arrière-scène. A* JULIETTE. *Fort)* Y devraient être icit. Y est déjà midi moins quart.

ANNONCEUR 1: And this float of the Road Runner pushing Wily Coyote off the cliff is always a favorite with the kids.

GÉRARD: *(Il revient au téléviseur.)* De coutume, y sont icit par dix heures et demi au moins. Les enfants watchent toujours les parades icit.

ANNONCEUR 2: *(Voix de femme)* And here's another float that's sure to go over big with the kids. As you can see, this one's animated. Watch how real Fred Flintstone's reaction is when BamBam hits him over the head with the club. And Pebble's laugh is really something else. Let's see if our microphone can pick it up.

GÉRARD: *(He gets up again and crosses to the window. To* JULIETTE. *Loud)* Juliette! Do you think I should call? *(No answer. Louder)* Juliette!

JULIETTE: *(From the kitchen. Loud)* What is it?

GÉRARD: Do you think I should try calling them?

JULIETTE: *(Comes into the living room with dishes of candy, chips, etc. that she puts down on tables in the room)* I wouldn't bother. They're probably on their way.

GÉRARD: But they've never gotten here this late.

JULIETTE: *(Half believing it)* Well, they got delayed somehow. That's all. *(She goes back into the kitchen.)*

GÉRARD: They should have called. It's not like them not to let us know what's going on. And they'd never miss the parades. The kids always watch the parades here.

JULIETTE: *(Coming in with more trays and dishes that she places on various tables)* You know how it is with four kids. They'll be here. Come and help me set the table.

JULIETTE *goes back to the kitchen.* GÉRARD *hesitates for moment while watching TV and then crosses to the kitchen. He starts setting the table but his heart is not in it.*

ANNOUNCER 1: Now, let's listen to the Wichita Falls, Kansas, marching band playing selections from Beethoven's Third Symphony . . . but this time with a disco beat.

GÉRARD *gets lost in thought. He comes back into the living room, looking increasingly nervous. He heads for the easy chair stage right but never succeeds in sitting down. He watches TV.* JULIETTE *enters with still more dishes of goodies that she places on various living room tables.*

GÉRARD: *(Il se lève de nouveau et va à la fenêtre à l'arrière-scène. A* JULIETTE. *Fort)* Juliette! Penses-tu que j'devrais appeler? *(Pas de réponse. Plus fort)* Juliette!

JULIETTE: *(De la cuisine. Fort)* Quoi c'est que tu veux?

GÉRARD: Penses-tu que j'devrais les appeler?

JULIETTE: *(Elle entre au salon avec des plats de bonbons, croustillantes, etc., qu'elle dépose sur les petites tables.)* Oh, ça sert à rien. Y sont probablement en chemin.

GÉRARD: Mais y sont jamais arrivés si tard que ça.

JULIETTE: *(Sans trop y croire)* Ah, ben y a quèque chose qui les a retardés, c'est tout. *(Elle retourne à la cuisine.)*

GÉRARD: Ben, y auraient dû téléphoner. C'est pas comme eux-autres de pas nous laisser savoir. Pi y manqueraient pas les parades. Les enfants watchent toujours les parades icit.

JULIETTE: *(Qui entre de nouveau avec d'autres plats qu'elle dépose sur des tables)* Tu sais comment que c'est avec leurs quatre enfants, Gérard. Y vont v'nir. Viens m'aider à mettre la table, là.

JULIETTE *retourne à la cuisine.* GÉRARD *hésite un instant en regardant la télévision et va ensuite à la cuisine. Il commence à mettre la table, mais sans trop d'enthousiasme.*

ANNONCEUR 1: Now, let's listen to the Wichita Falls, Kansas, marching band playing selections from Beethoven's Third Symphony . . . but this time with a disco beat.

GÉRARD *devient distrait. Il revient au salon. Il doit paraître de plus en plus nerveux. Il se dirige vers le fauteuil à droite, mais n'arrive pas à s'asseoir. Il regarde la télévision.* JULIETTE *entre avec d'autres plats qu'elle dépose sur des tables au salon.*

JULIETTE: Are you going to help me set the table or not?

GÉRARD: *(Distracted)* What?

JULIETTE: Are you going to help me set the table?

GÉRARD: Sure. I'll be right there.

We hear the sound of a car horn from outside. GÉRARD and JULIETTE both run to the window and look out. Pause. The two turn back to the room. They look disappointed. JULIETTE returns to the kitchen. GÉRARD crosses to the easy chair stage right and sits on the very edge of the chair. We continue to hear the sounds of the parade on TV. Pause

GÉRARD: They could have called, you know. Then, we wouldn't be worrying ourselves sick for nothing.

ANNOUNCER 1: And here's that wonderful moment . . . the moment that kids all over the world have been waiting for since last December twenty-fifth.

JULIETTE, who hears the TV, enters, crosses to the easy chair stage left, and sits.

ANNOUNCER 2: And us grown ups, too, Jack.

ANNOUNCER 1: That's certainly true, Shirley. The Christmas season holds magic for all of us.

JULIETTE: Well, that's it. The kids won't get a chance to see Santa Claus. *(Pause)* What a shame. They used to love to see all the reindeers. They'd jump up and down and get all excited. *(Pause)* Remember, Gérard? *(He nods.)*

ANNOUNCER 2: Have you made up your Christmas list yet, Jack?

ANNOUNCER 1: No, not yet, Shirley.

Juliette: Vas-tu m'aider à mettre la table, ou non?

Gérard: *(Distrait)* Hein?

Juliette: Vas-tu m'aider à mettre la table?

Gérard: Oui, oui. J'viens, là.

On entend le son d'un claxon du dehors. Gérard *et* Juliette *se précipitent vers la fenêtre à l'arrière-scène. Un temps. Les deux se tournent. Ils ont l'air déçus.* Juliette *retourne à la cuisine.* Gérard *se dirige vers le fauteuil à droite et s'assoit sur le bout du fauteuil. On entend toujours des sons de la parade à la télévision. Un temps*

Gérard: Y auraient ben pu nous appeler, t'sais. On passerait pas notre temps à s'occuper pour rien.

Annonceur 1: And here's that wonderful moment . . . the moment that kids all over the world have been waiting for since last December twenty-fifth.

Juliette, *qui a entendu, entre, se dirige vers le fauteuil à gauche, et s'assoit.*

Annonceur 2: And us grown ups, too, Jack.

Annonceur 1: That's certainly true, Shirley. The Christmas season holds magic for all of us.

Juliette: Tiens. Ça y est. Les p'tits vont manquer Santa Claus. *(Pause)* Pauvres p'tits enfants. Eux qui aimaient tant ça voir tous les reindeers. Y v'naient assez excités, que c'tait pas drôle. *(Pause)* T'en souviens-ti, Gérard? *(Il fait signe de tête que oui.)*

Annonceur 2: Have you made up your Christmas list yet, Jack?

Annonceur 1: No, not yet, Shirley.

ANNOUNCER 2: Well, knowing you . . . it'll sure be a biggie, won't it Jack?

ANNOUNCER 1: *(Fake laugh)* Well that could be, Shirley, but it won't be anywhere as big as that charming, overworked mouth of yours.

ANNOUNCER 2: *(Fake laugh)* Oh, Jack. You always know just what to say. That should come in handy when your wife finds out about Monica and that week-end in Lake Tahoe.

ANNOUNCER 1: *(Tries to continue as if nothing happened)* Well . . . here's that jolly old elf himself. Here's Santa Claus! *(Pause)* Yes, Santa Claus. What warm, pleasant memories that name brings back. And you know, Shirley, more than our lists and our presents, the things I remember most about Thanksgiving and Christmas are those good old down-home virtues that make this country so great. And if I could look into homes all across America right now, I'd see the smiling faces of men, women, and children . . . families together sharing each other's love. *(JULIETTE gets weepy. GÉRARD wipes his eyes. He'll do it a number of time during the announcer's speech.)* Oh, I'd see children talking happily about Santa Claus with their grand parents. I'd see mothers and daughters working together to put that wonderful Thanksgiving feast on the table. And I'd see fathers and sons talking about football. And by the way, stay tuned to this station right after the parades for the best of the Thanksgiving NFL games. Yep, that's what the holiday is for me, Shirley. It's families together . . . giving thanks for the very special things they have.

JULIETTE: *(She cries softly. Suddenly worried)* Gérard, you don't think that . . . that something happened to them, do you?

GÉRARD: *(Wiping his eyes)* Of course not.

JULIETTE: You never know when you travel. People today drive so fast and don't pay any attention at all to what they're doing.

ANNONCEUR 2: Well, knowing you . . . it'll sure be a biggie, won't it Jack?

ANNONCEUR 1: *(Rire faux)* Well that could be, Shirley, but it won't be anywhere as big as that charming, overworked mouth of yours.

ANNONCEUR 2: *(Même jeu)* Oh, Jack. You always know just what to say. That should come in handy when your wife finds out about Monica and that week-end in Lake Tahoe.

ANNONCEUR 1: *(Qui essaie de continuer comme si rien n'était)* Well . . . here's that jolly old elf himself. Here's Santa Claus! *(Pause)* Yes, Santa Claus. What warm, pleasant memories that name brings back. And you know, Shirley, more than our lists and our presents, the things I remember most about Thanksgiving and Christmas are those good old down-home virtues that make this country so great. And if I could look into homes all across America right now, I'd see the smiling faces of men, women, and children . . . families together sharing each other's love. *(JULIETTE commence à pleurnicher. GÉRARD s'essuie les yeux. Il le fera à plusieurs reprises au cours du discours suivant.)* Oh, I'd see children talking happily about Santa Claus with their grand parents. I'd see mothers and daughters working together to put that wonderful Thanksgiving feast on the table. And I'd see fathers and sons talking about football. And by the way, stay tuned to this station right after the parades for the best of the Thanksgiving NFL games. Yep, that's what the holiday is for me, Shirley. It's families together . . . giving thanks for the very special things they have.

JULIETTE: *(Elle pleure doucement. Soudain inquiète)* Gérard, tu penses pas que . . . qu'y a quèque chose qui est arrivé.

GÉRARD: *(S'essuyant les yeux)* Voyons, Juliette.

JULIETTE: *(Même jeu)* On l'sait jamais, t'sais, quand on voyage. Le monde aujourd'hui, ça conduit assez vite, pi ça fait pas attention.

GÉRARD: Don't worry, Juliette. *(Pause)* Is dinner ready?

JULIETTE: *(Wiping her eyes with her apron)* Yes, except for the turkey. That'll be ready in about a half hour. *(Pause)* Gérard, what'll we do if they don't come?

GÉRARD: *(Avoids the question)* Maybe I should get the drinks ready. That way, we'll be ready to eat sooner when they get here.

JULIETTE: Gérard . . .

GÉRARD: *(Still avoiding)* We could have drinks right away, and then sit right down at the table so things don't get cold.

JULIETTE: Gérard . . .

GÉRARD: *(Forced to listen)* What?

JULIETTE: What'll we do if they don't come?

GÉRARD: *(Tries to laugh it off)* You said so yourself the other day. We'll just eat a lot more turkey, that's all.

JULIETTE: That's not what I mean, Gérard. *(Pause. She starts to cry.)* I can't stay here all alone for Thanksgiving. I just can't. Understand?

GÉRARD: *(Trying to console her)* Don't worry, Juliette. Don't worry. They'll be here. You'll see.

JULIETTE: *(Bitterly)* No! They're not coming. I know that now.

GÉRARD: Don't say that, Juliette. *(Pause)* Listen, I'll go make us a drink. There no rule against getting a head start on them. *(Pause)* You're all upset, Juliette. You'll see. A drink will make you feel better.

GÉRARD: Voyons, Juliette. *(Pause)* L'diner est-ti tout prêt?

JULIETTE: *(S'essuyant les yeux avec son tablier)* Oui, à part du turkey. Pi lui, y va être prêt dans un quinzaine de minutes. *(Pause)* Gérard, quoi c'est qu'on va faire si y viennent pas?

GÉRARD: *(Qui essaie d'éviter de répondre)* J'devrais tedben préparer des drinks. Comme ça, ça prendra moins de temps mèque y arrivent.

JULIETTE: Gérard . . .

GÉRARD: *(Même jeu)* On pourra prendre notre drink tout de suite, pi s'asseoir à table pour pas que ça refroidisse trop.

JULIETTE: Gérard . . .

GÉRARD: *(Qui doit enfin écouter)* Hein?

JULIETTE: Quoi c'est qu'on va faire si y viennent pas?

GÉRARD: *(Essaie de plaisanter)* Ben, tu l'as dit toué même l'autre jour. On va manger plus de dinde, c'est tout.

JULIETTE: C'est pas ça que j'veux dire, Gérard. *(Pause. Elle commence à pleurer.)* Moué, là, j'peux pas rester tout seul icit à Thanksgiving. J'peux pas, comprends-tu?

GÉRARD: *(Essayant de la consoler)* Voyons, Juliette, voyons. Y vont v'nir, tu vas voir.

JULIETTE: *(Dur)* Non! Non, y viendront pas. J'l'sais, asteur.

GÉRARD: Mais voyons, Juliette. *(Pause)* Écoute, là, j'va aller nous faire une drink. Y a rien qui dit qu'on peut pas commencer un p'tit peu avant eux-autres. *(Pause)* T'es toute énervée, là, Juliette. Tu vas voir. Une drink, ça va t'faire filer mieux.

JULIETTE: *(Angrily)* I don't want any of your damned drinks. *(She bursts into tears.)* Will your damned drinks make them come? Will they make George and Normand come? Ach! Keep your damned drinks for yourself. Seems you can't do much without them, lately.

GÉRARD: *(Hurt)* Juliette . . .

JULIETTE: I think that's why they don't want to come any more. Their wives are fed up. Every time they come here, that's all you do. You drink and drink and drink. And then you all get together in the other room and you talk like REAL men. That's right. I tell you, it's quite a sight to see. And their wives and I are stuck with the dishes and the kids while you talk your BIG, important man talk.

GÉRARD: Don't, Juliette.

JULIETTE: I've asked you to be careful. I've asked you not to drink so much. But every time, it's the same damned thing. You don't listen worth a damn. I might as well be talking to the floor. *(Pause)* If you died, what do you think would happen to me? Did you ever think of that? All alone here, with no one to take care of me. It'd be a great life, I can tell you that! And the doctor told you to be careful. He even told you what could happen if you didn't. But does that mean anything to you? Bah! Not a thing. You're too busy having fun to care about what might happen to your wife. Well, you see what's going to happen after you're gone? I'll be all alone. Not one of those boys will be around to help me. And that'll be your fault . . . because the only thing you ever thought about your whole life was having fun . . . and because you never had the guts to make a man out of yourself!

GÉRARD: *(Who is visibly suffering)* Juliette!

JULIETTE: Don't start with the "Juliettes" now. It's too late.

Pause

JULIETTE: *(Dur)* J'n'en veux pas, de maudite drink. *(Elle éclate en sanglots.)* Ça va-ti les faire v'nir, ça, une maudite drink? Ça va-ti faire v'nir Georges pi Normand, une maudite drink? Garde les pour toué, tes maudites drinks. Ça d'l'air que tu n'as de besoin, de c'temps-cit.

GÉRARD: *(Blessé)* Juliette . . .

JULIETTE: Pour moué, c'est pour ça qui veulent pu v'nir. Leurs femmes sont tannées. A toutes les fois qui viennent icit, c'est rienque ça que vous faites, vous-autres. Ça boué, pi ça boué, pi ça boué. Pi après ça, vous vous mettez ensemble dans l'autre bord pi vous parlez comme des vrais hommes. Ah, oui. J'vous dis que c'est ben beau à voir. Pi moué pi leurs femmes, on reste pris avec la vaisselle pi les enfants pendant que vous-autres, là, vous parlez votre grand parlage d'hommes.

GÉRARD: Arrête donc, Juliette.

JULIETTE: J't'ai demandé de faire attention. J'te l'ai dit de pas en prendre trop, pourtant. Mais à toutes les fois, c'est la même maudite affaire. Tu m'écoutes pas une sacrée miette. *(Pause)* Si tu mourrais, là, quoi c'est que j'f'rais, moué? As-tu déjà pensé à ça, hein? Tout seul icit . . . j'te dis que ça s'rait une belle vie. Pi le docteur te l'a dit, hein? Y te l'a dit quoi c'est qui pourrait arriver si tu faisais pas attention. Mais ça pas l'air à te faire rien, toué. Non. Monsieur est ben trop occupé à avoir du fun pour penser à sa femme. Ben tu voué comment que ça va être, là, après que t'es parti? J'va être tout seule. Y aura pas un de ces gars-là qui va v'nir pour m'aider. Pi ça, ça va être à cause de toué . . . parce que la seule chose que t'as pensé dans vie, c'était d'avoir du fun . . . pi parce que t'as jamais eu assez de génie pour faire un homme de toué!

GÉRARD: *(Qui souffre perceptiblement. Angoissé)* Juliette!

JULIETTE: Commence pas à me "Julietter." Y est trop tard pour ça.

Pause

GÉRARD: *(Recovering a little. With difficulty)* You have no right to talk to me like that.

JULIETTE: I don't have the right?!?

GÉRARD: No, you don't have the right. Everything I did in life, I did for you. The only thing I ever wanted to do was make you happy. *(*JULIETTE *laughs bitterly.)* You don't have to believe me if you don't want to, but it's true. I never did anything without asking myself first if you'd like it or not. And if I thought you wouldn't like it, I didn't do it. Why do you think I never went to college after the war? Why do you think I agreed to buy that damned store? Why do you think I worked night and day, seven days a week, practically three hundred and sixty five days a year? Because I liked it? Because I didn't want to see my own kids grow up? Because I couldn't stand taking vacations? *(Doesn't let her answer)* Of course not! It's because I thought that's what you wanted. Do you remember, Juliette? Do you remember how desperately you wanted us to buy that store? "Think of how nice it'll be," you'd tell me. "A business of our own. No more bosses, no more layoffs. And look how much money store owners are making. We'll be able to have everything we've ever wanted." Remember? Well, we got some of the things we wanted. But they cost a lot more than you thought. And do you know who ended up paying for them all? Me . . . and I paid through the nose. But you seemed to want that so badly, Juliette. And I wanted to make you happy. *(Pause)* If it'd been up to me, I would have sold that damned thing after five years. But no. We had to keep on working . . . always harder . . . always longer. And why? So we could be all alone for Thanksgiving. *(Pause)* That's right, Juliette. You have no right to talk to me like that because if there's a reason those kids don't want to come here any more, it's because of you . . . not me. It's thanks to you that no one was ever home for them. It's thanks to you that I never had time to play with them or spend time with them. *(*JULIETTE *starts to cry.)* I couldn't even spend time with them on Sunday afternoons because I was too tired. So we'd all go out for an ice cream after supper. And those kids would get so excited. We thought it was because they liked ice cream so much. We should have known that it was the

GÉRARD: *(Qui se remet un peu. Avec un effort)* T'as pas le droit de m'parler comme ça, Juliette.

JULIETTE: *(Ironique)* Moué, j'ai pas le droit?!?

GÉRARD: Non, t'as pas le droit. Tout quoi c'est que j'ai fait dans vie, là, je l'ai fait à cause de toué. C'est la seule chose que j'voulais faire, ça, c'est de te faire plaisir. *(JULIETTE donne un petit rire ironique.)* Tu peux ben pas m'craire si tu veux, mais c'est vrai. J'ai jamais rien fait avant de penser pour voir si tu aimerais ça ou non. Pi si c'avait l'air à te déplaire, j'l'faisais pas. Pourquoi c'est que tu penses que chu pas allé au collège après la guerre? Pourquoi c'est que tu penses que j'ai acheté c'maudit magasin-là? Pourquoi c'est que tu penses que j'travaillais nuit et jour, sept jours par semaine, presque trois cent soixante et cinq jours par année? Parce que j'aimais ça? Parce que j'voulais pas voir grandir mes enfants? Parce que j'haïssais ça, prendre des vacances? *(Ne la laisse pas répondre)* Non. C'est parce que j'pensais que c'tait ça que tu voulais. T'en souviens-ti, Juliette? T'en souviens-ti comment tu voulais acheter ça, ce magasin-là? "On va-ti être ben," tu m'disais. "Notre magasin à nous-autres-mêmes. Pu d'boss, pu de layoffs. Pi regarde comment d'argent qui font, ceux qui ont des magasins. On va avoir tout ce qu'on veut." T'en souviens-tu? Ben on n'a eu des affaires qu'on voulait. Mais ça coûté ben plus cher que tu pensais. Pi sais-ti qui c'est que c'est qui a payé? C'est moué . . . pi j'ai payé cher. Mais t'avais d'l'air à vouloir ça tellement, Juliette. Pi moué, j'voulais tant te faire plaisir. *(Pause)* Si c'avait été ainque moué, j'aurais vendu ça après cinq ans, c'magasin-là. Mais non. Fallait continuer de travailler . . . toujours plus fort . . . toujours plus longtemps. Pi pourquoi? Pour qu'on reste icit tout seul à Thanksgiving. *(Pause)* Oui, Juliette, t'as pas le droit de m'parler comme ça, parce que si y a une raison que ces gars-là viennent pas, c'est à cause de toué . . . pas à cause de moué. C'est toué qui a arrangé ça pour qui ait jamais personne à maison. C'est toué qui a arrangé ça pour que j'aie jamais le temps de jouer avec eux-autres. *(JULIETTE se met à pleurer.)* J'pouvais même rien faire avec eux-autres le dimanche après-midi parce j'tais trop fatigué. Ça fait qu'on allait prendre un ice cream ensemble le soir. Pi ces gars-là, y étaient assez excités.

only time all week they had the chance to see us for more than two minutes. We never had time to pay attention to them Juliette. How can you expect them to pay attention to us now? I still remember when they'd ask us to go to some event at school. Like Normand's high school concert. They wanted so much for us to come. But no. We always had to work. Hockey games, football games, baseball games, plays . . . we always missed them because we were too busy making our big bucks. After a while, they gave up. They didn't even ask any more. Remember when you got so mad because Normand didn't fill us in about his graduation? You said he was inconsiderate and heartless. Remember? Well, he wasn't inconsiderate at all. He was just afraid that we wouldn't be interested in going. And all that on account of that damned store that you wanted so much. So don't try to blame me because those boys don't visit us any more. If we had spent time with them when they were young, they'd be here now . . . all of them. And we wouldn't have to go begging them, either.

JULIETTE: *(Still crying)* Sure. Go ahead. It's easy to criticize your wife. It's easy to put the whole blame on me. But remember that if we hadn't had that store, we'd be even worse off than we are. Besides, hard work never hurt anyone . . . and there's no one who can get by without it. If we hadn't worked our fingers to the bone, if I hadn't pushed and pulled, and pleaded and begged, and told you what to do, we'd have never gotten anywhere at all. We'd still be living in an apartment in one of those damned three-deckers by the river. And if I worked, it wasn't for my benefit. It's because I wanted those kids to have the chances we never had. It's not a sin to work hard, you know. And if I had had a little more help from you, we wouldn't have had as much trouble as we did. If you had only listened to me when I wanted us to sell our own homemade sandwiches . . .

GÉRARD: Don't start on that again.

JULIETTE: Why not? We could have made lots of money on those

On pensait que c'tait parce qu'y aimaient ça, l'ice cream. On aurait du savoir que c'tait parce qu'y avaient la chance de nous voir pour plus que deux minutes pour la seule fois pendant la semaine. On s'est pas occupé d'eux-autres pour une vingtaine d'années, Juliette. Comment veux-tu qui s'occupent de nous-autres asteur? J'm'en souviens encore quand y v'naient nous demander d'aller à quèque chose à l'école. Tu t'en souviens du concert à Normand à high school? Y voulait assez qu'on vienne. Mais non. Fallait travailler. Des games de hockey, pi de football, pi de baseball . . . on manquait toujours ça, parce qu'on était trop occupé à faire notre grosse argent. Après une secousse, y s'sont découragés. Y nous demandaient même pu. Tu t'en souviens quand tu t'es fâchée parce que Normand nous avait pas parlé de sa graduation. Tu l'as traité de p'tit sans-coeur. T'en souviens-ti? Ben, y était pas sans-coeur pantoute. Y avait ainque peur qu'on s'rait pas intéressé. Pi tout ça, à cause du maudit magasin que tu voulais tant. Ça fait que là, essaie pas de me blâmer parce que ça vient pu, nos gars. Si on avait passé plus de temps avec eux-autres quand y étaient jeunes, y s'raient icit . . . toutes icit . . . pi sans se faire prier, non plus.

JULIETTE: *(Qui pleure toujours)* Ah, oui. Vas-y, là. C'est ben facile de critiquer ta femme, hein? C'est ben facile de mettre tout ça sur mon dos. Mais souviens-toué que si on l'avait pas eu, c'magasin-là, on s'rait encore pire qu'on est aujourd'hui. Pi travailler, y a personne dans le monde qui a pas besoin de travailler. Si on avait pas travaillé comme des fous, si j't'avais pas poussé, pi si j't'avais pas dit quoi faire, on aurait crevé ben net y a ben longtemps. On resterait encore dans un maudit loyer au troisième étage dans un gros bloc près d'la rivière. Pi si j'ai travaillé, c'tait pas pour moué. C'tait pour que ces gars-là aient toutes les chances qu'on a pas eu, nous-autres. C'est pas péché, travailler, tu sais. Pi si j'avais eu un peu plus d'aide de toué, on aurait pas toujours eu d'la misère comme on a eu. Si tu m'avais écouté, là, quand j'voulais qu'on commence à vendre nos sandwichs à nous-autres . . .

GÉRARD: Ah, ben, commence pas là-dessus encore.

JULIETTE: Pourquoi pas, hein? Tu sais qu'on aurait fait d'l'argent avec

sandwiches. All the other stores in town only sold grinders or those cardboard-tasting things.

GÉRARD: Well, maybe you didn't mind spending three hours after work every night making sandwiches for the next day, but I did.

JULIETTE: It wouldn't have taken that long. And it would have brought in people from the mills and the college kids . . . but no. You didn't want to. So we bought the cardboard sandwiches and the microwave oven, and made nothing at all. People tasted those things once and never came back.

GÉRARD: But can't you see I did that for you? I didn't want any sandwiches at all. We didn't need any damned sandwiches. We were getting along fine without them.

JULIETTE: You call not having enough money to pay your bills "getting along fine?"

GÉRARD: Stop it, Juliette. We always paid our bills. And we didn't go without much either.

JULIETTE: Well, we always had enough to eat, that's for sure. We ate everything that we couldn't sell. And at the end, we ate a lot.

GÉRARD: So what was the answer? What should we have done? Go ahead. Tell me.

ces sandwichs-là. Toutes les autres magasins en ville, y vendaient ainque des grinders ou ben des maudits sandwichs de carton qui avient été faits la semaine passée.

GÉRARD: Ben tedben que t'aurais aimé ça, passer trois heures chaque soir après l'ouvrage pour faire des sandwichs pour le lendemain, mais pas moué.

JULIETTE: Ça aurait pas pris si longtemps que ça. Pi ça aurait attiré des gars du moulin, pi des jeunes du collège . . . mais non. Tu voulais pas, toué. Ça fait qu'on a acheté des sandwichs en carton, pi le p'tit fourneau, pi on a niaisé avec ça. Le monde goûtait ça pi y revenait pu, j'te l'dis!

GÉRARD: Mais tu voué pas que j'ai fait ça pour toué? Des sandwichs, là moué, j'en voulais pas pantoute. On n'avait pas de besoin, des maudits sandwichs. On s'arrangeait ben comme c'tait-là.

JULIETTE: T'appelles ça s'arranger ben, ça, crever?

GÉRARD: On crevait pas.

JULIETTE: Ah, ben, excuse. Moué, j'ai toujours pensé que quand le monde a pas assez d'argent pour payer leurs "bills," on appelle ça crever.

GÉRARD: Voyons, Juliette. On les payait toujours, nos "bills," pi on se passait pas de grand'chose, non plus.

JULIETTE: Ben, on avait toujours assez à manger, ça c'est certain. On mangeait toute la viande qui se vendait pas. Pi à fin, là, on mangeait d'la viande en masse.

GÉRARD: Quoi c'est qu'on aurait dû faire, hein, Juliette? Dis-moué ça! Quoi c'est qu'on aurait dû faire?!?

JULIETTE: We should have worked harder . . . or else we should have sold the damned thing as fast as possible and gone on welfare.

GÉRARD: Well, I'll take that one step further. I never wanted to buy that damned store in the first place. And I still say we shouldn't have bought it.

JULIETTE: Sure. You would have liked that. We could have gone on welfare right away. You wouldn't have had to work a day in your life.

GÉRARD *goes to say something but stops himself. He gets up quickly, crosses to the door up center, and exits. The telephone rings. It should ring four or five more times.* GÉRARD *comes back in. He's wearing a winter coat and a hat. He crosses to the phone and answers it.*

GÉRARD: Hello? *(Pause)* Oh hello, Paul. Where in heaven's name are you? *(Pause)* Ah. *(Pause)* Ah. *(Pause)* Well, we were expecting you, but . . . *(Pause)* No, no, they didn't come this year. *(Pause)* Well, George wanted to spend Thanksgiving in their new house . . . and Normand and Elaine both have to work tomorrow, and they thought it was too far to drive for just one day. *(Pause)* No, no, we haven't eaten yet. We were waiting for you. And when you didn't call . . . *(Pause)* Unhuh. *(Pause)* Ah . . . so will you be coming later on? *(Pause)* Unhuh. *(Pause)* Sure, that's understandable. *(Pause)* Oh, not too bad for a couple of old relics. And you? *(Pause)* How about Cécile and the kids? *(Pause)* What do you think of this weather? I've never seen anything like it. We haven't . . . *(he stops for a moment, realizing that he's falling onto the old pattern he always uses to talk to his sons. He finishes slowly and without conviction)* . . . had a November this bad in a long time. *(Pause)* Listen, do you want to talk to your mother? *(Pause)* Ah. *(Pause)* Ah, okay then. *(Pause)* Yep, and happy Thanksgiving to all of you, too. *(Pause)* Bye. *(Pause.* GÉRARD *hangs up the phone. To* JULIETTE*)* They went to a restaurant.

JULIETTE: Ah.

JULIETTE: On aurait dû travailler plus fort . . . ou ben on aurait dû vendre c't'affaire-là aussi vite que possible pi aller collecter sur l'welfare.

GÉRARD: Ben moué, j'va aller plus loin que toué! Moué, j'voulais jamais l'acheter, ce maudit magasin-là. Pi j'dis encore qu'on aurait jamais dû l'acheter.

JULIETTE: Ouais. T'aurais ben aimé ça. On aurait pu se mettre sur l'welfare tout de suite. Comme ça, t'aurais pas eu besoin de travailler pantoute!.

GÉRARD *va pour dire quelque chose, mais hésite. Il se lève brusquement, se dirige vers la porte à l'arrière-scène et sort. Le téléphone sonne. Il doit sonner encore quatre ou cinq fois.* GÉRARD *rentre. Il porte un manteau d'hiver. Il se dirige vers le téléphone et répond.*

GÉRARD: Allô? *(Pause)* Ah allô, Paul. Où c'est que vous êtes, donc? *(Pause)* Ah. *(Pause)* Ah. *(Pause)* Oui, on vous attendait, mais . . . *(Pause)* Non, non, y sont pas venus c't'année. *(Pause)* Ben chez Georges voulaient passer Thanksgiving dans leur nouvelle maison . . . pi Normand pi Élaine travaillent toutes les deux demain, pi y pensaient que c'tait trop loin à venir pour ainque une journée. *(Pause)* Non, non, on a pas mangé encore. On vous attendait. Pi quand vous avez pas appelé . . . *(Pause)* Oui. *(Pause)* Ah . . . comme ça, allez-vous v'nir plus tard? *(Pause)* Ah. *(Pause)* Oui, ça se comprend. *(Pause)* Ah, pas pire pour des vieux. Pi toué? *(Pause)* Pi Cécile pi les enfants? *(Pause)* Fait pas beau, hein? Ça pas de bon sens. Ça fait longtemps qui . . . *(il s'arrête pour un moment. Il se rend compte qu'il répète sa phrase banale. Il finit lentement et sans conviction)* . . . qu'on a pas eu un novembre comme ça. *(Pause)* Écoute, veux-tu parler à ta mère, là? *(Pause)* Ah. *(Pause)* Ah, okay comme ça. *(Pause)* Oui, pi happy Thanksgiving à vous-autres, étou. *(Pause)* Bye. *(Pause. Gérard raccroche le téléphone. Pause. À* JULIETTE*)* Y sont allés à un restaurant.

JULIETTE: Ah.

GÉRARD: Paul thought that Cécile had called us.

JULIETTE: Ah.

GÉRARD: And Cécile thought that Paul had called us from the office last week to tell us.

JULIETTE: Ah.

GÉRARD: It's only when they got to the restaurant that they realized.

JULIETTE: Ah.

GÉRARD: They won't be able to stop by later, either, because Paul's boss is throwing a party. *(Silence)* He wanted to talk to you, but their food had just arrived and he didn't want it to get cold. *(Silence)* They all wish us a happy Thanksgiving.

Silence

JULIETTE: *(Noticing that* GÉRARD *has his coat on)* Where are you going?

GÉRARD: I don't know. I thought that maybe I'd . . . I don't know.

Silence

JULIETTE: Gérard?

GÉRARD: What?

JULIETTE: What are we going to do?

GÉRARD: There's nothing we can do. They're not coming. That's it!

JULIETTE: That's not what I mean. You and me, the two of us . . . what are we going to do? I can't go on living this way.

GÉRARD: Paul pensait que Cécile nous avait appelés.

JULIETTE: Ah.

GÉRARD: Pi Cécile pensait que Paul nous avait appelés de l'office.

JULIETTE: Ah.

GÉRARD: C'est rienque quand y sont arrivés au restaurant qui ont réalisé.

JULIETTE: Ah.

GÉRARD: Y pourront pas v'nir plus tard non plus, parce qui vont chez le boss à Paul pour un party. *(Silence)* Y aurait voulu te parler mais leur manger arrivait pi y voulait pas que ça refroidisse. *(Silence)* Y nous souhaitent tous un happy Thanksgiving.

Silence

JULIETTE: *(Qui s'aperçoit que* GÉRARD *porte son manteau)* Où c'est que tu vas?

GÉRARD: J'l'sais pas. J'pensais tedben . . . j'l'sais pas.

Silence

JULIETTE: Gérard?

GÉRARD: Hein?

JULIETTE: Quoi c'est qu'on va faire?

GÉRARD: Y a rienqu'on peut faire. Y viennent pas, c'est tout.

JULIETTE: C'est pas ça que j'veux dire, Gérard. Nous-autres, là . . . quoi c'est qu'on va faire? J'peux pas continuer à vivre comme ça.

GÉRARD: *(Crosses slowly to the easy chair stage right and sits. To himself)* It must have been an awful sin. An awful, terrible sin.

JULIETTE: *(To herself)* We haven't got a clue, that's for sure.

Silence

GÉRARD: Listen, Juliette. If we did like Paul. If we went out to eat, seems it would do us some good. It's been years since we went out to eat at a nice restaurant.

JULIETTE: You can't be serious. We just can't leave all this food here. We'll have trouble enough eating it all as it is. *(Pause)* It's true that it would do us some good to get out. *(Pause)* Maybe we could go to the movies after we eat. I think I'd like to see a good movie.

GÉRARD: There's no such thing as a good movie any more. It's all a bunch of killings and swearing and sex. Besides, two months after they're in the theaters, we can see them on TV for nothing. *(Pause)* But we really should do something, huh, Juliette. *(Pause)* You know what looks like fun to me when I see it on TV? Bowling.

JULIETTE: *(Chuckles a little)* Right! We'd look real cute trying to bowl at our age. Can you see me trying to bowl? I can't see enough to find a number in the phone book. What a joke. *(She gets up.)* Come carve the turkey. We might as well eat before it gets too late. *(She crosses to the kitchen.)* There's gotta be something we can do.

GÉRARD: *(Gets up, crosses to the door up center and exits. He comes back with two TV trays that he opens and places in front of the two easy chairs. He has taken off his coat and hat.)* That's right. We've got a head on our shoulders. We'll think of something, you'll see. What do people do these days when they want to have fun and pass the time away?

GÉRARD: *(Se dirige lentement vers le fauteuil à droite et s'assoit. Il parle plutôt à lui-même qu'à* JULIETTE.*)* Ça d'vait être un ben gros péché. Ben gros.

JULIETTE: *(Même jeu)* On a pas l'tour, ça c'est certain.

Silence

GÉRARD: Écoute, Juliette. Si on faisait comme Paul. Si on sortait manger, me semble que ça nous f'rait du bien. Ça fait des années qu'on est pas sorti ensemble manger à un beau restaurant.

JULIETTE: Voyons, Gérard. On est pas pour laisser tout c'manger-là icit. On va avoir assez de misère à finir tout ça comme c'est là. *(Pause)* C'est vrai que ça nous f'rait du bien de sortir. *(Pause)* Tedben qu'après dîner, on pourrait aller aux vues. Me semble que ça s'rait le fun de voir un bon portrait.

GÉRARD: Y n'en font pu, des bons portraits. C'est rienque du tuage pi du sacrage. A part de ça, deux mois après qui viennent au théâtre, on les voué à TV pour rien. *(Pause)* Mais on devrait vraiment faire quèque chose, hein, Juliette? *(Pause)* Sais-ti c'qui me paraît le fun? T'sais à TV, quand y ont du bowling.

JULIETTE: *(Qui rit un peu)* Ouais. On aurait d'l'air ben cute aller bowler à notre âge. Me voué-ti bowler ... moué qui peut pas même voir assez pour trouver un numéro dans le telephone book? Ça, ça s'rait drôle. *(Elle se lève.)* Viens couper la dinde, là. On est aussi ben de manger avant qui soit trop tard. *(Elle va à la cuisine.)* Y devrait avoir quèque chose qu'on pourrait faire.

GÉRARD: *(Se lève, se dirige vers la porte à l'arrière-scène, et sort. Il revient presqu'aussitôt avec deux "TV trays" qu'il ouvre et place devant les deux fauteuils. Il a enlevé son manteau et son chapeau.)* Ben oui. On est pas si bête que ça, nous-autres. On va trouver quèque chose, tu vas voir. Quoi c'est que ça fait, le monde, quand ça veut avoir du fun, pi passer le temps?

JULIETTE: *(Enters with napkins and glasses)* Well, some people like to read.

GÉRARD: But that's not something you can do together.

JULIETTE: I know . . . and it doesn't do much to get us out of the house, either.

GÉRARD: *(Heading for the kitchen)* There's always cards. *(He goes into the kitchen and starts carving the turkey.)*

JULIETTE: Forget it! That's all I do. I've played so many games of solitaire that I've got aces coming out my ears. *(Pause. She becomes lost in thought.)* You know what the Livingstons would do? Almost every weekend, we'd go skiing. Now that was fun! There's nothing prettier than a beautiful winter's day. The snow was so white . . . and when the sun was shining, it was like being in heaven. And as we'd ski down the mountain, the cold air would hit our faces until we practically couldn't feel a thing. *(Pause)* We'd spend all day outside. At night, we were so tired that we'd go to bed at eight.

GÉRARD: *(Coming back to the living room)* Well, I hate to tell you this, but you're not getting me on a pair of skis.

JULIETTE: *(Laughs a little)* No, no. *(Suddenly serious)* Especially with your heart. But it was a lot of fun just the same.

GÉRARD: I've carved the turkey.

JULIETTE: *(Who was day-dreaming)* What? Oh, right. I guess we're ready to eat, then. *(She goes to the kitchen.)*

GÉRARD: *(Crosses to the easy chair stage right and sits. Loud, to* JULIETTE*)* How about taking karate lessons? *(He laughs.)* Can you see the two of us? *(He tries a few karate chops.)* Hai! Hup! Haaaaaa!

JULIETTE: *(From the kitchen. Loud)* Easy on the blood pressure, there.

JULIETTE: *(Qui entre avec des serviettes et des verres)* Ben, y en a qui lisent.

GÉRARD: Oui, mais ça se fait pas ensemble, ça.

JULIETTE: J'l'sais . . . pi ça nous fait pas diable sortir, non plus.

GÉRARD: *(Se dirige vers la cuisine)* On peut toujours jouer aux cartes. *(Il va à la cuisine et commence à couper la dinde.)*

JULIETTE: Parle-moué pas des maudites cartes! C'est rienque ça qu'on fait. Moué, j'joue assez de jeux de patience que ça m'sort par les oreilles. *(Pause. Elle devient rêveuse.)* Sais-ti quoi c'est qu'on faisait chez les Livingston? Presque tous les fins de semaines, là, on allait skier. Ça, c'tait le fun. Y avait rien si beau que ça dans des belles journées d'hiver. La neige était assez blanche . . . pi quand le soleil frappait ça, on dirait que c'tait un vrai paradis. Pi quand on descendait, là, on sentait l'air froide qui nous frappait le visage. *(Pause)* On passait toute la journée dehors. Le soir, on était assez fatigué qu'on se couchait à huit heures.

GÉRARD: *(Il entre de la cuisine.)* Ben, t'es pas pour me mettre sur des skis, toué.

JULIETTE: *(Qui rit un peu)* Ah, non. *(Plus sombre)* Surtout avec ton coeur, là. Mais c'tait l'fun, quand même.

GÉRARD: J'ai coupé le turkey.

JULIETTE: *(Qui rêvait)* Ah? Ah, oui. On est prêt comme ça. *(Elle se rend à la cuisine.)*

GÉRARD: *(S'assoit sur le fauteuil à droite. Fort. A* JULIETTE*)* Tedben qu'on devrait prendre des leçons de karate. *(Il rit doucement.)* Nous voué-ti? *(Il fait des gestes de karaté.)* Hai! Hup! Haaaaaa!

JULIETTE: *(De la cuisine. Fort)* Commence pas à t'exciter, toué!

GÉRARD: How about aerobics?

JULIETTE *enters with two plates full of food, crosses to the easy chairs, and puts a plate on each TV tray.*

JULIETTE: Oh, sure. All you'd do is stand around and watch the girls jiggle. *(Pause)* Gérard, remember what Lucien and Georgette did when they retired?

GÉRARD: *(Grandiose)* They worked for world peace.

JULIETTE: Come on. Be serious. Don't you remember. They started playing golf.

GÉRARD: Oh, right.

JULIETTE: And they really seemed to like it. Georgette used to tell me it was real easy. *(Pause)* Come to think of it, I remember when Mister Livingston used to go play golf. He was always so well dressed. We went to pick him up a couple of times at the country club. Boy, I tell you it was snazzy. I thought those people were so lucky to be able to play golf. They were outside, in the fresh air. They'd be nice and tan after just an afternoon. Seems it was so good and healthy for them. *(Getting more enthusiastic)* And with those little electric carts they have now, you almost don't have to walk at all. Besides, a little exercise would probably do you some good, Gérard. You know what the doctor said. I think it's just what you need.

GÉRARD: *(Trying to convince himself)* Right. And they say that the new town golf course isn't expensive at all.

JULIETTE: They even let you rent your clubs. That's what Georgette used to do. That way, you don't have to spend all that money to buy them.

GÉRARD: And it can't be all that hard to hit a little ball into a little hole. *(Semi-joking)* Will you be able to see the thing, at least?

GÉRARD: Ou ben faire des aerobics.

JULIETTE *entre avec deux assiettes pleines de manger, se dirige vers les fauteuils, et dépose une assiette sur chaque TV tray.*

JULIETTE: Ouais. Si j'te connais, tu irais là pi tu resterais planté à regarder les belles filles. *(Pause)* Gérard, t'en souviens-ti quoi c'est que Lucien pi Georgette ont fait, eux-autres, quand y sont retirés?

GÉRARD: Si j'm'en rappelle ben, y ont niaisé.

JULIETTE: Voyons, Gérard. Sois sérieux, là. Tu t'en souviens pas? Y ont commencé à jouer au golf.

GÉRARD: Ah, oui.

JULIETTE: Pi c'avait d'l'air qui aimaient ben ça. Georgette me disait que c'tait ben facile. *(Pause)* Quand j'y pense, là, j'm'en souviens quand Monsieur Livingston allait jouer au golf. Y était toujours assez ben habillé. On est allé le chercher un couple de fois au club. J'te dis que c'tait swell. Me semble que c'tait assez ben, c'monde-là, de pouvoir jouer au golf. Y étaient dehors, à bonne air. Y passaient rienque une journée, pi y étaient toutes bruns. Me semble que ça d'vait être si bon pour eux-autres. *(Elle devient de plus en plus enthousiasmée.)* Pi tu sais, avec les p'tites machines qui ont asteur, t'aurais presque pu besoin de marcher. Pi un peu d'exercice, ça te f'rait du bien, Gérard. Tu sais quoi c'est que l'docteur t'as dit, hein? Pour moué, ça s'rait juste quoi c'est qui te faut.

GÉRARD: *(Essayant de se convaincre)* Ouais. Pi on dit que ça coûte pas cher au nouveau golf course.

JULIETTE: On peut même louer les golf clubs. C'est ça que Georgette faisait, elle. Comme ça, on aurait pas besoin d'en acheter.

GÉRARD: Pi ça devrait pas être si dur que ça, frapper une p'tite boule dans un p'tit trou. Vas-tu pouvoir la voir, au moins?

JULIETTE: I'll get some new glasses if I can't. *(Pause)* Gérard, that champagne you bought . . . do you think it's cold yet?

GÉRARD: It certainly should be.

JULIETTE: Well bring it out here and let's celebrate.

GÉRARD: What's the occasion?

JULIETTE: We're going to play golf.

GÉRARD: There's six inches of snow on the ground.

JULIETTE: Not now. In the spring!

GÉRARD *gets up and crosses to the kitchen. The TV gets louder.*

ANNOUNCER: Now both of you understand our simple contest rules, right? If either one of you answers the question correctly, you get your choice of the box, the curtain, or the lovely case that Tina's holding in her beautifully manicured hands. If you choose the box . . .

GÉRARD *comes back with the bottle of champagne and two glasses. He swings the bottle a little like a golf club.*

JULIETTE: *(Watching him)* What on earth are you doing?

GÉRARD: Practicing my swing.

They laugh. GÉRARD *crosses to the easy chairs and uncorks the bottle.*

ANNOUNCER: . . . and you forfeit all the prizes you've won during our preliminary round. You do get to keep your cash, though, if you can reach and ring our buzzer before the end of the elapsed time on our wacky studio clock right there on the wall.

JULIETTE: J'm'achèterai des nouvelles lunettes, s'il le faut. *(Pause)* Gérard, la champagne que t'as acheté, a est-ti frette?

GÉRARD: Ah, oui.

JULIETTE: Ben va la chercher. On va célébrer.

GÉRARD: Quoi c'est qu'on célèbre?

JULIETTE: On va jouer au golf.

GÉRARD: Y a six pouces de neige sur le lawn.

JULIETTE: Pas c't'hiver. Au printemps, voyons.

GÉRARD *se lève et va à la cuisine. Le son du téléviseur devient plus fort.*

ANNONCEUR: Now both of you understand our simple contest rules, right? If either one of you answers the question correctly, you get your choice of the box, the curtain, or the lovely case that Tina's holding in her beautifully manicured hands. If you choose the box . . .

GÉRARD *entre avec la bouteille de champagne et deux verres. Il se sert de la bouteille un peu comme un bâton de golf.*

JULIETTE: *(Et l'aperçoit)* Quoi c'est que tu fais là, donc?

GÉRARD: J't'après pratiquer mon swing.

Ils rient. GÉRARD *se dirige vers son fauteuil et commence à déboucher la bouteille.*

ANNONCEUR: . . . and you forfeit all the prizes you've won during our preliminary round. You do get to keep your cash, though, if you can reach and ring our buzzer before the end of the elapsed time on our wacky studio clock right there on the wall.

GÉRARD *pours champagne into the two glasses.*

ANNOUNCER: And here's the really good news. If you ring our zany buzzer within one and a half seconds, you keep your money AND you get your opponent's selection of prizes the next time he answers a question correctly.

GÉRARD *and* JULIETTE *look at each other for a moment.*

JULIETTE: *(Lifting her glass)* To golf!

GÉRARD: To us, Juliette. To us.

The two drink and start to eat while watching TV.

ANNOUNCER: But if you're late . . . if you ring that craaaazy buzzer within five to ten seconds, your opponent gets your money, I get your prizes, and the audience gets a chance to send you to our contestant penalty zone. And we all know what that means, don't we folks? That's riiiiight. It means that your next three correct answers will be disregarded and you'll be allowed to win prizes for your opponent if . . . and only if . . . he has chosen the curtain or the case or Tina, but not all three. If not, then you're out of the preliminary round, but you do automatically qualify for the final round and our grand prize of . . . ONE HUNDRED THOUSAND DOLLARS! I'm sure you'll get the rest of the rules as we go along. Now, it's time for our two contestants to give me their answers. Jessica, you're up first. Do you want to win to lose . . . or would you rather lose to win? Think it over carefully, Jessica, but I need your answer right now.

The TV gets softer. Tableau.

Curtain

GÉRARD *débouche la bouteille et verse de la champagne dans les deux verres.*

ANNONCEUR: And here's the really good news. If you ring our zany buzzer within one and a half seconds, you keep your money AND you get your opponent's selection of prizes the next time he answers a question correctly.

GÉRARD *et* JULIETTE *se regardent un instant.*

JULIETTE: *(Elle lève son verre.)* Au golf!

GÉRARD: A nous–autres, Juliette. A nous–autres.

Les deux boivent. Il se mettent à manger en silence en regardant le TV.

ANNONCEUR: But if you're late . . . if you ring that craaaazy buzzer within five to ten seconds, your opponent gets your money, I get your prizes, and the audience gets a chance to send you to our contestant penalty zone. And we all know what that means, don't we folks? That's riiiiight. It means that your next three correct answers will be disregarded and you'll be allowed to win prizes for your opponent if . . . and only if . . . he has chosen the curtain or the case or Tina, but not all three. If not, then you're out of the preliminary round, but you do automatically qualify for the final round and our grand prize of . . . ONE HUNDRED THOUSAND DOLLARS! I'm sure you'll get the rest of the rules as we go along. Now, it's time for our two contestants to give me their answers. Jessica, you're up first. Do you want to win to lose . . . or would you rather lose to win? Think it over carefully, Jessica, but I need your answer right now.

Le son du téléviseur s'adoucit. Tableau.

Rideau